THE REFERENCE SHELF

Volume XVI

No.
1. Representative American Speeches: 1941-1942. A. C. Baird. $1.25.
2. Plans for a Postwar World. J. E. Johnsen. $1.25.
3. Independence for India. J. E. Johnsen. $1.25.

No.
5. World Peace Plans. J. E. Johnsen. $1.25.
6. Representative American Speeches: 1942-1943. A. C. Baird. $1.25.
7. Reconstituting the League of Nations. J. E. Johnsen. $1.25.

Volume XV

No.
1. Representative American Speeches: 1940-1941. A. C. Baird. $1.25.
2. Universal Military Service. R. E. Summers and H. B. Summers. $1.25.
3. Federal Regulation of Labor Unions. J. V. Garland. $1.25.

No.
6. Wages and Prices. R. E. Summers. $1.25.
7. The Closed Shop. J. E. Johnsen. $1.25.
9. Permanent Price Control Policy. J. E. Johnsen. $1.25.
10. A Federal Sales Tax. E. R. Nichols. $1.25.

Volume XIV

No.
1. Representative American Speeches: 1939-1940. A. C. Baird. $1.50.
2. Interstate Trade Barriers. J. E. Johnsen. $1.25.
6. Compulsory Military Training. J. E. Johnsen. $1.25.

No.
8. International Federation of Democracies. J. E. Johnsen. $1.25.
9. Debate Index. Supplement. J. E. Johnsen. 75c.

Volume XIII

No.
4. Europe: Versailles to Warsaw. R. S. Kain. $1.25.
5. Public Housing in America. M. B. Schnapper. $1.25.
6. United States Foreign Policy (Supplement) J. E. Johnsen. 75c.

No.
9. The National Labor Relations Act. Should It Be Amended? J. E. Johnsen. $1.25.
10. Trade Unions and the Anti-Trust Laws. J. E. Johnsen. $1.25.

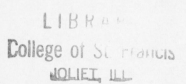

THE REFERENCE SHELF

Vol. 21   No. 2

REPRESENTATIVE AMERICAN SPEECHES: 1948-1949

Edited, and with introductions,
by
A. CRAIG BAIRD
Department of Speech, State University of Iowa

THE H. W. WILSON COMPANY
NEW YORK   1949

PREFATORY NOTE

REPRESENTATIVE AMERICAN SPEECHES: 1948-1949 is the twelfth in this annual series. Each volume includes some twenty-five speeches of "representative" public speakers of the United States. These twelve volumes contain more than three hundred addresses by some two hundred and twenty-five orators.

The speeches are grouped according to content, such as International Politics, Industry and Labor, Political Campaign, and Education. For those who prefer a different arrangement, the classification may be according to speech types or occasions, such as addresses on Statecraft, Congressional Debates, Inaugural Addresses, Radio Commentaries, Sermons, University Commencement addresses.

These divisions of content and speech types obviously overlap. The groupings are functional, for the reader's convenience, rather than for demonstration of scientific classification.

The editor again disavows any implication that these are the "best" speeches of the year. They are merely "important" and are selected to illustrate special techniques or points of view.

The Introduction to this volume suggests a method both of evaluating thought or ideas as one of the elements in a public address and of developing the thought pattern for the student's own speeches. For principles of good speaking and guides to methods of speech preparation and delivery, consult the introductions to the previous annual editions.

The brief introductory note to each speech gives background facts and may stimulate the reader "to probe more fully into the speaking methods; into the occasion and audience; and into the immediate and later effects of the address as clues for judging the total effectiveness." Each speech is viewed as a social force and the collection as a whole is regarded as a mirror of the thinking and communicative techniques of 1948-1949.

The biographical notes in the Appendix may encourage the investigator to explore more fully the intellectual resources, personality, and previous speaking record of the representative.

The Table of Contents of each annual edition and the Cumulative Author Index at the end of this volume are further means of reviewing the issues and speakers of the past twelve years. Such an over-all survey will give the student perspective and will demonstrate the intimate connection between speech making and events. The twelve volumes, it is hoped, provide insight into the forces behind the cultural and political history of these years.

This volume, like the earlier ones, is a reference source for the study of contemporary American problems; a partial record of the history of recent months; a collection of material for courses in debate and extempore speaking; a series of speeches for the systematic study of contemporary American public address; and a series of examples of how to proceed with one's own speech composition. Each volume, then, in addition to its services as a library reference, is especially recommended to students of extempore speaking, communication, debate, social sciences, history, and general public speaking.

This editor is grateful to the authors of these speeches for their cooperation in furnishing authentic texts and permitting their publication; and to publishers and organizations that have cooperated in granting permission to reprint. Specific acknowledgment is made in the footnote accompanying each speech.

June 1, 1949

A. CRAIG BAIRD

CONTENTS

SCIENCE

BUSINESS AND LABOR

EDUCATION

RELIGION

INTRODUCTION

How Shall We Judge the Thought Or Ideas of a Speech?

How shall we judge the thought or ideas contained in speeches?

Students of speech-making have long agreed that the principal components of an effective speech include (1) thought or ideas, (2) structure or organization, (3) language or style, and (4) delivery.

I propose here to make certain suggestions about thought or ideas as one of the elements of a speech. How will you develop *the thought* in your own speeches? How will you criticize that of the speech to which you listen or which you read?

1. *Thought should be selected and developed with a view to its influence on or relationship to a specific audience.* Ideas in speech-making are not abstract concepts for the thinker himself. They consist of *thought in process—in application to hearers.* The basic principle of all speech preparation and presentation is that speech is social adaptation; that communication is effective only when it adapts itself to the comprehension, interests and attitudes of those who listen; that audience response is the test of a superior speech. This principle is especially important as it applies to the speaker's thought. The most brilliant ideas have value to a crowd only when the group is able and willing to grasp and apply what is uttered. Thus the subject itself, the main and sub-ideas, and the arguments and evidence should be selected and presented with an eye to the demands of the place, the hour, and the human beings assembled.

2. *The speech should have one central idea.* This nucleus is the theme or thesis. The speaker may not state it directly. Or he may reserve concrete statement of it until the very end of his remarks. Whether or not he says, "This is my thesis," you

should be able to recognize it, and to phrase it as a main proposition. If you are unable to do so, the speaker has presumably been foggy in his thinking, or he has treated several unrelated ideas that should properly have been handled in separate addresses. Eisenhower, for example, in his appeal for the Red Cross, has this theme: Your voluntary support of the Red Cross will vindicate your individual responsibility and will prove that you are worthy of your heritage and are ready to sacrifice for it. He has one central idea and excludes all else.

3. *This central idea should be an important one.* The outstanding speaker discriminates between the essential and the unessential. He has the capacity to focus on the more significant ideas.

4. *This central proposition is usually a synthesis of several sub-propositions or ideas.* These related statements make up the fabric of the speaker's thought. If you outline one of your speeches already given or those of another, you will have before you an objective demonstration of how the speaker's mind has worked in a single address.

5. *The ideas are clearly defined.* The superior speaker, as a thinker, is at home with meanings. He is a definition maker. He keeps his audience and himself free from semantic pitfalls. Sometimes he gives an entire discourse to his explanation of a term. The Supreme Court argument, *Terminiello v. Chicago*, as presented by Justices Douglas and Jackson, deals at length with the questions, What is "free speech"? and What is "present danger"?

6. *The central ideas in the superior speech are based upon a sound analysis of the subject.* Analysis has to do with the division of the subject. It is frequently expressed by preliminary questions or "main issues," the answers to which are the "propositions" or "points to be developed." Dean Acheson, in reporting on the North Atlantic Pact, thus states the issues: "I think the American people will want to know the answers to three principal questions about the pact: How did it come about and why is it necessary? What are its terms? Will it accomplish its purpose?"

Even though these main questions may not be stated, the speaker often announces the three or four steps or points he would expand during the rest of his talk. These points represent his method of analyzing or dividing the subject. You, as critic, are to decide why he picked his topics and whether they are the most appropriate ones. President Truman in his inaugural address proceeds: "In the coming years, the program for peace and freedom will emphasize four major courses of action." Why does he single out these specific "courses"? Are they the four choices for national action in the foreign field, most urgent as of January 1949?

7. *These main and sub-ideas should all be relevant to the central theme.* They should unitedly make a harmonious pattern. Churchill, at Boston, seemingly gave two speeches in one: (1) the political and military history of Britain since 1900; and (2) the future political and military policies of the Anglo-American nations. A close examination of the entire address, however, will make clear the thematic unity. The chronological or time order of development predominates. The distributive (topical or classificational) and logical methods determine the amplification of Churchill's sub-points.

8. *The ideas of the speech should have internal consistency.* Sound thinking over a period may evolve and so contradict initial points of view. Within a single ten minute speech, however, one point should not seem to deny another. Such logical distortions confuse the listeners and destroy their confidence in the intellectual integrity of the platform leader.

The political campaigner, even in a given address, may present contradictory ideas. Dewey, Truman, and Wallace, in persuasive stump appeals, were each inclined to advocate programs that economically or politically contradicted other propositions in the same speech. Review the political speeches in the campaign of 1948 for evidence of such logical inconsistencies.

9. *The ideas or thought in a given speech should have originality.* A fresh point of view, a new approach to an old problem, should pervade the talk. If the topic is argumentative, the theses should be less superficial and more basic than those

mentioned by scores of other orators. The superior speaker gets to the bottom of the case. If the ideas are informative, then the facts and generalizations should add to the audience's knowledge. Superior speakers are Conant, Hancher, Churchill, Gannon, and others in this volume. In their analysis they have gone beyond the conventional.

10. *The ideas of the superior speech, as a demonstration of logical thinking, often deal with problem solving.* The speaker's mind focuses on problem and solution. The thinking is reflective. The speaker recognizes clearly the disturbing problem; views fully the nature of the problem as it reflects the economic or other movements and backgrounds; suggests ideas most applicable to a sound solution; examines by his reasoning the practical import of each solution; and verifies his judgment by adequate interpretation of the most feasible solution.

11. *The ideas of the superior speech as logical units deal with causes and results.* Lowell Thomas, immediately after Truman's election, explained over the air the apparent causes for the startling results. Does he hit upon the major or real causes?

12. *The ideas of the superior speech often form a deductive chain of reasoning.* Major premise or assumption, minor premise, and conclusion are evident. They may not always be expressed in more than enthymeme form. Often the syllogisms are telescoped into a series of propositions, each dependent on the preceding one. Conant, in his baccalaureate message to the Harvard students, develops such a mode of thinking: (1) As a nation we have much good fortune. (2) This good fortune suggests our responsibilities. (3) One of these responsibilities is that of world leadership. (4) Such leadership in turn is based upon our ability to make democracy work at home and to conduct our foreign affairs with wisdom, understanding, and courage. (5) The successful realization of these goals will depend upon our national solidarity. (6) This national solidarity, in turn, is based upon a sound philosophy. (7) Such philosophy will depend upon our application of the ideals of equality of

opportunity and of social justice. (8) These ideals rest upon spiritual unity. (9) Spiritual unity will be based upon the unifying doctrines of religious tolerance and a recognition of the sanctity of each human soul and the duty of the "social good." (10) These postulates, in turn, rest upon the concept of the sacredness of human life. ("Each individual is related to the structure of the universe.")

13. *The main ideas should be supported by logical argument and evidence.* The ideas, whether inductively or deductively unfolded, should be interpreted and substantiated by analogies, comparisons, cases, illustrations (real or hypothetical), statistics, enumeration of details that make up a transaction or event, and testimony of witnesses or authorities who express opinions or confirm facts. To such argumentative details and the accompanying evidence you are to apply the tests of inference and of evidence. Both competent critics and composers of superior speeches should familiarize themselves with these representative forms of support and the criteria by which their validity may be affirmed or denied. Speech ideas are to be subjected to the principles of straight thinking.

14. *Ideas are a reflection of the speaker's thinking and experience.* Ideas are related to the education, occupation, and environment of the speaker. Originality and force of thought with the accompanying details of subject matter are traceable not simply to the intellectual acuity of the speaker but to his previous contact with literature, history and other reading. The good speaker-thinker has inherited something of the riches of great minds. Furthermore, his direct educational development, whether through schools and colleges or individual self-discipline, affects his observations and judgments. His contacts with life, his experience as soldier, salesman, journalist, pedagogue, or statesman, furnish clues to his mental processes and his choice of materials.

15. *The ideas of the superior speech are integrated with the emotional and reflective thinking of the audience.* Whether the speaker engages in direct debate or merely expounds a controversial idea, he analyzes the attitudes of the hearers and interprets his thinking accordingly. He removes inhibitions, antici-

pates objections, and, on occasion, offers direct reply to counter arguments. Subtle or more obvious refutation accompanies most speeches on current problems. Much of the material in the present collection, whether delivered before educational, religious, political, or other groups, was framed to diminish prejudice, reassure, enlighten, convince, and persuade.

16. *Speech ideas are to be gauged according to the impress they make on contemporary and later society.* The thinking must do more than demonstrate accuracy and inference. Intellectual expression must be measured also by the social effect. Do the ideas work? Do they create only a ripple? Do they set in motion wider currents and affect civilization? Does later history vindicate the judgment of the speaker? The test is pragmatic.

Certainly in our description of speech effectiveness, it is hard to separate thought from voice, language, and other factors. As best we can, nevertheless, we are called upon to do so. Some one hundred speech instructors in November 1948, mentioned most frequently as representative living American speakers Harry S. Truman, Thomas E. Dewey, Harold E. Stassen, Norman Thomas, Robert M. Hutchins, Arthur H. Vandenberg, Henry A. Wallace, Harry Emerson Fosdick, Eleanor A. Roosevelt, Dwight D. Eisenhower, Eric A. Johnston, George C. Marshall, and Fulton J. Sheen. Will any of these, as far as ideas in public address are concerned, be more than a half-forgotten name fifty years from now? Living within the events, we view as best we can their influence. Through the receding months and years, we continue to evaluate their record.

17. *Ideas are to be measured ultimately by their contribution to truth.* What is truth? As critics we confess our inability to grapple with such metaphysical subtleties. Yet our assumption is that those ideas are most enduring and permanent that approximate high standards of value for mankind. As best we can, we formulate ultimate goals and measure the orator's contribution by such standards. We offer no assured guarantee on the truth of the orator's arguments. The great orator recognizes the limitations of his art and his materials. He admittedly relies upon the probability of his Truth. Progressive

and repeated examination of his judgments, he hopes, will justify them. From such approach do we as critics and speechmakers evaluate thought in oral discourse.

SPEECH TYPES

The speeches in this volume might be classified according to type of speech. Many of them might, of course, be put in more than one classification. Some of the types are:

Speeches on Affairs of State: Dean Acheson's The North Atlantic Pact; President Harry Truman's Inaugural Address; Winston Churchill's address at Massachusetts Institute of Technology; Francis B. Sayre's speech on United States foreign policy at the Conference on Public Affairs at Ohio State University.

Political Campaign Speeches: The addresses by President Truman and Thomas E. Dewey at Madison Square Garden; Henry Wallace's acceptance speech at Philadelphia.

Congressional Debate: The speeches by Speaker Sam Rayburn and members of the House of Representatives, on the repeal of the Taft-Hartley Labor Act.

Speeches at Conferences: David Lilienthal on The Spirit of Democracy at Rochester University; Ruth Alexander's "Which Way America?"; Churchill at Massachusetts Institute of Technology; Sayre at Ohio State University; Harrison Brown on "Social Responsibility of Science," at the New York *Herald Tribune* forum; and John Foster Dulles on "The Church and International Disorder," at Amsterdam, Holland.

Radio Commentary and Debate: Lowell Thomas's comments on the election of President Truman; the Town Meeting of the Air debate on, "Are We Educating for the Needs of the Common Man?"

Commencement Addresses: President James Bryant Conant's "A National Philosophy"; President Virgil Hancher's "The Art of Contemplation."

Addresses of Tribute and Response: Hoover's "The Meaning of America"; and Vandenberg's tribute to Alben Barkley and Barkley's response.

Judicial Decisions: William O. Douglas and Robert H. Jackson on "Freedom of Speech."

Fund Raising Speeches: Dwight D. Eisenhower's plea for the American Red Cross.

INTERNATIONAL POLICIES

THE NORTH ATLANTIC PACT [1]

DEAN ACHESON [2]

Dean Acheson, Secretary of State, broadcast this address over the combined networks of the Columbia and Mutual broadcasting systems, at 10:30, E.S.T., on Friday, March 18, 1949. The eastern CBS television network carried this speech.

Earlier that day the official text of the treaty was released. The Secretary of State's radio talk attempted to explain to the public the general plan and to develop public opinion favorable to the later ratification of the Pact by the Senate.

The treaty, a twenty year pact, was obviously aimed to contain Russia, to present a solid front to the immense Communist world, to prepare for a possible war, and to make possible concerted action if one came. The core of the document was expressed in the declaration that "an armed attack on any of them, in Europe or North America, will be considered an attack on all of them." The treaty itself, some 1040 words, with a preamble and fourteen articles, reaffirmed the obligations of the signatories under the United Nations. It proposed the creation of a North Atlantic Council and a Military Staff Committee.

This Acheson address was a model of organization, with well defined introduction, main divisions, and conclusion. The introduction explained the cause for discussion, gave a brief history, and stated directly the issues to be developed. The main body developed the principal ideas of (1) necessity for the treaty, (2) its provisions, and (3) its expected results. The swift conclusion reinforced the preceding argument and appealed for action. Each sub-idea was supported by authority, analogy, and historical detail. The argumentative mode of development included anticipatory refutation of objections bound to arise in and out of the United States Senate. Students of debate will profit by analysis of this speech that was designed both to inform the nation and to remove their inhibitions against abandoning the traditional policy of no alliances.

Mr. Acheson has an excellent radio voice. Critics of this broadcast suggested that the speaker's voice reminded them of Ronald Colman

---

[1] Text supplied through the courtesy of Miss Margaret R. T. Carter, Chief of the Division of Public Liaison, Department of State.

[2] For biographical note, see Appendix.

or even Winston Churchill. The voice was relaxed, resonant, cultivated, yet free from vocal artifice or obviousness. The positive inflections, even though accompanied by a measured rate, were well suited to the persuasive and yet restrained temper of the discourse itself. The lack of acerbity, the logical consistency of ideas, and ethical proof furnished partly by the speaker's successful leadership in implementing this historic treaty, gave the speech unusual persuasiveness.

Twelve nations, Great Britain, the United States, Canada, France, Belgium, the Netherlands, Luxembourg, Norway, Italy, Portugal, Denmark, and Iceland, signed the pact. Later each government was to ratify it. Congress set about approving some one billion dollars for distribution among these allies for their immediate defense. The debate in the Senate for formal ratification was to be delayed "for several months." As of June 1, 1949, it was widely predicted that such endorsement would follow and that thus this nation would reverse its historic policy of no permanent military commitments to European countries.

The text of the proposed North Atlantic Pact was made public today. I welcome this opportunity to talk with my fellow citizens about it. It has taken many months to work out this text with the representatives of the other nations involved. First Mr. Lovett and then I met with the Ambassadors of Canada, Britain, France, Belgium, the Netherlands and Luxembourg. Recently the Ambassador of Norway joined in these discussions. These talks had to be conducted in private and in confidence, so that each of us could speak frankly and fully on matters of vital importance to our countries. It is for this compelling reason that public discussion of the text of the Pact by your representatives has not been possible up to this time.

That restraint no longer applies. The treaty and its implications can now be fully discussed. Public opinion can now be formed on the basis of complete information. Only in this way can your government have what former Secretary of State Stimson has termed "the understanding support . . . of the American people," which is essential to the success of any policy.

I think the American people will want to know the answers to three principal questions about the Pact: How did it come about and why is it necessary? What are its terms? Will it accomplish its purpose?

The paramount purposes of the Pact are peace and security. If peace and security can be achieved in the North Atlantic area, we shall have gone a long way to assure peace and security in other areas as well.

The achievement of peace and security means more than that in the final outcome we shall have prevented war and brought about the settlement of international disputes by peaceful means. There must be conviction of people everywhere that war *will* be prevented and that disputes *will* be settled peacefully. In the most practical terms, true international peace and security require a firm belief by the peoples of the world that they will not be subjected to unprovoked attack, to coercion and intimidation, to interference in their own affairs. Peace and security require confidence in the future, based on the assurance that the peoples of the world will be permitted to improve their conditions of life, free from fear that the fruits of their labor may be taken from them by alien hands.

These are goals of our own foreign policy which President Truman has emphasized many times, most recently in his inaugural address when he spoke of the hope that we could help create "the conditions that will lead eventually to personal freedom and happiness for all mankind." These are also the purposes of the United Nations, whose members are pledged "to maintain international peace and security" and to promote "the economic and social advancement of all peoples."

These purposes are intimately related to the origins of the United Nations. As the second World War neared its end, the peoples who bore the brunt of the fighting were sick of the horror, the brutality, the tragedy of war. Out of that revulsion came the determination to create a system that would go as far as humanly possible in insuring international peace and security.

The United Nations seeks to maintain peace and security by enjoining its members from using force to settle international disputes. Moreover, it insists that they acknowledge tolerance and cooperation as the guiding principles for the conduct of nations.

The members are expected to settle differences by the exercise of reason and adjustment, according to the principles of justice and law. This requires a spirit of tolerance and restraint on the part of all the members.

But, as in any other institution which presupposes restraint, violence or obstruction can be used to defeat the basic undertaking. This happens in personal relations, in families, communities, churches, politics, and everywhere in human life. If the system is used in ways it was not intended to be used, there is grave danger that the system will be disrupted.

That applies to the United Nations. The system is not working as effectively as we hoped because one of its members has attempted to prevent it from working. By obstructive tactics and the misuse of the veto, the Soviet Union has seriously interfered with the work of the Security Council in maintaining international peace and security.

But the United Nations is a flexible instrument. Although the actions of the Soviet Union have disturbed the work of the United Nations, it is strong enough to be an effective instrument for peace. It is the instrument by which we hope world peace will be achieved. The Charter recognizes the importance of regional arrangements consistent with the purposes and principles of the Charter. Such arrangements can greatly strengthen it.

The Atlantic Pact is a collective self-defense arrangement among the countries of the North Atlantic area. It is aimed at coordinating the exercise of the right of self-defense specifically recognized in Article 51 of the United Nations Charter. It is designed to fit precisely into the framework of the United Nations and to assure practical measures for maintaining peace and security in harmony with the Charter.

It is the firm intention of the parties to carry out the Pact in accordance with the provisions of the United Nations Charter and in a manner which will advance its purposes and principles.

Already one such arrangement under the Charter has been established with U. S. participation. The twenty-one American republics in reorganizing their regional system have specifically brought it within the framework of the United Nations Charter. We are now joining in the formation of a second arrangement, pertaining to the North Atlantic area, likewise within the framework of the United Nations.

It is important to keep in mind that the really successful national and international institutions are those that recognize and express underlying realities. The North Atlantic community of nations is such a reality. It is based on the affinity and natural identity of interests of the North Atlantic powers.

The North Atlantic treaty which will formally unite them is the product of at least three hundred and fifty years of history, perhaps more. There developed on our Atlantic coast a community, which has spread across the continent, connected with Western Europe by common institutions and moral and ethical beliefs. Similarities of this kind are not superficial, but fundamental. They are the strongest kind of ties, because they are based on moral conviction, on acceptance of the same values in life.

The very basis of western civilization, which we share with the other nations bordering the North Atlantic, and which all of us share with many other nations, is the ingrained spirit of restraint and tolerance. This is the opposite of the Communist belief that coercion by force is a proper method of hastening the inevitable. Western civilization has lived by mutual restraint and tolerance. This civilization permits and stimulates free inquiry and bold experimentation. It creates the environment of freedom, from which flows the greatest amount of ingenuity, enterprise and accomplishment.

These principles of democracy, individual liberty and the rule of law have flourished in this Atlantic community. They have universal validity. They are shared by other free nations and find expression on a universal basis in the Charter of the United Nations; they are the standards by which its members have solemnly agreed to be judged. They are the elements out of which are forged the peace and welfare of mankind.

Added to this profoundly important basis of understanding is another unifying influence—the effect of living on the sea. The sea does not separate people as much as it joins them, through trade, travel, mutual understanding and common interests.

For this second reason, as well as the first, North America and Western Europe have formed the two halves of what is in reality one community, and have maintained an abiding interest in each other.

It is clear that the North Atlantic Pact is not an improvisation. It is the statement of the facts and lessons of history. We have learned our history lesson from two world wars in less than half a century. That experience has taught us that the control of Europe by a single aggressive, unfriendly power would constitute an intolerable threat to the national security of the United States. We participated in those two great wars to preserve the integrity and independence of the European half of the Atlantic community in order to preserve the integrity and independence of the American half. It is a simple fact, proved by experience, that an outside attack on one member of this community is an attack upon all members.

We have also learned that if the free nations do not stand together, they will fall one by one. The stratagem of the aggressor is to keep his intended victims divided or better still, set them to quarreling among themselves. Then they can be picked off one by one without arousing unified resistance. We and the free nations of Europe are determined that history shall not repeat itself in that melancholy particular.

As President Truman has said: "If we can make it sufficiently clear, in advance, that any armed attack affecting our national security would be met with overwhelming force, the armed attack might never occur."

The same thought was expressed by the Foreign Relations Committee of the Senate last year in its report recommending approval of Senate Resolution 239. "The Committee is convinced," the report said, "that the horrors of another world war can be avoided with certainty only by preventing war from starting. The experience of World War I and World War II suggests that the best deterrent to aggression is the certainty that immediate and effective counter-measures will be taken against those who violate the peace." That resolution, adopted by an overwhelming vote of the Senate, expressly encourages the development of collective self-defense and regional arrangements within the United Nations framework and the participation of the United States in these arrangements.

What are the principal provisions of the North Atlantic Pact? I should like to summarize them.

First, the Pact is carefully and conscientiously designed to conform in every particular with the Charter of the United Nations. This is made clear in the first Article of the Pact, which reiterates and reaffirms the basic principle of the Charter. The participating countries at the very outset of their association state again that they will settle all their international disputes, not only among themselves but with any nation, by peaceful means in accordance with the provisions of the Charter. This declaration sets the whole tone and purpose of this treaty.

The second Article is equally fundamental. The associated countries assert that they will preserve and strengthen their free institutions and will see to it that the fundamental principles upon which free institutions are founded are better understood everywhere. They also agree to eliminate conflicts in their economic life and to promote economic cooperation among themselves. Here is the ethical essence of the treaty—the common resolve to preserve, strengthen and make understood the very basis of tolerance, restraint and freedom—the really vital things with which we are concerned.

This purpose is extended further in Article 3, in which the participating countries pledge themselves to self-help and mutual aid. In addition to strengthening their free institutions, they will take practical steps to maintain and develop their own capacity and that of their partners to resist aggression. They also agree to consult together when the integrity or security of any of them is threatened. The treaty sets up a council, consisting of all the members, and other machinery for consultation and for carrying out the provisions of the Pact.

Successful resistance to aggression in the modern world requires modern arms and trained military forces. As a result of the recent war, the European countries joining in the Pact are generally deficient in both requirements. The treaty does not bind the United States to any arms program. But we all know that the United States is now the only democratic nation with the resources and the productive capacity to help the free nations of Europe to recover their military strength.

Therefore, we expect to ask the Congress to supply our European partners some of the weapons and equipment they need to be able to resist aggression. We also expect to recommend military supplies for other free nations which will cooperate with us in safeguarding peace and security.

In the compact world of today, the security of the United States cannot be defined in terms of boundaries and frontiers. A serious threat to international peace and security anywhere in the world is of direct concern to this country. Therefore it is our policy to help free peoples to maintain their integrity and independence, not only in Western Europe or in the Americas, but wherever the aid we are able to provide can be effective. Our actions in supporting the integrity and independence of Greece, Turkey and Iran are expressions of that determination. Our interest in the security of these countries has been made clear, and we shall continue to pursue that policy.

In providing military assistance to other countries, both inside and outside the North Atlantic Pact, we will give clear priority to the requirements for economic recovery. We will carefully balance the military assistance program with the capacity and requirements of the total economy, both at home and abroad.

But to return to the treaty, Article 5 deals with the possibility, which unhappily cannot be excluded, that the nations joining together in the Pact may have to face the eventuality of an armed attack. In this Article, they agree that an armed attack on any of them, in Europe or North America, will be considered an attack on all of them. In the event of such an attack, each of them will take, individually and in concert with the other parties, whatever action it deems necessary to restore and maintain the security of the North Atlantic area, including the use of armed force.

This does not mean that the United States would be automatically at war if one of the nations covered by the Pact is subjected to armed attack. Under our Constitution, the Congress alone has the power to declare war. We would be bound to take promptly the action which we deemed necessary to restore and maintain the security of the North Atlantic area. That decision would be taken in accordance with our Constitutional procedures. The factors which would have to be considered would be, on the one side, the gravity of the armed attack; on the other, the action which we believed necessary to restore and maintain the security of the North Atlantic area. That is the end to be achieved. We are bound to do what in our honest judgment is necessary to reach that result. If we should be confronted again with a calculated armed attack such as we have twice seen in the Twentieth Century, I should not suppose that we would decide any action other than the use of armed force effective either as an exercise of the right of collective self-defense or as necessary to restore the peace and security of the North Atlantic area. That decision will rest where the Constitution has placed it.

This is not a legalistic question. It is a question we have frequently faced, the question of faith and principle in carrying out treaties. Those who decide it will have the responsibility for taking all appropriate action under the treaty. Such a responsibility requires the exercise of will—a will disciplined by the undertaking solemnly contracted to do what they decide is necessary to restore and maintain the peace and security of the North Atlantic area. That is our obligation under this Article 5. It is equally our duty and obligation to the security of our own country.

All of these provisions of the Pact are subject to the over-riding provisions of the United Nations Charter. Any measures for self-defense taken under the treaty will be reported to the Security Council of the United Nations. These measures will continue only until the Security Council, with its primary responsibility, takes the necessary action to restore peace and maintain security.

The treaty has no time limit, but after it has been in effect twenty years any member can withdraw on one year's notice. It also provides that after it has been in existence ten years, it will be reviewed in the circumstances prevailing at that time. Additional countries may be admitted to the Pact by agreement of all parties already signatories.

These are the principal provisions of the treaty.

Will the Pact accomplish its purpose?

No one can say with certainty. We can only act on our convictions. The United States Government and the governments with which we are associated in this treaty are convinced that it is an essential measure for strengthening the United Nations, deterring aggression, and establishing the sense of security necessary for the restoration of the economic and political health of the world.

The nations joining in the Pact know that war does not pay. Others may not be as deeply convinced of this as we are. The North Atlantic treaty should help convince them also that war does not pay.

It seems absurd that it should be necessary, in this era of popular education and highly developed communications, to deal with allegations which have no relation to the truth and could not stand even the crudest test of measurement against realities. Nevertheless, the power and persistence with which the lie is today employed as a weapon of international policy is such that this cannot always be avoided.

I refer here to the allegations that this treaty conceals aggressive designs on the part of its authors with respect to other countries. Any one with the most elementary knowledge of the processes of democratic government knows that democracies do not and cannot plan aggressive wars. But for those from whom such knowledge may have been withheld I must make the following categoric and unequivocal statement, for which I stand with the full measure of my responsibility in the office I hold:

This country is not planning to make war against anyone. It is not seeking war. It abhors war. It does not hold war to be inevitable. Its policies are devised with the specific aim of bridging by peaceful means the tremendous differences which beset international society at the present time.

Allegations that aggressive designs lie behind this country's signature of the Atlantic Pact can rest only on a malicious misrepresentation or a fantastic misunderstanding of the nature and aims of American society. It is hard to say which of these attitudes is more irresponsible and more dangerous to the stability of international life. For misunderstanding on a question so vital to world progress and so easily susceptible of clarification could only be willful or the product of a system that imprisons the human mind and makes it impervious to facts. It is the duty of all those who seriously and realistically wish for peace to refuse to be misled by this type of falsehood and to prevent it from poisoning the atmosphere in which the quest of a happier world must be conducted.

This treaty is designed to help toward the goal envisioned by President Truman when he said:

> As our stability becomes manifest, as more and more nations come to know the benefits of democracy and to participate in growing abundance, I believe that those countries which now oppose us will abandon their delusions and join with the free nations of the world in a just settlement of international differences.

To bring that time to pass, we are determined, on the one hand, to make it unmistakably clear that immediate and effective counter-measures will be taken against those who violate the peace, and on the other, to *wage peace* vigorously and relentlessly.

Too often peace has been thought of as a negative condition—the mere absence of war. We know now that we cannot achieve peace by taking a negative attitude. Peace is positive, and it has to be waged with all our thought, energy and courage, and with the conviction that war is *not* inevitable.

Under the leadership of President Truman, the United States is waging peace with a vigor and on a scale without precedent. While the war was being fought, this country took the initiative in the organization of the United Nations and related agencies for the collective and cooperative conduct of international affairs. We withdrew our military forces, except those required for occupation duties, and quickly reduced our military establishment to about one tenth its wartime size. We contributed generously to postwar relief and rehabilitation.

When events called for firmness as well as generosity the United States waged peace by pledging its aid to free nations threatened by aggression, and took prompt and vigorous action to fulfill that pledge. We have actively sought and are actively seeking to make the United Nations an effective instrument of international cooperation. We proposed, and with the eager cooperation of sixteen other nations, put into effect a great concerted program for the economic recovery and spiritual reinvigoration of Europe. We joined the other American republics, and we now join with Western Europe, in treaties to strengthen the United Nations and insure international peace and security.

The United States is waging peace by promoting measures for the revival and expansion of world trade on a sound and beneficial basis. Continuance of the Reciprocal Trade Agreements program and ratification by the United States of the Charter of the International Trade Organization are essential to the success of our foreign trade policies. We are preparing to carry out an energetic program to apply modern skills and techniques to what President Truman has called the "primitive and stagnant" economies of vast areas, so that they will yield a better and richer life for their people.

The United States is waging peace by throwing its full strength and energy into the struggle, and we shall continue to do so.

We sincerely hope we can avoid strife, but we cannot avoid striving for what is right. We devoutly hope we can have genuine peace, but we cannot be complacent about the present uneasy and troubled peace.

A secure and stable peace is not a goal we can reach all at once and for all time. It is a dynamic state, produced by effort and faith, with justice and courage. The struggle is continuous and hard. The prize is never irrevocably ours.

To have this genuine peace we must constantly work for it. But we must do even more. We must make it clear that armed attack will be met by collective defense, prompt and effective.

That is the meaning of the North Atlantic Pact.

INAUGURAL ADDRESS [3]

HARRY S. TRUMAN

President Harry S. Truman, the thirty-second president, delivered this inaugural message on the steps of the Capitol on Thursday, January 20, 1949, in the most impressive inaugural ceremonies in American history. He took the oath of office before an immediate crowd of about a hundred thousand in Capitol Plaza, and to a huge world-wide audience by radio, short wave and television. (The television audience alone, the first such in American history, was estimated at ten million.)

The President, abandoning a general discourse, outlined concretely and frankly the American foreign policy. He analyzed the major issue before him—the threat of communism—and outlined his four-fold program: (1) unqualified support of the United Nations and its agencies, (2) complete and continued commital to the program for economic strengthening of Western Europe, (3) the formulation of a North Atlantic pact to resist communism, and (4) a "fair deal" non-imperialistic program for the rest of the world through a sharing of our industrial and scientific skills and resources.

Similar in significance were Washington's First Inaugural April 30, 1789, dedicating this country to national unity and liberty; Lincoln's First Inaugural, March 4, 1861, with his warning to the South; or F. D. Roosevelt's, on March 4, 1933, sounding the philosophy and program of the New Deal.

Although Truman condemned communism, belligerency was absent. The tone throughout was one of dignity and of statesmanship. Truman, the highly personal political stump speaker, had well adjusted his style and delivery to the solemn hour.

The immediate audience applauded warmly and repeatedly. National opinion also was generally favorable. Official opinion in world capitols (outside the Soviet world) was highly laudatory and presaged the North Atlantic alliance. Criticism centered chiefly in the proposal of economic and other help to backward nations. By January 1949, the Communists had triumphed in China. Did the President's message imply that our military and economic weight would also be so distributed as to somehow minimize that Far Eastern catastrophe? Did he also propose strong economic support of South American countries as well as of India, the Middle East and Africa?

[3] Text furnished through the courtesy of Charles G. Ross, Secretary to the President.

[4] For biographical note, see Appendix.

Mr. Vice President, Mr. Chief Justice, and Fellow Citizens: I accept with humility the honor which the American people have conferred upon me. I accept it with a deep resolve to do all that I can for the welfare of this nation and for the peace of the world.

In performing the duties of my office, I need the help and prayers of every one of you. I ask for your encouragement and your support. The tasks we face are difficult, and we can accomplish them only if we work together.

Each period of our national history has had its special challenges. Those that confront us now are as momentous as any in the past. Today marks the beginning not only of a new Administration, but of a period that will be eventful, perhaps decisive, for us and for the world.

It may be our lot to experience, and in large measure to bring about, a major turning point in the long history of the human race. The first half of this century has been marked by unprecedented and brutal attacks on the rights of man, and by the two most frightful wars in history. The supreme need of our time is for men to learn to live together in peace and harmony.

The peoples of the earth face the future with grave uncertainty, composed almost equally of great hopes and great fears. In this time of doubt, they look to the United States as never before for good will, strength and wise leadership.

It is fitting, therefore, that we take this occasion to proclaim to the world the essential principles of the faith by which we live, and to declare our aims to all peoples.

The American people stand firm in the faith which has inspired this nation from the beginning. We believe that all men have a right to equal justice under law and equal opportunity to share in the common good. We believe that all men have the right to freedom of thought and expression. We believe that all men are created equal because they are created in the image of God.

From this faith we will not be moved.

The American people desire, and are determined to work for, a world in which all nations and all peoples are free to govern themselves as they see fit and to achieve a decent and satisfying life. Above all else, our people desire, and are determined to work for, peace on earth—a just and lasting peace—based on genuine agreement freely arrived at by equals.

In the pursuit of these aims, the U. S. and other like-minded nations find themselves directly opposed by a regime with contrary aims and a totally different concept of life.

That regime adheres to a false philosophy which purports to offer freedom, security and greater opportunity to mankind. Misled by this philosophy, many peoples have sacrificed their liberties only to learn to their sorrow that deceit and mockery, poverty and tyranny, are their reward.

That false philosophy is communism. Communism is based on the belief that man is so weak and inadequate that he is unable to govern himself, and therefore requires the rule of strong masters.

Democracy is based on the conviction that man has the moral and intellectual capacity, as well as the inalienable right, to govern himself with reason and justice.

Communism subjects the individual to arrest without lawful cause, punishment without trial, and forced labor as the chattel of the state. It decrees what information he shall receive, what art he shall produce, what leaders he shall follow and what thoughts he shall think.

Democracy maintains that government is established for the benefit of the individual, and is charged with the responsibility of protecting the rights of the individual and his freedom in the exercise of his abilities.

Communism maintains that social wrongs can be corrected only by violence.

Democracy has proved that social justice can be achieved through peaceful change.

Communism holds that the world is so deeply divided into opposing classes that war is inevitable.

Democracy holds that free nations can settle differences justly and maintain lasting peace.

These differences between communism and democracy do not concern the United States alone. People everywhere are coming to realize that what is involved is material well-being, human dignity and the right to believe in and worship God.

I state these differences, not to draw issues of belief as such, but because the actions resulting from the Communist philosophy are a threat to the efforts of free nations to bring about world recovery and lasting peace.

Since the end of hostilities, the United States has invested its substance and its energy in a great constructive effort to restore peace, stability and freedom to the world.

We have sought no territory and we have imposed our will on none. We have asked for no privileges we would not extend to others.

We have constantly and vigorously supported the United Nations and related agencies as a means of applying democratic principles to international relations. We have consistently advocated and relied upon peaceful settlement of disputes among nations.

We have made every effort to secure agreement on effective international control of our most powerful weapon, and we have worked steadily for the limitation and control of all armaments.

We have encouraged, by precept and example, the expansion of world trade on a sound and fair basis.

Almost a year ago, in company with sixteen free nations of Europe, we launched the greatest cooperative economic program in history. The purpose of that unprecedented effort is to invigorate and strengthen democracy in Europe, so that the free people of that continent can resume their rightful place in the forefront of civilization and can contribute once more to the security and welfare of the world.

Our efforts have brought new hope to all mankind. We have beaten back despair and defeatism. We have saved a number of countries from losing their liberty. Hundreds of millions of people all over the world now agree with us, that we need not have war—that we can have peace.

The initiative is ours.

We are moving on with other nations to build an even stronger structure of international order and justice. We shall have as our partners countries which, no longer solely concerned with the problem of national survival, are now working to improve the standards of living of all their people. We are ready to undertake new projects to strengthen the free world.

In the coming years, our program for peace and freedom will emphasize four major courses of action.

First, we will continue to give unfaltering support to the UN and related agencies, and we will continue to search for ways to strengthen their authority and increase their effectiveness. We believe that the UN will be strengthened by the new nations which are being formed in lands now advancing toward self-government under democratic principles.

Second, we will continue our programs for world economic recovery. This means, first of all, that we must keep our full weight behind the European Recovery Program. We are confident of the success of this major venture in world recovery. We believe that our partners in this effort will achieve the status of self-supporting nations once again. In addition, we must carry out our plans for reducing the barriers to world trade and increasing its volume. Economic recovery and peace itself depend on increased world trade.

Third, we will strengthen freedom-loving nations against the dangers of aggression. We are now working out with a number of countries a joint agreement designed to strengthen the security of the North Atlantic area. Such an agreement would take the form of a collective defense arrangement within the terms of the United Nations Charter. We have already established such a defense pact for the Western Hemisphere by the treaty of Rio de Janeiro.

The primary purpose of these agreements is to provide unmistakable proof of the joint determination of the free countries to resist armed attack from any quarter. Each country participating in these arrangements must contribute all it can to the common defense. If we can make it sufficiently clear, in advance, that any armed attack affecting our national security would be met with overwhelming force, the armed attack might never occur. I hope soon to send to the Senate a treaty respecting the North Atlantic security plan. In addition, we will provide military advice and equipment to free nations which will co-operate with us in the maintenance of peace and security.

Fourth, we must embark on a bold new program for making the benefits of our scientific advances and industrial progress available for the improvement and growth of underdeveloped areas. More than half the people of the world are living in conditions approaching misery. Their food is inadequate. They are victims of disease. Their economic life is primitive and stagnant. Their poverty is a handicap and a threat both to them and to more prosperous areas. For the first time in history, humanity possesses the knowledge and the skill to relieve the suffering of these people.

The United States is preeminent among nations in the development of industrial and scientific techniques. The material resources which we can afford to use for the assistance of other peoples are limited. But our imponderable resources in technical knowledge are constantly growing and are inexhaustible. I believe that we should make available to peace-loving peoples the benefits of our store of technical knowledge in order to help them realize their aspirations for a better life. And in cooperation with other nations, we should foster capital investment in areas needing development.

Our aim should be to help the free peoples of the world, through their own efforts, to produce more food, more clothing, more materials for housing, and more mechanical power to lighten their burdens. We invite other countries to pool their technological resources in this undertaking. Their contributions will be warmly welcomed. This should be a cooperative enterprise in which all nations work together through the United Nations and its specialized agencies wherever practicable. It must be a world-wide effort for the achievement of peace, plenty and freedom. With the cooperation of business, private capital, agriculture and labor in this country, this program can greatly increase the industrial activity in other nations and can raise substantially their standards of living.

Such new economic developments must be devised and controlled to benefit the peoples of the areas in which they are established. Guarantees to the investor must be balanced by guarantees in the interest of the people whose resources and whose labor go into these developments. The old imperialism—exploitation for foreign profit—has no place in our plans. What we envisage is a program of development based on the concepts of democratic fair dealing.

All countries, including our own, will greatly benefit from a constructive program for the better use of the world's human and natural resources. Experience shows that our commerce with other countries expands as they progress industrially and economically. Greater production is the key to prosperity and peace. And the key to greater production is a wider and more vigorous application of modern scientific and technical knowledge. Only by helping the least fortunate of its members to help themselves can the human family achieve the decent, satisfying life that is the right of all people.

Democracy alone can supply the vitalizing force to stir the peoples of the world into triumphant action, not only against their human oppressors, but also against their ancient enemies—hunger, misery and despair.

On the basis of these four major courses of action we hope to help create the conditions that will lead eventually to personal freedom and happiness for all mankind. If we are to be successful in carrying out these policies, it is clear that we must have continued prosperity in this country and we must keep ourselves strong. Slowly but surely we are weaving a world fabric of international security and growing prosperity.

We are aided by all who wish to live in freedom from fear—even by those who live today in fear under their own governments. We are aided by all who want relief from the lies of propaganda—who desire truth and sincerity. We are aided by all who desire self-government and a voice in deciding their own affairs. We are aided by all who long for economic security—for the security and abundance that men in free societies can enjoy. We are aided by all who desire freedom of speech, freedom of religion and freedom to live their own lives for useful ends. Our allies are the millions who hunger and thirst after righteousness.

In due time, as our stability becomes manifest, as more and more nations come to know the benefits of democracy and to participate in growing abundance, I believe that those countries which now oppose us will abandon their delusions and join with the free nations of the world in a just settlement of international differences.

Events have brought our American democracy to new influence and new responsibilities. They will test our courage, our devotion to duty and our concept of liberty. But I say to all men, what we have achieved in liberty, we will surpass in greater liberty. Steadfast in our faith in the Almighty, we will advance toward a world where man's freedom is secure. To that end we will devote our strength, our resources and our firmness of resolve. With God's help, the future of mankind will be assured in a world of justice, harmony and peace.

UNITED WE STAND SECURE [5]

WINSTON S. CHURCHILL [6]

The Right Honorable Winston S. Churchill, leader of the Opposition, British House of Commons, delivered this address at the Mid-Century Convocation of the Massachusetts Institute of Technology, Boston, Massachusetts, on March 31, 1949.

This visit was Mr. Churchill's fifth to the United States since the entry of this country into World War II. On December 26, 1941, he addressed a joint session of Congress.[7] On May 19, 1943, he again spoke to Congress, this time to assure America that Great Britain would stand firmly for united victory not only in Europe and Africa but also against Japan.[8] At Harvard, on September 6, 1943, on his third wartime trip to this country, he talked before Harvard University. Here he suggested that the British-American partnership be made permanent, and that the League of Nations, or some equivalent organization, should emerge.[9] In a fourth appearance in America, Churchill, who retired as Prime Minister in 1945, spoke at Westminster College, Fulton, Missouri, on March 5, 1946.[10] Here he bluntly advocated close accord between the two nations, a "fraternal association." He brought on his head much American criticism for his alleged proposal of an Anglo-American alliance.

The address of March 31, 1949, he delivered before an audience of almost fourteen thousand alumni and guests at Boston Garden, the largest sports arena in that city. Radio networks, television, and short wave enlarged his audience to several millions. Mr. Bernard Baruch, his American host on this trip, introduced him. On the platform were also Dr. Karl Compton, retiring president of Massachusetts Institute of Technology, and Dr. James Killian, who assumed the office of president of that institution on April 2.

Just as each previous visit of Churchill served an obvious political purpose, so this one was apparently timed to strengthen American public opinion in support of the North Atlantic Pact, signed four days later in Washington (April 4, 1949).

[5] This authoritative text as handed out by Mr. Churchill and later amended as the speech was broadcast was furnished with permission to reprint through the courtesy of Mr. D'Arcy Edmondson, of the British Information Services, 30 Rockefeller Plaza, New York.

[6] For biographical note, see Appendix.

[7] See *Representative American Speeches*: 1941-1942, p19-29.

[8] See *Representative American Speeches*: 1942-1943, p30-45.

[9] See *Representative American Speeches*: 1943-1944, p27-36.

[10] See *Representative American Speeches*: 1945-1946, p20-32.

The speech was in two distinct parts; the first, historical and analytical, to provide a background for the present Anglo-American policy; the second, to justify the treaty and to prophesy future accomplishments by these Western European allies. Forthright and unqualified was his denunciation of communism and the Kremlin leaders, coupled with his observation that "Europe would have been communized like Czechoslovakia and London under bombardment some time ago but for the deterrent of the atomic bomb in the hands of the United States."

The Churchillian ideas, language, and mode of presentation in this address had by no means diminished in their power despite the speaker's seventy-four years. He was ably expressing the traditions of Anglo-Saxon and Western European civilization. The historical resume was penetrating in its interpretation of events after 1900. Here as in his previous speeches was bluntness; humor ("I just had to pick up a few things as I went along"); his vindication of England; his high tribute to America; his confidence in the outcome despite his frank view of the major China disaster; his freedom from the usual oratorical platitudes; his concreteness; his use of literary allusions and Biblical expressions; his constant adjustment to his audience; and the climactic development of his discourse. The religious and philosophical overtone ("The flame of Christian ethics is still our highest guide") distinguishes the address.

The speaker embarked for England a few days later. The Boston address failed to evoke notable world-wide comment, either favorable or unfavorable, perhaps because the Washington treaty signing absorbed the press, radio, and current American thinking. Churchill at Boston, nevertheless, gave one of the strongest utterances of his career as political orator.

I am honored by your wish that I should take part in the discussions of the Massachusetts Institute of Technology. We have suffered in Great Britain by the lack of colleges of university rank in which engineering and the allied subjects are taught. Industrial production depends on technology and it is because the Americans, like the prewar Germans, have realized this and created institutions for the advanced training of large numbers of high-grade engineers to translate the advances of pure science into industrial technique, that their output per head and consequent standard of life are so high. It is surprising that England, which was the first country to be industrialized, has nothing of comparable stature. If tonight I strike other notes than those of material progress, it implies no want of admiration for all the work you have done and are doing. My aim, like yours, is to be guided by balance and proportion.

The outstanding feature of the twentieth century has been the enormous expansion in the numbers who are given the opportunity to share in the larger and more varied life which in previous periods was reserved for the few and for the very few. This process must continue at an increasing rate. If we are to bring the broad masses of the people in every land to the table of abundance, it can only be by the tireless improvement of all our means of technical production, and by the diffusion in every form of education of an improved quality to scores of millions of men and women. Even in this darkling hour I have faith that this will go on.

I rejoice in Tennyson's celebrated lines:

> Men, my brothers, men, the workers, ever reaping
> something new;
> That which they have done but earnest of the things
> that they shall do.

I was, however, a little disquieted, I must admit, that you find it necessary to debate the question, to quote Dr. Burchard's opening address, "whether the problem of world production yielding at least a minimum living to the whole population can be solved, and whether man has so destroyed the resources of his world that they may be doomed to die of starvation." If, with all the resources of modern science, we find ourselves unable to avert world famine, we shall all be to blame, but a peculiar responsibility would rest upon the scientists. I do not believe that they will fail, but if they do, or perhaps were not allowed to succeed, the consequences would be very unpleasant because it is quite certain that mankind would not agree to starve equally, and there might be some very sharp disagreements about how the last crust was to be shared. This would simplify our problem, as our greatest intellectual authorities here will readily admit, in an unduly primordial manner.

Ladies and Gentlemen, I feel somewhat overawed in addressing this vast scientific and learned audience on the subjects which your panels are discussing. I have no technical and no university education, and have just had to pick up a few things as I went along. Therefore I speak with a diffidence, which I hope to overcome as I proceed, on these profound scientific, social and philosophic issues, each of which claims a life-long study for itself, and are now to be examined, as schoolmen would say, not only in their integrity but in their relationship, meaning thereby not only one by one but all together.

I was so glad that in the first instance you asked me to talk about the past rather than to peer into the future because I know more about the past than I do about the future, and I was well content that the President of the United States, whose gift of prophecy was so remarkably vindicated by recent electoral results, should have accepted that task. We all regret that his heavy state duties prevent him from being here tonight. I shall therefore have to do a little of the peering myself.

Ladies and Gentlemen, for us in Britain the nineteenth century ended amid the glories of the Victorian era, and we entered upon the dawn of the twentieth in high hope for our country, our empire and the world. The latter and larger part of the nineteenth century had been the period of liberal advance (liberal with a small "l" please). In 1900 a sense of moving hopefully forward to brighter, broader and easier days was predominant. Little did we guess that what has been called the Century of the Common Man would witness as its outstanding feature more common men killing each other with greater facilities than any other five centuries put together in the history of the world. But we entered this terrible twentieth century with confidence. We thought that with improving transportation, nations would get to know each other better. We believed that as they got to know each other better they would like each other more, and that national rivalries would fade in a growing international consciousness. We took it almost for granted that science would confer continual boons and blessings upon us, would give us better meals, better garments and better dwellings for less trouble, and thus steadily shorten the hours of labor and leave more time for play, and culture. In the name of ordered but unceasing progress, we saluted the Age of Democracy, democracy ever expressing itself ever more widely through parliaments freely and fairly elected on a broad or universal franchise. We saw no reason why men and women should not shape their own home life and careers without being cramped by the growing complexity of the state, which was to be their servant and the protector of their rights. You had the famous American maxim "Governments derive their just powers from the consent of the governed," and we both noticed that the world was divided into peoples that owned the governments and governments that owned the peoples. At least I heard all this around that time and liked some of it very much.

I was a Minister in the British Liberal Government (large "L" this time please), returned with a great majority in 1906. That new Liberal Government arrived in power with much of its message already delivered and most of its aims already achieved. The days of hereditary aristocratic privilege were ended or numbered. The path was opened for talent in every field of endeavor. Primary education was compulsory, universal and free, or was about to become so. New problems arising from former successes awaited the new administration. The independence of the proletariat from thralldom involved at least a minimum standard of life and labor and security for old age, sickness, and the death of the family breadwinner. It was to these tasks of social reform and social insurance that we addressed ourselves. Ladies and Gentlemen, the name of Lloyd George will ever be associated in Great Britain with this new departure. I am proud to have been his lieutenant in this work and also later as a Conservative Chancellor of the Exchequer and later still as head of the wartime National Coalition to have carried these same themes further forward on a magnified scale. That is how we began the century.

Science presently placed novel and dangerous facilities in the hands of the most powerful countries. Humanity was informed that it could make machines that would fly through the air and vessels which could swim beneath the surfaces of the seas. The conquest of the air and the perfection of the art of flying fulfilled the dream which for thousands of years had glittered in human imagination. Certainly it was a marvellous and romantic event. Whether the bestowal of this gift upon an immature civilization composed of competing nations whose nationalism grew with every advance of democracy and who were as yet devoid of international organization, whether this gift was a blessing or a curse has yet to be proved. On the whole I remain an optimist. For good or for ill air mastery is today the supreme expression of military power, and fleets and armies, however vital and important, must accept a subordinate rank. This is a memorable milestone in the march of man.

The submarine, to do it justice, has never made any claim to be a blessing or even a convenience. I well remember when it became an accomplished military fact of peculiar military significance to the British Isles and to the British navy, there was a general belief even in the Admiralty where I presided, that no nation would ever be so wicked as to use these under-water vessels to sink merchantmen at sea. How could a submarine, it was asked, provide for the safety of the crews of the merchant ships it sank? Public opinion was shocked when old Admiral Fisher bluntly declared that this would be no bar to the submarines being used by the new and growing German navy in a most ruthless manner. His prediction was certainly not stultified by what was soon to happen.

Here, then, we have these two novel and potent weapons placed in the hands of highly nationalized sovereign states in the early part of the twentieth century, and both of them dwell with us today for our future edification.

A third unmeasured sphere opened to us as the years passed, which, for the sake of comprehensive brevity, I will describe as radar. This radar, with its innumerable variants and possibilities, has so far been the handmaiden of the air, but it has also been the enemy of the submarine and in alliance with the air may well prove its exterminator.

But we see the changes which were brought upon our century. In the first half of the twentieth century, fanned by the crimson wings of war, the conquest of the air affected profoundly human affairs. It made the globe seem much bigger to the mind and much smaller to the body. The human biped was able to travel about far more quickly. This greatly reduced the size of his estate, while at the same time creating an even keener sense of its exploitable value. In the nineteenth century, Jules Verne wrote "Round the World in Eighty Days." It seemed a prodigy. Now you can get round it in four; but you do not see much of it on your way. The whole prospect and outlook of mankind grew immeasurably larger, and the multiplication of ideas also proceeded at an incredible rate. This vast expansion was unhappily not accompanied by any noticeable advance in the stature of man, either in his mental faculties, or his moral character. His brain got no better, but it buzzed the more. The scale of events around him assumed gigantic proportions while he remained about the same size.

By comparison therefore he actually became much smaller. We no longer had great men directing manageable affairs. Our need was to discipline an array of gigantic and turbulent facts. To this task we have certainly so far proved unequal. Science bestowed immense new powers on man and at the same time created conditions which were largely beyond his comprehension and still more beyond his control. While he nursed the illusion of growing mastery and exulted in his new trappings, he became the sport and presently the victim of tides and currents, of whirlpools and tornadoes amid which he was far more helpless than he had been for a long time.

Hopeful developments in many directions were proceeding in 1914 on both sides of the Atlantic and they seemed to point to an age of peace and plenty when suddenly violent events broke in upon them. For more than twenty years there had been no major war in Europe. Indeed since the Civil War in the United States, there had been no great struggle in the West. A spirit of adventure stirred the minds of men and was by no means allayed by the general advance of prosperity and science. On the contrary prosperity meant power, and science offered weapons. We read in the Bible "Jeshurun waxed fat and kicked." For several generations Britannia had ruled the waves—for long periods at less cost annually than that of a single modern battleship.

History, I think, Ladies and Gentlemen, will say that this great trust was not abused. American testimony about the early period of the Monroe Doctrine is upon record. There was the suppression of the slave trade and piracy. During our prolonged period of naval supremacy undeterred by the rise of foreign tariffs, we kept our ports freely opened to the commerce of the world. Our colonial and oriental empire, even our coastal trade, was free to the shipping of all the nations on equal terms. We in no way sought to obstruct the rise of other states or navies. For nearly the whole of the nineteenth century the monopoly of sea power in British hands was a trust discharged faithfully in the general interest. But now in the first decade of the twentieth century with new patterns of warships, naval rivalries became acute and fierce. Civilized governments began to think in dreadnoughts. It was in such a setting very difficult to prevent the first World War. Far more difficult than it would have been to prevent the second.

There was of course one way—one way then *as now*—the creation of an international instrument, strong enough to adjust the disputes of nations and enforce its decisions against an aggressor. Much wisdom, eloquence and earnest effort was devoted to this theme in which the United States took the lead, but we only go as far as the World Court at the Hague and improvements in the Geneva Convention. The impulses towards a trial of strength in Europe were far stronger at this time. Germany, demanding her "place in the sun," was faced by a resolute France with her military honor to regain. England, in accordance with her foreign policy of three hundred years, sustained the weaker side. France found an ally in the Russia of the Czars and Germany in the crumbling empire of the Hapsburgs. The United States, for reasons which were natural and traditional, but no longer so valid as in the past, stood aloof and expected to be able to watch as a spectator, the thrilling, fearful drama unfold from across what was then called "the broad Atlantic." These expectations, as you perhaps may remember, were not borne out by what happened.

After four and a half years of hideous mechanical slaughter, illuminated by infinite sacrifice, but not remarkably relieved by strategy or generalship, high hopes and spacious opportunities awaited the victorious allies when they assembled at Versailles. War, stripped of every pretention of glamor or romance had been brought home to the masses of the peoples and brought home in forms never before experienced except by the defeated.

To stop another war was the supreme object and duty of the statesmen who met as friends and allies around the peace table. They made great errors. The doctrine of self-determination was not the remedy for Europe, which needed then above all things, unity and larger groupings. The idea that the vanquished could pay the expenses of the victors was a destructive and crazy delusion. The failure to strangle bolshevism at its birth and to bring Russia, then prostrate, by one means or another, into the general democratic system lies heavy upon us today. Nevertheless the statesman at Versailles, largely at the inspiration of President Wilson, an inspiration implemented effectively by British thought, created the League of Nations. This is their defense before history, and had the League been resolutely sustained and used, it would have saved us all.

This was not to be. Another ordeal even more appalling than the first lay before us. Even when so much else had failed we could have obtained a prolonged peace, lasting all our lives at least, simply by keeping Germany disarmed in accordance with the Treaty, and by treating her with justice and magnanimity. This latter condition was very nearly achieved at Locarno in 1925, but the failure to enforce the disarmament clauses and above all to sustain the League of Nations, both of which purposes could easily have been accomplished, brought upon us the second World War. Once again the English speaking world gloriously but narrowly emerged, bleeding and breathless, but united as we never were before. This unity is our present salvation, because after all our victories, we are now faced by perils, both grave and near, and by problems more dire than have ever confronted Christian civilization, even in this twentieth century of storm and change.

There remains, however, a key of deliverance. It is the same key which was searched for by those who labored to set up the World Court at the Hague in the early years of the century. It is the same conception which animated President Wilson and his colleagues at Versailles, namely the creation of a world instrument capable at least of giving to all its members security against aggression. The United Nations organization which has been erected under the inspiring leadership of my great wartime friend, President Roosevelt, that organization which took the place of the former League, has so far been rent and distracted by the antagonism of Soviet Russia and by the fundamental schism which has opened between communism and the rest of mankind. But we must not despair. We must persevere, and if the gulf continues to widen, we must make sure that the cause of freedom is defended by all the resources of combined forethought and superior science. Here lies the best hope of averting a third world struggle, and a sure means of coming through it without being enslaved or destroyed.

One of the questions which you are debating here is defined as "the failure of social and political institutions to keep pace with material and technical change." Scientists should never underrate the deep-seated qualities of human nature and how, repressed in one direction, they will certainly break out in another. The *genus homo*—if I may display my Latin, I have some, not much—is a tough creature who has traveled here by a very long road. His nature has been shaped and his virtues ingrained by many millions of years of struggle, fear and pain, and his spirit has, from the earliest dawn of history, shown itself upon occasion capable of mounting to the sublime, far above material conditions or mortal terrors. He still remains—man still remains —as Pope described him two hundred years ago:

> Placed on this isthmus of a middle state
> A being darkly wise and rudely great
> Created half to rise and half to fall
> Great lord of all things, yet a prey to all.
> Sole judge of truth in endless error hurled
> The glory, jest and riddle of the world.

In his introductory address, Dr. Burchard, the Dean of Humanities, spoke with awe of "an approaching scientific ability to control men's thoughts with precision." I shall be very content, personally, if my task in this world is done before that happens. Laws just or unjust may govern men's actions. Tyrannies may restrain or regulate their words. The machinery of propaganda may pack their minds with falsehood and deny them truth for many generations of time. But the soul of man thus held in a trance or frozen in a long night can be awakened by a spark coming from God knows where, and in a moment the whole structure of lies and oppression is on trial for its life. Peoples in bondage need never despair. Let them hope and trust in the genius of mankind. Science no doubt could if sufficiently perverted exterminate us all, but it is not in the power of material forces at present or in any period which the youngest here tonight need take into practical account, to alter permanently the main elements in human nature or restrict the infinite variety of forms in which the soul and genius of the human race can and will express itself.

How right you are, Dr. Compton, in this great institution of technical study and achievement to keep a Dean of Humanities and give him so commanding a part to play in your discussions! No technical knowledge can outweigh knowledge of the humanities in the gaining of which philosophy and history walk hand in hand. Our inheritance of well-founded, slowly conceived codes of honor, morals and manners, the passionate convictions which so many hundreds of millions share together of the principles of freedom and justice, are far more precious to us than anything which scientific discoveries could bestow. Those whose minds are attracted or compelled to rigid and symmetrical systems of government should remember that logic, like science, must be the servant and not the master of man. Human beings and human societies are not structures that are built or machines that are forged. They are plants that grow and must be tended as such. Life is a test and this world a place of trial. Always the problems, or it may be the same problem, will be presented to every generation in different forms. The problems of victory may even be more baffling than those of defeat. However much the conditions change, the supreme question is how we live and grow and bloom and die, and how far each human life conforms to standards which are not wholly related to space or time.

And here I speak not only to those who enjoy the blessings and consolation of revealed religion but also to those who face the mysteries of human destiny alone. I say that the flame of Christian ethics is still our highest guide. To guard and cherish it is our first interest, both spiritually and materially. The fulfillment of spiritual duty in our daily life is vital to our survival.

Only by bringing it into perfect application can we hope to solve for ourselves the problems of this world and not of this world alone.

Ladies and Gentlemen, I cannot speak to you here tonight without expressing to the United States—as I have perhaps some right to do—the thanks of Britain and of Europe for the splendid part America is playing in the world. Many nations have risen to the summit of human affairs, but here is a great example where new-won supremacy has not been used for self-aggrandisement but only for further sacrifice.

Three years ago I made a speech at Fulton under the auspices of President Truman. Many people here and in my own country were startled and even shocked by what I said. But events have vindicated and fulfilled in much detail the warnings which I deemed it my duty to give at that time.

Today there is a very different climate of opinion. I am in cordial accord with much that is being done. We have, as dominating facts, the famous Marshall Aid, the new unity in Western Europe and now the Atlantic Pact. How has this tremendous change in our outlook and policy been accomplished? The responsible ministers in all the countries concerned deserve high credit. There is credit enough for all. In my own country the Foreign Secretary, Mr. Bevin, who has come here to sign the Atlantic Pact, has shown himself indifferent to mere party popularity in dealing with these great national issues. He has shown himself, like many American public men, above mere partisan interest in dealing with these national and world issues. No one could, however, have brought about these immense changes in the feeling of the United States, of Great Britain, and of Europe, but for the astounding policy of the Russian Soviet Government. We may well ask, "Why have they deliberately acted so as to unite the free world against them?" It is certainly not because there are not very able men among them. Why then have they done it? I will offer you my own answer to this strange conundrum. It is because they fear the friendship of the West more than its hostility. They cannot afford to allow free and friendly intercourse to grow up between the vast area they control and the civilization of the West. The Russian people must not see what is going on outside, and the world must not see what goes on inside the Soviet domain. Thirteen men in the Kremlin, holding down hundreds of millions of people and aiming at the rule of the world, feel that at all costs they must keep up the barriers. Self-preservation, not for Russia but for themselves, lies at the root and is the explanation of their sinister and malignant policy.

In consequence of the Soviet conduct the relations of Communist Russia with the other great powers of the world are without precedent in history. Measures and counter-measures have been taken on many occasions which in any previous period could only have meant or accompanied armed conflict. The situation has been well described by distinguished Americans as the "cold war." And the question is asked, "Are we winning the cold war?" Well, this cannot be decided by looking at Europe alone. We must also look at Asia. The worst disaster since our victory has been the collapse of China under Communist attack and intrigue. China, in which the United States has always taken a high interest, comprises an immese part of the population of the world. The absorption of China and of India into the Kremlin-controlled Communist empire, would certainly bring measureless bloodshed and misery to eight or nine hundred million people.

On the other hand the position in Europe has so far been successfully maintained. The prodigious effort of the Berlin Air Lift has carried us through the winter. Time, though dearly bought, has been gained for peace. The efficiency of the American and British Air Forces has been proved and improved. Most of all the spectacle of the British and Americans trying to feed the two million Germans in Berlin, in their zone in Berlin, while the Soviet Government was trying to starve them, has been an object lesson to the German people far beyond anything that words could convey. I trust that small and needless provocations of German sentiment may be avoided by the Western powers. The revival and union of Europe cannot be achieved without the earnest and freely given aid of the German people. This has certainly been demonstrated by the Berlin Air Lift which has fully justified itself. Nevertheless fear and its shadows brood over Western Europe today. A month ago in Brussels I spoke to a meeting of thirty thousand Belgians. I could feel at once their friendship and their anxiety. They have no Atlantic Ocean, no English Channel, between them and the Russian Communist armored divisions. Yet they bravely and ardently support the cause of United Europe. I admire them. I was also conscious of the hope and faith which they, like the Greek people, place in the United States. I can see the movement of this vast crowd when I spoke of the hands, strong hands, stretched out across the ocean. You have great responsibilities there for much faith is placed upon you.

We are now confronted with something quite as wicked, but in some ways more formidable than Hitler, because Hitler had only the Herrenvolk pride and anti-Semitic hatred to exploit. He had no fundamental theme. But these thirteen men in the Kremlin have their hierarchy and a church of Communist adepts, whose missionaries are in every country as a Fifth Column, obscure people but awaiting the day when they hope to be the absolute masters of their fellow-countrymen and pay off old scores. They have their anti-God religion and their Communist doctrine of the entire subjugation of the individual to the state. And behind this stands the largest army in the world, in the hands of a government pursuing imperialist expansion, as no Czar or Kaiser had ever done.

I must not conceal from you the truth as I see it. It is certain that Europe would have been communized in Czechoslovakia and London under bombardment some time ago but for the deterrent of the atomic bomb in the hands of the United States.

Another question is also asked. Is time on our side? That is not a question that can be answered except within strict limits. We have certainly not an unlimited period of time before a settlement should be achieved. The utmost vigilance should be practiced but I do not think myself that violent or precipitate action should be taken now. War is not inevitable. The Germans have a wise saying, "The trees do not grow up to the sky." Often something happens to turn or mitigate the course of events. Four or five hundred years ago Europe seemed about to be conquered by the Mongols. Two great battles were fought almost on the same day near Vienna and in Poland. In both of these the chivalry and armed power of Europe was completely shattered by the Asiatic hordes—mounted archers. It seemed that nothing could avert the doom of the famous continent from which modern civilization and culture have spread throughout the world. But at the critical moment something happened— the Great Khan died. The succession was vacant and the Mongol armies and their leaders trooped back on their ponies across the seven thousand miles which separated them from their capital in order to choose a successor. They never returned—till now.

We need not abandon hope or patience. Many favorable processes are on foot. Under the impact of communism all the free nations are being welded together as they never have been before and never could be, but for the harsh external pressure to which they are being subjected. We have no hostility to the Russian people and no desire to deny them their legitimate rights and security. I hoped that Russia, after the war, would have access, through unfrozen waters, into every ocean, guaranteed by the World Organization of which she would be a leading member; I hoped that she would have the freest access, which indeed she has at the present time, to raw materials of every kind; and that the Russians everywhere would be received as brothers in the human family. That still remains our aim and ideal. We seek nothing from Russia but good will and fair play. If, however, there is to be a war of nerves let us make sure our nerves are strong and are fortified by the deepest convictions of our hearts. If we persevere steadfastly together, and allow no appeasement of tyranny and wrong-doing in any form, it may not be our nerve or the structure of our civilization which will break; something else may happen and peace may yet be preserved.

This is a hard experience in the life of the world. After our great victory, which we believed would decide the struggle for freedom for our time at least, we thought we had deserved better of fortune. But unities and associations are being established by many nations throughout the free world with a speed and reality which would not have been achieved perhaps for generations. Of all these unities the one most precious to me, to use an expression I used first at Harvard six years ago, is the fraternal association between the British Commonwealth of Nations and the United States. Do not, my friends I beg you, underrate the strength of Britain. As I said at Fulton, "Do not suppose that half a century from now you will not see seventy or eighty millions of Britons spread about the world and united in defense of our traditions, our way of life, and the world causes which you and we espouse." United we stand secure.

Let us then move forward together in discharge of our mission and our duty, fearing God and nothing else.

MAJOR PROBLEMS IN THE UNITED STATES
FOREIGN POLICIES [11]

FRANCIS B. SAYRE [12]

The honorable Francis B. Sayre gave this address at the Third Annual Conference on Public Affairs, at Ohio State University, Columbus, Ohio, on March 5, 1949.

This conference, under the auspices of the Speech Department of Ohio State University, was typical of the intercollegiate discussional programs sponsored by speech departments after the close of World War II. The conference subject focussed on major problems of United States foreign policy in 1949. Some fifty colleges participated. There were open hearings with statements by some eleven authorities on phases of foreign policy. These were supplemented by party caucuses of the Right of Center, Center, and Left of Center groups. Steering committees functioned. The conference concluded with extended general assemblies and an all-conference luncheon, at the Deshler-Wallick Hotel, on which occasion Mr. Sayre spoke.

The students in this three-day program thus came to grips with significant aspects of foreign policy; had direct contact with the ideas and personalities of important leaders, both civil and military; had considerable experience in applying discussion techniques related to cooperative thinking and action; had experience in debating and persuasive speaking in the public assemblies; practiced parliamentary law; and, in general, demonstrated the application of general education to the exercise of social and political responsibility.

Francis B. Sayre, at the time of this speech, represented the United States Delegation to the Third General Assembly of the United Nations. He had had wide experience in diplomatic assignments both in Europe and the Orient. Back of his address at Columbus was a long and active record in dealing with international problems.

Comments Dr. H. F. Harding, of Ohio State University:

> Mr. Sayre impresses you as a speaker who has spent long years in a college lecture hall. He was, as you know, professor of criminal law at Harvard Law School for about fifteen years before he entered the diplomatic service. His voice is strong and his projection is excellent. He has a way of emphasizing and varying the voice so that it is not at all difficult to under-

[11] Text supplied through the courtesy of Dr. H. F. Harding and permission to reprint given by Francis B. Sayre.

[12] For biographical note, see Appendix.

stand him. The total impression is that of a scholarly person who is sure of his data and has taken great pains to present all details in proper relation to the central idea. The essential characteristics of Sayre as a speaker center around simplicity of statement, logical structure, excellent choice of examples and to use the legal phrase the doctrine of *res ipsa loquitur*—the facts speak for themselves.[13]

It is an honor and a privilege to be invited to meet with you, representatives from some fifty colleges, in this Conference on Major Problems in United States Foreign Policy. I am particularly delighted to have the chance of discussing these problems with you; for America has a right to look to her college trained men for wise leadership and help in the days ahead. As frankly and as simply as I can, I want to lay before you the fundamental issues as I see them.

We are living in an age of problems because we are in an age of revolutionary change. Sometimes I am sure you feel, as I do, that there is not a corner of the world that is not boiling today with unprecedented events. Our country's relationships with over fifty different nations present over fifty different problems, some small and some great. But there is only one today that is really paramount. It overshadows and colors and generally distorts every other one with which we have to deal.

The supreme problem of our time is the struggle between Communists and freedom-loving peoples. The issue depends upon whether communism constitutes, as claimed by the Soviet Government and its followers in other countries, a means of deliverance and of human progress, or whether it marks the pathway to human bondage, the inevitable concomitant of the police state. What shall be America's attitude and what her concrete program? The answer to this fundamental issue must inevitably determine and shape during our time the foreign relationships between the Soviet Union and its satellites on the one hand, and all democratic and free countries on the other.

Our Western world, endowed with the priceless heritage of Greco-Roman civilization, for centuries has fought and sacrificed in the age-old struggle for human freedom. We have come to

[13] Letter to this editor, May 24, 1949. Quoted by permission. For further comment on Francis B. Sayre, see *Representative American Speeches*: 1941-1942, p179-89.

believe in this as one of the most precious things in life. Today our western civilization is struggling to defend against virulent attack human liberty, the rights of small nations, the rule of law and of right and of conscience as opposed to might.

The Soviet leaders, whatever their professions, have in their concrete deeds violated and denied the right of freedom. Emerging from the second World War, Soviet Russia has brought under its rule some five hundred million people of over twelve countries by methods of terrorism and fear. Human freedom no longer exists among those peoples who once formed the independent states of Latvia, Esthonia and Lithuania, but who now are living repressed under Soviet rule. Human freedom, as we understand it, no longer exists in Poland, or Czechoslovakia, in Hungary or Bulgaria, or in the other countries behind the Iron Curtain. The Soviet Government is seeking by every ruthless means to extend this rule. Its followers are attempting to overrun China. It is seeking, like an octopus, to envelop Greece and Korea. It is attempting, through its agents, to work its way into Indonesia. It is attempting to threaten Norway and Sweden and Italy and every country where weakness offers opportunity. Those whom it has enveloped have lost freedom of speech, freedom of religion, and even in many cases freedom of movement.

The head-on conflict between these two great forces,—communism against free democracy—is the supreme issue of our day. Make no mistake about it. The forces of communism are bent upon wrecking those countries which uphold western civilization and the philosophy upon which it is built; and, although the Communists may not be putting soldiers in the field, they are just as surely waging active war against western civilization with all the forces and methods at their command. The Communists, in truth, are today working out new tactics for gaining their objective of world mastery which, unless effectively combated, are potentially more deadly than the old-fashioned method of battleships and guns. Our supreme problem of foreign policy is how we, in our own self-interest, can best assist those who, like us, are determined to defend human liberty and the noble heritage of western civilization against the insidious attack of communism.

The fundamental conflict, you see, is not between two great peoples. It is a struggle between two fundamentally conflicting philosophies—belief in a world of moral law and ordered justice as against a world of terrorism and the rule of sheer force. In this there is nothing new. From time immemorial this struggle has been going on; and it is only because peoples through the years have felt that human freedom and a rule of law are more precious than life itself and have again and again been willing to fight and die, if need be, in their defense that western civilization as we know it has evolved.

How are we to meet this paramount problem of our day? What practical and concrete steps are we to take? Two opposite courses have been advocated, the one a policy of compromise, the other a policy of war.

Those who support the first course point out the undeniable fact that we cannot rid ourselves of the problem. We have to learn to live together, whether we like it or not. Therefore, they say, there is compelling necessity for us to work out some kind of compromise.

But the experience of the last few years, and particularly the experience at Paris last autumn in the General Assembly, shows the futility of trying to reach a compromise with the policies at present being followed by the Soviet Government. As long as these are pursued, the differences are too radical and too basic.

You cannot, for instance, compromise on the issue of freedom of religion. Either you have it or you do not have it. Restraints and curbs, even though partial, spell denial of freedom. A secret police with despotic power, even though that power is curbed, is still a secret police subject to all of its abuses. Government, unchecked by constitutional safeguards of law and by courts freely accessible to all, is, and always will be, despotism. The trial of Cardinal Mindszenty in Hungary and the trials currently being staged in Bulgaria reveal the hollowness and the mockery of so-called justice when the decisions of courts depend not upon law but upon orders from state dictators. The philosophy that the state is supreme over everything else cannot possibly be reconciled with a philosophy built upon the supreme value of human personality.

With the great masses of Russian people we have no quarrel. But, unhappily, we have no way of reaching them. For centuries they have been kept in ignorance and darkness, largely cut off from vital contacts with other peoples. They were scarcely touched by the great civilization of Rome. The Renaissance and the humanistic movements of the fifteenth and sixteenth centuries, sweeping across Western Europe, never reached the rank and file of Russian people. Their present government is still keeping them separated from the warm currents of human intercourse flowing outside. The Soviet Government is isolating itself in the world as it is isolating itself in the United Nations. Manifestly, it is either not yet alive to the international responsibilities of the twentieth century world, or, if it is, it has determined that such responsibilities are in conflict with its own ambitions.

There should be no insoluble problem standing between East and West. The Russian people fought valiantly as our Allies during the last war and helped to win the victory. Between our two peoples there has always been a strong tradition of friendship.

If the Soviet Government makes clear by action rather than by words her respect for fundamental human rights and her willingness to cooperate in the building of a world based upon law and human freedom, the United States stands always ready to meet her more than half way. A simple change of conduct in Berlin or at Lake Success would pave the way. Then we would have not compromise, but cooperation.

A second and very different policy from that of compromise is a frank recourse to arms. As already suggested, our experience of the past two years makes it clear that compromise with the present policies being pursued by the Soviet Government is impossible. It is equally clear that the Soviet Government is bent upon aggressive action; and, since the appeal to reason has proved utterly unavailing, it is argued that there is only one practical way to stop the Russian advance—superior physical force. Therefore, the conclusion is reached that since American foreign policy must above all else be realistic, the only course open to us is the protection of our nation and our civilization by armed force. The United Nations, it is argued, has again and again manifested its impotency and its inability to prevent Soviet aggression. Czechoslovakia cried to the United Nations. But Czechoslovakia is in chains and Jan Marsaryk is dead. Hence, it is said, armed force is the only answer. That is the only language the Russians understand. Let us be realistic.

But the trouble is that such a policy assumes that a smashing victory over Russia would destroy communism. That is not true. The conflict is not between two peoples but between two fundamentally opposed philosophies. It is not as simple as if we were back in the nineteenth century fighting an enemy within their own borders. Our real enemy is communism. Ideas cannot be downed by force. War is not a practical way to stop the spread of communism. Communism battens on war.

Moreover, a third World War could only be a tragic catastrophe to the civilization we would give our lives to protect. Out of the ghastly ruins of such a war communism or something uglier would lift its head.

The scrapping of the United Nations by the resort to arms therefore offers no positive solution to the problem now facing us; nor does it assure the real protection of western civilization.

In what direction, then, must we turn?

All of the western world is looking to the United States for leadership. Our vast preponderance in wealth, in natural resources, and in population, and also our history and present strategic position thrust upon us, whether we like it or not, responsibility for leadership. Once before the youthful American nation, consecrated to the ideal of human liberty, was the hope of the world. Now, in a far more crucial struggle, the eyes of all who believe in human liberty and democracy are again upon us. Grounded in the faith of our fathers, believing passionately in human freedom and in the brotherhood of man as taught by the Christian religion, we dare not fail. But which way shall we lead?

Since a genuine solution is to be found neither in compromising with the present policies of the Soviet Government nor in the opposite course of a resort to arms, wise leadership, it seems clear, must struggle to find some middle course other than compromise and other than war. Such a program the United States is boldly developing. Its main points are these:

First, we must consecrate ourselves wholeheartedly and unswervingly to the support of the United Nations.

The nineteenth century world of separate and more or less isolated national units is gone. That was a world which knew nothing of modern electricity or airplanes or radios; when it took more than a week to get news across the Atlantic Ocean. Out of such a world were naturally evolved theories of national sovereignty absolute in its nature and practices based upon the geographical fact of comparative isolation. But under the facts of today nations can no longer live separate, isolated existences, competing each for selfish, superior power over rivals. We have reached an age when, whether we like it or not, if our civilization is to survive, collaboration among peoples for the service of humanity must take the place of power politics for selfish national ends. Call it humanitarianism—the service of humanity —or call it by the Christian name of brotherhood—this is the goal toward which our twentieth century world is moving, and must move, if we are to survive.

The nation which plays a lone hand for stakes of selfish power is bound to lose in the twentieth century world. The dice are heavily loaded against her. The United States, dreaming of economic self-sufficiency, attempted a long-range policy of selfish isolation in the years between the two World Wars. In spite of our matchless power and wealth, the attempt ended in utter failure. The Iron Curtain is another attempt. It also will end in failure.

Since the second World War a new world is emerging, a world built upon global concepts of international obligation.

The international trusteeship system is an instance of this twentieth century trend. Under the United Nations the old nineteenth century colonialism is being supplanted in the trust territories by a new machinery, to prevent every form of human exploitation, and to promote the political, economic, social and educational advancement of some sixteen million inhabitants.

Or, again, take the recent resolution now before the Economic and Social Council to find practical means for raising the standards of living in underdeveloped areas by providing needed technological and other assistance.

Under twentieth century realities we are coming to realize that unless we can achieve uninterrupted and effective international collaboration, our present civilization, built upon the increasing interdependence of all peoples and races, cannot possibly progress. And the United Nations is today the *only* organized governmental world machinery in existence for making possible effective international collaboration. It is the hope of the world.

I well realize the current feeling of frustration in many minds about the United Nations. But the United Nations is a growing organism. For one so young, it has displayed a surprising and unexpected vitality and strength. Its very imperfections are a challenge to your generation. It can be improved.

The one chance of winning Russia to reason is through the debates within the United Nations.

If I may digress for a moment I would like to tell you what happened last autumn during the General Assembly meeting in Paris. In spite of the pessimistic reports that went out, the meeting achieved telling and substantial results. The chief protagonists were talking and not fighting. Each was forced to lay before the bar of public opinion its actions and its policies and to find justification for them insofar as possible. The votes taken at Paris were highly significant.

First of all, the General Assembly approved the International Control Plan developed by the Atomic Energy Commission. The vote was forty to six, only the Soviet bloc voting against it. One may hope that, as a result of this overwhelming expression of world opinion, the Soviet Union may find a way to reconsider its position so as to permit atomic energy to be controlled for peace.

Another important vote was taken on the armaments question. The Soviet proposal to reduce armaments by one third, without any system of effective international inspection and verification, convinced practically everyone of the insincerity and hypocrisy of Soviet aims. The Assembly, instead, passed a constructive resolution looking towards the checking and publication of full information with regard to existing armaments by an international organ of control. The vote was forty-three in favor and only the Soviet bloc against.

Next, the General Assembly, over the protest of the Soviet Government and its satellites, voted forty-seven to six to place the guilt for the border disturbances in Greece squarely upon Albania, Yugoslavia, and Bulgaria. Although the Greek case is not settled, the Balkan Commission has been reconstituted for another year. It is doubtful if Greece would be independent today were it not for the United Nations.

A fourth important vote, forty-eight to six this time, declared in unequivocal terms the legality of the Government of the Republic of Korea which had been set up with the assistance of a United Nations Commission.

From these examples you can see how the debates at Paris helped to consolidate and unify the policies of those countries genuinely seeking world peace, as they illumined the hypocrisy of those nations seeking purely selfish ends. The practical unanimity recorded in vote after vote, with only the Soviet bloc voting in opposition, was convincing proof of solid achievement. The Kremlin cannot afford to ignore what happened in Paris.

The recent achievement of a truce in Palestine was brought about through the patient striving of the United Nations. Were it not for the United Nations there seems little doubt but that Jew and Arab would be fighting on the plains of Palestine today. Indeed, without the United Nations the area of sanguinary fighting by this time might well be extended in the Middle East considerably beyond the confines of Palestine.

To consolidate and unify the policies and thus to strengthen the action of those countries seeking a world peace based upon law, it is a cardinal principle of American foreign policy to fortify and wholeheartedly support the United Nations.

Second, the United States will continue to throw its full weight behind the program for European economic recovery. As a result of the most disastrous and destructive conflict in history, the nations of Western Europe were left at the end of the second World War economically prostrate. Unemployment and economic ruin stared them in the face.

Since the end of the war already much has been accomplished in the way of industrial rehabilitation. But much remains to be done. Unless the countries of Western Europe can be successfully assisted to their feet so as to permit again the effective functioning of their machinery of production and thus enable them to regain their economic strength, it will be most difficult for them to withstand Russia's advance or contribute to the defense of western civilization.

We have heard the Soviet propaganda that the shipments of American machinery and industrial goods to Europe are being made to dump unneeded surpluses for the economic advantage of the United States. But the fact that large proportions of these goods are in short supply and vociferously demanded by important American industrial and agricultural groups gives the lie to such a smear campaign. It is sheer nonsense to claim that such shipments are a phase of economic imperialism to gain an American strangle-hold over European industry. The American objective is manifestly not to weaken, but to strengthen the European economy and to assist in building it again into a highly productive and self-reliant economy. The Marshall Plan is built upon the hard-headed realization that in our twentieth century civilization no nation can live unto itself alone, that we all sink or swim together, that not even the wealthiest nation can prosper if large populations are desperately hungry and in need in other parts of the world, that the wisest and most rewarding, if not the only safe, national policy today is a humanitarian policy. As part of the project, so that these deliveries will not lead to pauperization and permanent dependency, the shipments are being made on the express condition that the receiving nations themselves collaborate in determining what their own contributions shall be, each to the other, in order to build up a unified Europe, and in planning the organization of a European economy which will become at the earliest date possible independent of further American aid.

The United States is equally concerned in the proposed "regional arrangement" of Western Europe, the so-called Western European Union. The objective of this cooperative enterprise is not the setting up of a military alliance to threaten the security of other states. It is not a move for selfish power to impose its will through armed force on unwilling peoples. It is rather a cooperative movement by free peoples, through common effort and collaboration, to crash through much of the outlived political and economic nationalism which once held them apart. It is a movement of great promise and of hope. It is an effort in the spirit of the twentieth century to give to peoples a freer and more spacious life and at the same time a higher degree of security under which to work.

It is one of the fundamentals of United States policy to support and, in so far as possible, to assist in those "regional arrangements," set up under Chapter VIII of the Charter, for the strengthening of peace foundations to make possible a more gracious life for men and women everywhere.

Third, although, as I have already suggested, superior armed force alone will not afford to twentieth century life the security which is necessary if our civilization is to progress, nevertheless, as long as the present East-West conflict continues, we cannot afford to strip ourselves of our defenses. In frontier days men of peace often found it necessary to build stockades against attack. Both for our own sake and for that of freedom everywhere we must keep our nation strong to resist aggression.

Western Europe and the United States have the heritage of a common civilization to defend. It is to the very manifest interest of the United States to make common cause with Western Europe in lessening the chance of Soviet attack. If the United States can strengthen the capacity and the will of freedom-loving nations to defend themselves against aggression, it thereby increases to that extent the power of the United Nations, in the words of the Charter, "to save succeeding generations from the scourge of war."

The organization of a well-armed North Atlantic Security Pact is not a resort to arms. Its purpose is precisely the opposite

—to prevent war by making the Soviet Government realize the futility of attack.

In the formulation of a proposed North Atlantic Pact it has been made unmistakably clear that the purpose of the Pact is defense and not offense. A North Atlantic Security Pact must be understood as part of a program not to supplant, but to operate *under*, the United Nations.

Fourth, more important than all else must be a policy of aggressive activity throughout the world for the establishment and the strengthening of the fundamental principles in which we believe—human freedom, justice, genuine world brotherhood. We must be missionaries for human freedom.

The ultimate issue between the forces of communism and democracy will be decided not by armies and atomic bombs. Those philosophies and those basic ideas will ultimately triumph which contain within themselves the inherent power to capture the imaginations and stir the deep desires of men and women throughout the world. How vital is man's faith in human freedom? If this be his ultimate desire, no communistic aggression, no hypocritical propaganda, no terrorism or trickery, can ultimately capture the citadel of man's soul.

Again and again history has proved that ideas and ideals are more powerful than armies—that no dictator can make himself supreme master of the world by force alone.

Western democracy has swept the world because in our experience men and women have believed in human freedom and justice and democracy so passionately that they have been willing to die for them. These will surely triumph over communism too if only we aggressively and passionately carry them into the four corners of the world. History down through the centuries has proved again and again that there can be but one outcome to a struggle for selfish power against forces fighting to protect and advance human rights. Those genuinely serving humanity always emerge ultimately triumphant.

Our task then must be to find a way to prevent war from blazing up, and to spread the faith of democracy and human liberty. Our policy toward Russia must be one of firmness, but at the same time one of understanding and of tolerance. We need Russia's assistance and cooperation in reconstructing Europe and in the gigantic job of building a lasting peace. We must win the Russian people's help if we can. We have no right to conclude that this is impossible.

America is a Christian nation. American foreign policy must be foundationed essentially upon Christian fundamentals. Upon that path we must go forward unflinchingly and unafraid. Otherwise, we must forfeit our leadership.

In conclusion, then, may I recapitulate in summary form the four cardinal points in American foreign policy:

First, to build up and fortify in every way possible the youthful and developing United Nations organization;

Second, to continue our full support to ERP and to the movement toward a Western European Union so as to help unify and strengthen the countries of Western Europe;

Third, to assist in establishing an effective North Atlantic Security Pact under the Charter of the United Nations in order to make strong the bastions of human freedom and thus to lessen the likelihood of war;

Fourth, to find ways and means of aggressive action to spread and strengthen the basic principles upon which rests our civilization. America, as a Christian nation, must base its policy unswervingly upon right and justice and humanity. We must believe, in the words of Lincoln, that "right makes might"; and in that faith we "must dare to do our duty as we understand it."

I often think of the verse of Martin Luther, that doughty old fighter, who could not be downed:

> And though this world with devils filled
> Should threaten to undo us,
> We will not fear for God hath willed
> His truth to triumph through us.

With closer political and economic understanding among the free peoples of the world may come a great upsurge of the forces of democracy. The consequences could be electric. Democracy, foundationed upon the deep desires and will of the great masses of mankind, is an unconquerable force.

The time is big with opportunity. Destiny is in the making. The issues call for men of vision and men of courage.

NATIONAL ATTITUDES

THE SPIRIT OF DEMOCRACY [1]

David E. Lilienthal [2]

David E. Lilienthal, chairman of the Atomic Energy Commission, gave this address at Rochester, New York, on January 16, 1949. He talked to an audience of three thousand in the Eastman Theatre of the University of Rochester, under the joint auspices of the university and the Temple B'Rith Kodesh, celebrating its hundredth year.

Departing from his prepared text, he criticized the House Committee on Un-American Activities for treating Dr. Edward Condon, director of the United States Bureau of Standards, with "cynical dis-regard of fairness."

The address was significant in its warning that trust in the atomic bomb alone would be dangerous. His exposition of the moral and religious tenets and principles underlying America's strength was reminiscent of his "credo" expressed before the Joint Congressional Committee on Atomic Energy, February 4, 1947.

Mr. Lilienthal is a dominating speaker, invariably extempore de-spite his occasional use of a manuscript, pleasing in vocal quality, rate, intensity, and inflection. His pronunciation is standard American. He is adept at concrete, closely organized speech composition. Note in this address the semi-colloquial ease.

At DePauw University, he was debater and member of Delta Sigma Rho, honorary forensic society. He had training under Dr. Harry B. Gough, for many years prominent national speech director at DePauw.[3]

I wish to speak to you this afternoon about this country we love so deeply, about the sources of her strength. And the theme of what I shall say to you is simply this: that it is in the spirit of the American people that our great strength is found, that the foundation of the Republic is in the moral sense of her people, a sense of what is right and what is wrong, in short, that the faiths we hold are the chief armament of our democracy.

[1] Text supplied by David Lilienthal and, through his courtesy, permission to reprint.

[2] For biographical note, see Appendix.

[3] For additional comment on Mr. Lilienthal and additional examples of his speaking, see *Representative American Speeches: 1946-1947*, p113-43.

There are those who take quite a different view. I refer to those among us who have been bewitched by the atomic bomb. They see that we now have a weapon of fantastic power; they know that we are in the forefront of the whole world in the further development of this revolutionary weapon. They have come to believe—these bewitched ones—that the real power of America is to be found in the possession of this incredibly powerful instrument of war.

I would be perhaps the last one in this country to make the mistake of underestimating the destructive power of the atom bomb, either the ones the world has seen in action, or those which the Commission on which I serve has developed and is in process of further developing. One who lives with atomic weapons night and day, as I do, is not likely to deprecate them.

But neither the atomic weapon nor any other form of power and force constitutes the true source of American strength. Nothing could be more misleading, nothing could be farther from reality, nothing could be more dangerous to the future security of our nation or the peace of the world than this myth.

For if we embrace this myth of the atomic bomb we will drift into the belief—some people already have such a belief —that we Americans are safe in the world, safe and secure, because we have this devastating weapon. We will then tend to relax, when we need to be eternally vigilant and constantly alert. We will come to believe that for our nation to be secure in a troubled world all we need is this powerful weapon.

The myth will cause us to fall into an even deeper pit of error. We will grow forgetful of the true sources of America's strength. We will be misled into believing that America can be strong by military force alone, when in truth the foundation of our strength and amazing vitality is not in material things, but rather in the spirit of this nation, in the faiths we cherish.

We are a people with a faith in each other, and when we lose that faith we are weak, however heavily armed. We are a people with a faith in reason, and the unending pursuit of new knowledge; and when we lose that faith we are insecure, however heavily armed. We are a people with a faith in God, with a deep sense of stewardship to our Creator, the Father of us all; and when that is no longer strong within us we are weak and we are lost, however heavily armed with weapons—even atomic weapons—we may be.

To carry the burdens of world leadership that now rest upon us we need strength in great measure. That strength I believe we have; but it is not the strength of force or of power, but of the spirit, a strength that is nourished by those ethical and moral precepts that have become a part of the living tissue of everyday life in America. It is these ethical principles and indeed religious faiths that distinguish and exemplify the spirit of American democracy. These are the things I wish to talk over with you this afternoon.

Generally speaking it's not a good idea for an individual to think too much about himself. He can become so occupied with how his digestion is getting along that just fussing about it will get it out of fix. Perfectly healthy people can give themselves the jitters by paying too much attention to their nerves and their mental processes. The advice "Let your mind alone," has a lot to be said for it.

I have a feeling that much the same thing applies to nations, and particularly to a nation as healthy and high spirited as the United States of America. But a certain amount of national self-examination is inescapable, and indeed at this juncture in world events, it is not only inevitable but wholesome. The eyes of the world's people are upon us these days. Everything we do (and a good many things we don't do) and much of what we say, in this wonderfully talkative and uninhibited land of ours, occupy the attention of hundreds of millions of people in England, in France and the Lowlands, in Italy and the Balkans, in Latin America, in the vast reaches of Soviet Russia. Even though we might prefer not to talk about our own health, about what it is that makes us so fit, or about that occasional headache, the times just won't permit.

Each day all over the world, we, the people of the United States, are given a physical and mental appraisal by the people of other lands. Whether the looking over we are getting around the world is sincere and temperate—as it often is—or deliberately false, and incredibly mean—as it sometimes is—the justification for this constant appraisal of America is clear enough. For we no longer say: Our way is good enough for us; please go away and don't bother us with your problems.

Upon a world-wide stage we stand today as the exemplars and the active protagonists of certain heroic principles of human life, about which we feel so deeply that we are prepared to stake everything upon keeping them alive and flourishing. We assert that the principles by which we live are basically opposed to, and demonstrably superior to, those modern versions of tyranny over men that first enslaved and then destroyed the German and Japanese people; that now threaten the peoples of all Europe and of Asia, and that may in time—how long a time is uncertain—actually endanger the free men and women of America itself.

If I understand the essence of our evolving foreign policy, it is based largely upon what we believe to be the peculiar merits and the superior qualities of our way of living together here at home. The anxious peoples of the world are bedeviled and often confused by many voices in their own lands, telling them just what America is like, what our motives are. The confusion abroad is natural enough. But we should take care that we ourselves do not get confused about the sources of our strength, about what it is that makes America strong and that will keep her strong.

Many years ago Walt Whitman used to wander along the Atlantic seaboard celebrating America. In words that ring he told his countrymen of the great strength and vigor and beauty of America. He sang of a stout and powerful land— strong, and bragging of its strength. Old Walt shouted to the universe that this was the greatest country ever heard of. That was true then; it is even more clearly true today.

I wish Walt Whitman were alive today to continue his immortal song. We need to talk about what a wonderful land and people we are. We must not allow ourselves to develop a kind of national jitters, we must not become a bunch of Nervous

Nellys. We do face danger, there is no doubt about that. But jitters and long faces at a time of danger are not in the American tradition. Whitman would have roared his disapproval. The pioneers met danger with steady nerves and sure hands; from their trials they gathered strength. Another trial must now be met: a worldwide propaganda assault upon our democratic way of life, with a long period of tension and alarms and provocation. It is a time again for steady nerves. Here is another test of mettle, another opportunity to grow in strength.

We do have weaknesses and they must be carefully assessed, but it is also important to remember how strong we are. It is of our strength and the source of that strength that I want to speak today.

America is today the first nation of the world. There is no close second.

This has become the first nation by almost every measure one can apply:

First in productiveness: more things; more telephones, more steel, more chemicals.

First in military.

First in the conditions of human life; the best medical care; the best fed and clothed and housed people on earth.

First in technical resources and scientific facilities.

First in freedom for our citizens: the freest by all odds to bellyache about our government or our grocer or our employer.

First in spirit: the most generous people anywhere in their treatment of others less fortunate; first in ethical standards.

First in sense of responsibility for the peace of the world: one of the least nationalistic of big nations.

First of the peoples of the world in strengthening the instruments that discourage aggression and promote the peace: among those instruments of peace that we strengthen are, on the one hand, a stockpile of atomic weapons, and, on the other, the United Nations and the European Recovery Program.

What is the source and the foundation of our American strength? The answer most commonly heard is: our economic system. The "system" is variously referred to as the capitalist system, or democratic capitalism, or the system of free enterprise, or some similar expression.

The central role of free, competitive, private enterprise in the life of America can hardly be exaggerated. But neither this nor any other answer in economic terms can explain our basic vitality.

The basic source of the strength of American civilization does not lie in an "economic system." The well-springs of our vitality are not economic. They go deeper still: they are ethical and spiritual. Our society in America is founded, not upon the cold and bloodless "economic man" of the Marxist, but upon a faith in man as an end in himself.

We believe in man. We believe in men not merely as production units, but as the children of God. We believe that the purpose of our society is not primarily to assure the "safety of the state," but to safeguard human dignity and the freedom of the individual. We are a people who have built upon a faith in the spirit of man, who conceive that the development and happiness of the individual is the purpose and goal of American life. I judge that we are not ready to "trade in" this luminous concept of a people's purpose for the notion that the America of the Bill of Rights, of Walt Whitman and Justice Holmes and Abraham Lincoln, is simply a highly productive economic system.

What we have, actually, is not a system at all, but almost its opposite; that is, a society of the greatest imaginable diversity and flexibility, taking things as they come, deciding how to handle situations by the facts of each situation itself—"doing what comes naturally." The only way in which it can be said to be a "system" is to say that our "system" is to have no system.

The vitality of our distinctive institutions of production and distribution of goods, ultimately depends, not upon rigid and fixed economic principles, but upon ethical and moral assumptions and purposes.

Our unparalleled productivity and standard of living are not the consequences of an economic system but rather the other way round. Our economic success and our flourishing economic institutions are the consequences of our ethical and moral standards and precepts, of our democratic faith in man.

We have ethical guide lines in this country. We have developed rather highly a sense of what is right and what is wrong, of what is fair and decent, and what is just crude use of arbitrary power. A cynical labor leader or business giant, a cynical politician or public official—those who conceive of American society as nothing more than a jungle in which the most ruthless prevails—may fool us for a time by a mask of pretense. And, sometimes, we are slow to repudiate cynical disregard of our democratic faith. But that faith is always there, the foundation of our buying and selling, our hiring and firing, our political and financial institutions. No factory can be operated, not a carload of wheat sold, not a labor dispute negotiated, not an election held, without these ethical, legally unenforceable precepts being part of the transaction.

I do not see how our kind of society could flourish in any other way. A highly interdependent country, one capable of producing more than 200 billion dollars' worth of goods a year, is too complex for rigid planning and the enforcement of detailed plans by law. We must function in a loose, informal way under sanctions that are largely ethical and moral, based upon commonly accepted standards of fair plan and respect for human integrity. This is the way we do function, by and large, and this is why we flourish.

Some would have us believe that because we excel in making millions of the same kind of useful gadgets, therefore we are free men. No; that has the cart before the horse. It is because freedom and fairness are primary ethical concerns of ours that we do so well in making gadgets and raising food and doing successfully many other things—among them the winning of wars.

We ourselves should be very clear about American fundamentals, as we move into the most fateful role we have ever played in world affairs. For our leadership in large part depends upon our continued capacity to demonstrate how superior, in human terms, is our way of living. If I am right in what I have been saying, then it is important—desperately important—that we be clear in our own minds about the true sources of our strength; that we nourish and safeguard the ethical principles that make us strong.

In Whitman's time it was common enough to celebrate our nation, its area, its power, its opportunities, the character and spirit of its people. Then something happened. Our novels, our plays, began to make fun of our boasting. The American traveler abroad who was always telling about what a great country this was became a standard joke. We began to apologize for ourselves, for our Babbitts, for our failure to cultivate the arts and graces.

We even became apologetic—or some Americans did—for being the strongest and most dramatically beautiful land on earth. No great national spirit can be built up by wearing a hair shirt and sitting in the ashes of our shortcomings. In a period of emergency this morbid faultfinding can sap our strength. The armaments of a democracy must include pride and confidence.

I am not one who underestimates the prophylaxis of criticism. I know the danger of complacency; I know we have our slums in city and country, our depressed areas, and many other things that are ugly and evil. We have the highest standard of living in the world; but you and I know it is unevenly distributed. But of this I am sure: if we spend our energies wailing and moaning, we shall find our courage badly depleted at the very time when we need to be confident, steady, and sure.

The song of America is more than one of steel and oil and murals and automobiles; more than of material things. We have a solidarity, a unity of spirit and purpose that we can brag about. Now and then we hear the fear expressed that we face disunity in our country—that we are in danger of being torn into opposing classes. That seems to me to be simply nonsense. We can boast with truth that nowhere on the face of the earth in any period of human history has there been a vast nation less cursed with deep class divisions. Here there are no fixed classes as in Europe; no landed gentry, no bowing and scraping. If you call an American worker a member of the proletariat you may get a black eye for your pains. Nor has there ever been a vast nation in which the different national and racial groups have been so readily assimilated. The melting pot has really melted. That is something to be proud about.

But this is not all. What is most important is that in America what is right matters to the average citizen, and the truth matters. A man's reputation among his fellows as a truthful and kindly human being means more in the long run than anything else. Compare this standard with that of the countries where there is now a premium on lying; a premium on brutality.

The song of America is a song of great horizons; of "a new order of the ages"; of a new way of life under the sun. We can boast that in the United States we have created the most luminous concepts of the objects of human society that any people has ever dedicated itself to: "life, liberty, and the pursuit of happiness"; government of the people, by the people, for the people";
"We hold these truths to be self-evident, that all men are created equal"; "one nation, indivisible with liberty and justice for all."
We in America have no need for the slogans of other lands when on our banner are inscribed such imperishable cries of the human spirit as these.

To us the individual human spirit comes first—and this it is that is the well-spring of our strength; this it is that is the spirit of our democracy. Let us celebrate this great and shining fact in the stirring words of old Walt Whitman:

> It is not the earth, it is not
>   America who is so great,
> It is I who am great or to be great,
>   it is You up there, or any one,
> It is to walk rapidly through
>   civilization, governments, theories,
> Through poems, pageants, shows,
>   to form individuals.
> Underneath all, individuals, I swear
>   nothing is good to me now that
>   ignores individuals.

AMERICAN RED CROSS [4]

DWIGHT D. EISENHOWER [5]

General Dwight D. Eisenhower gave this speech at the Medinah Temple, in Chicago, Illinois, on Monday, February 28, 1949, on the annual "kick off" program of the American Red Cross fund campaign. The speech, delivered to a face-to-face audience of five thousand, was carried over the American Broadcasting Company network.

On the program with General Eisenhower were James Stewart, Helen Hayes, and Wayne King and his orchestra in a dramatic narrative illustrating the work and history of the American Red Cross. During the last five minutes of the program President Truman made his appeal from the White House. He designated March as Red Cross month and urged each citizen to contribute to the proposed fund of $60 million (it was over subscribed).

The copy of this speech, as provided by Eisenhower, was titled "notes for address." The speaker, however, adhered verbatim to the text as distributed to Mr. Sterritt. It was a striking example of an effective salestalk, giving a vivid picture of the past services of the Red Cross, the present need, future benefits and the necessity that everyone join in the campaign. Said Eisenhower, "Whether we give ten cents, ten dollars, or ten thousand dollars, we are equal partners in this glorious work, so long as we give what we can."

The address, however, was much more than a cleverly organized salestalk. It was a highly personal reflection of Eisenhower's own experience and life-long philosophy, couched in language unhackneyed, direct, and convincing. Undoubtedly the General's immense prestige, coupled with the fact that the public was currently reading his *Crusade in Europe*, provided powerful ethical proof for the listeners. The composition itself, however, and the direct, vocally decisive yet calm tones of the speaker were in themselves strongly persuasive instruments in this Red Cross appeal. General Eisenhower is considered one of the leading representative American speakers.[6]

In every village, town, city—in every home of our country— this March of 1949 is a month of test. In the next thirty-one days we Americans, by our deeds, can prove again that gen-

[4] Text supplied through the courtesy of Charles R. Sterritt, chief, radio and television division of the American National Red Cross, Washington, D. C.

[5] For biographical note, see Appendix.

[6] For further reference to Dwight Eisenhower as a speaker, see *Representative American Speeches: 1944-1945*, p. 114-22.

erosity, greatness of heart and individual acceptance of responsibility are truly characteristic of this nation. The American Red Cross, dedicated to voluntary humanitarian service, needs our unstinted help.

Before me in this hall are five thousand men and women who during the month ahead will give freely of their time and effort that the American Red Cross may continue its mission. Joined with them in similar meetings, across the face of the country, are many other thousands, girding themselves for the March campaign. Together, they constitute an army whose objective is assurance of relief and aid for those who are stricken.

Soon they will bring to millions upon millions of Americans opportunity to show ourselves worthy of our heritage—a heritage that requires each of us to look upon individual and community misfortune as the business of each of us—not merely the responsibility of an overpowering central government.

The American Red Cross is the warm heart of a free people.

With millions of other men and women in the Armed Forces, I am a witness to its magnificent wartime spirit and achievements. I shall never forget the sight, often repeated, of Red Cross women moving into a battered town, lately held by the enemy, to take over a shattered building and get down on their hands and knees to scrub it to spotless cleanliness. There they worked far into the night so that by morning our men would find in that foreign land a bit of home, a touch of the United States, a wealth of friendly American welcome.

Behind the groups that worked so hard and enthusiastically in the field was a vast organization of supporting citizens. Millions of you, by giving of your blood to Red Cross banks, made sure that fighting men, stricken in their country's defense, might win new life and health. There were the volunteers, too, who in hospitals throughout this country and abroad lightened the weary days of our sick and wounded. And there were millions of women, busy with the tasks of house and family or office and factory, who set aside all their hours of leisure, that in some Red Cross-sponsored enterprise they might aid those who were in the country's service.

Truly, the American Red Cross in war was a manifestation of American teamwork and American spirit. No compulsion of combat dictated membership in its ranks. No decree of government regimented those who formed it. No physical power on earth could have enlisted in so splendid a way the hearts and bodies and minds of America. It sprang from a sense of oneness within our people and it was rooted deep in the neighborliness, in the fundamental acceptance of all men as brothers and members of one family, that is uniquely characteristic of the American way of life. Its strength was of the spirit and, therefore, its success, even by the most material measure, was unbounded. It was the America of our fathers in action—to abandon or neglect it would stamp us as unworthy of the freedoms that made possible this kind of voluntary cooperation. Our neglect would justify and even compel a governmental intervention in a field where government has no business in a free country. By that much, then, would we cease to be free.

For those of us in the fighting services, the campaigns of Asia, Africa and Europe of World War II are over. But the Red Cross is always at war—at war against suffering, privation, disaster. And part of its work is still for the victims of America's wars. Today, thousands of veterans, not yet recovered from the wounds of battle, look to the American Red Cross worker for a multitude of services no other organization can give. Hundreds of thousands of veterans' families are assured a fuller reconversion to a peaceful life at home because the American Red Cross is at their call. Moreover, a million and a half men in the Armed Forces, standing guard against any new aggression, depend on the American Red Cross every day of their service.

Every contributor is an active participant in this great work. More than that, every one of us may some day owe his life to the American Red Cross. Disaster by fire or flood or disease is no respecter of persons, of power or of wealth. In crisis, when action must be quick and trained and abundant, no agency of our people is so well fitted as the American Red Cross to care for the injured, to feed the hungry, to clothe the naked and to house the homeless. Whether it be a devastating fire, or a flood that endangers hundreds of thousands, each of us who contributes to the American Red Cross is on the scene of action in the work of mercy. Moreover, whether we give ten cents, ten dollars or ten thousand dollars, we are equal partners in this glorious work, so long as we give what we can.

As a soldier and a plain citizen of this greatest of all nations, I carry the conviction that when we support the American Red Cross

> We vindicate individual responsibility and combat degradation of the individual to a state ward and dependent.

> We demonstrate the mighty effectiveness of voluntary effort and we silence those who preach "only government can do this job."

> We prove ourselves in our day worthy of our heritage and devoted to it, ready to sacrifice so that all who share that heritage with us, even in misfortune and disaster, will know that we are all members of a single, free, responsible citizenship.

> In short, we defeat regimentation; we support freedom.

FREEDOM OF SPEECH: TERMINIELLO vs. CITY OF CHICAGO [7]

WILLIAM O. DOUGLAS, ROBERT H. JACKSON [8]

On Monday, May 16, 1949, the Supreme Court of the United States, by a vote of five to four, reversed, on constitutional grounds, the conviction of the Reverend Arthur W. Terminiello.

On February 7, 1946, Gerald L. K. Smith, of America First, held a rally in Chicago. On the speaking program was the Reverend A. W. Terminiello, a Roman Catholic priest from Birmingham, Alabama. At that time he was under suspension (later cancelled) by his Bishop for utterances "detrimental to the Church and the unity of our country."

According to the testimony, Father Terminiello's speech was inflammatory. The crowd, estimated at fifteen hundred, constituted, according to the evidence, "a surging, howling mob hurling epithets at those who would enter and trying to tear their clothes off." Father Terminiello, in his speech, attacked "atheistic, communistic Jewish or Zionist Jews," and used similar epithets. The crowd shouted "Fascists, Hitlers," and threw bricks and stench bombs. Some twenty-eight windows were broken. The police were unable to control the mob.

After the meeting, Father Terminiello was arrested, tried, and fined a hundred dollars for disorderly conduct, according to the City of Chicago Code, on the ground that his speech had "stirred the public to anger" and created a "disturbance." The conviction was appealed. Mr. Justice Douglas' majority opinion is reprinted below in full. Concurring with him were Justices Hugo W. Black, Wiley B. Rutledge, Frank Murphy, and Stanley F. Reed.

In the minority were Chief Justice Fred M. Vinson, Felix Frankfurter, Robert H. Jackson, and Harold H. Burton. Justices Vinson, Frankfurter and Jackson each wrote dissenting opinions. The limits of this volume permit reprinting only the closing section of Mr. Jackson's extended argument upholding the conviction. The student should analyze in detail the evidence preceding the concluding argument.[9]

The issue thus raised is a persistent one. Shall the United States tolerate the "widest latitude in the expression of opinion"? Or should the extremists be restrained lest they destroy the very democracy under

---

[7] Text supplied through the courtesy of Justice William O. Douglas and of Justice Robert H. Jackson.

[8] For biographical notes, see Appendix.

[9] See Supreme Court of the United States, no272, October Term, 1948. Arthur Terminiello, Petitioner, *v.* City of Chicago.

which they exercise their freedoms? What constitutes "clear and present danger"? [10]

Mr. Justice Douglas delivered the opinion of the Court:

Petitioner after jury trial was found guilty of disorderly conduct in violation of a city ordinance of Chicago and fined. The case grew out of an address he delivered in an auditorium in Chicago under the auspices of the Christian Veterans of America. The meeting commanded considerable public attention. The auditorium was filled to capacity with over eight hundred persons present. Others were turned away. Outside of the auditorium a crowd of about one thousand persons gathered to protest against the meeting. A cordon of policemen was assigned to the meeting to maintain order; but they were not able to prevent several disturbances. The crowd outside was angry and turbulent.

Petitioner in his speech condemned the conduct of the crowd outside and vigorously, if not viciously, criticized various political and racial groups whose activities he denounced as inimical to the nation's welfare.

The trial court charged that "breach of the peace" consists of any "misbehavior which violates the public peace and decorum"; and that the "misbehavior may constitute a breach of the peace if it stirs the public to anger, invites dispute, brings about a condition of unrest, or creates a disturbance, or if it molests the inhabitants in the enjoyment of peace and quiet by arousing alarm." Petitioner did not take exception to that instruction. But he maintained at all times that the ordinance as applied to his conduct violated his right of free speech under the Federal Constitution. The judgment of conviction was affirmed by the Illinois Appellate Court (332 Ill. App. 17, 74 N. E. 2d 45) and by the Illinois Supreme Court (396 Ill. 41, 71 N. E. 2d 2, 400 Ill. 23, 79 N. E. 2d 39). The case is here on a petition for *certiorari* which we granted because of the importance of the question presented.

[10] For comments on R. H. Jackson as a speaker, see *Representative American Speeches: 1939-1940*, p233-4; *1945-1946*, p60-1. For comments on W. O. Douglas as a speaker, see *Representative American Speeches: 1940-1941*, p225; *1947-1948*, p207.

The argument here has been focused on the issue of whether the content of petitioner's speech was composed of derisive, fighting words, which carried it outside the scope of the constitutional guarantees. (See *Chaplinsky* v. *New Hampshire*, 315 U. S. 568; *Cantwell* v. *Connecticut*, 310 U. S. 296, 310.) We do not reach that question, for there is a preliminary question that is dispositive of the case.

As we have noted, the statutory words "breach of the peace" were defined in instructions to the jury to include speech which "stirs the public to anger, invites dispute, brings about a condition of unrest, or creates a disturbance. . . ." That construction of the ordinance is a ruling on a question of state law that is as binding on us as though the precise words had been written into the ordinance. (*See Hebert* v. *Louisiana*, 272 U. S. 312, 317; *Winters* v. *New York*, 333 U. S. 507, 514.)

The vitality of civil and political institutions in our society depends on free discussion. As Chief Justice Hughes wrote in *De Jonge* v. *Oregon* (299 U. S. 353, 365) it is only through free debate and free exchange of ideas that government remains responsive to the will of the people and peaceful change is effected. The right to speak freely and to promote diversity of ideas and programs is therefore one of the chief distinctions that sets us apart from totalitarian regimes.

Accordingly a function of free speech under our system of government is to invite dispute. It may indeed best serve its high purpose when it induces a condition of unrest, creates dissatisfaction with conditions as they are, or even stirs people to anger. Speech is often provocative and challenging. It may strike at prejudices and preconceptions and have profound unsettling effects as it presses for acceptance of an idea. That is why freedom of speech, though not absolute (*Chaplinsky* v. *New Hampshire, supra*, p. 571-2) is nevertheless protected against censorship or punishment, unless shown likely to produce a clear and present danger of a serious substantive evil that rises far above public inconvenience, annoyance, or unrest. (See *Bridges* v. *California*, 314 U. S. 252, 262; *Craig* v. *Harney*, 331 U. S. 367, 373.) There is no room under our Constitution for a more restrictive view. For the alternative would lead to standardization of ideas either by legislatures, courts, or dominant political or community groups.

The ordinance as construed by the trial court seriously invaded this province. It permitted conviction of petitioner if his speech stirred people to anger, invited public dispute, or brought about a condition of unrest. A conviction resting on any of those grounds may not stand.

The fact that petitioner took no exception to the instruction is immaterial. No exception to the instructions was taken in *Stromberg* v. *California* (283 U. S. 359). But a judgment of conviction based on a general verdict under a state statute was set aside in that case, because one part of the statute was unconstitutional. The statute had been challenged as unconstitutional and the instruction was framed in its language. The Court held that the attack on the statute as a whole was equally an attack on each of its individual parts. Since the verdict was a general one and did not specify the ground upon which it rested, it could not be sustained. For one part of the statute was unconstitutional and it could not be determined that the defendant was not convicted under that part.

The principle of that case controls this one. As we have said, the gloss which Illinois placed on the ordinance gives it a meaning and application which are conclusive on us. We need not consider whether as construed it is defective in its entirety. As construed and applied it at least contains parts that are unconstitutional. The verdict was a general one; and we do not know on this record but what it may rest on the invalid clauses.

The statute as construed in the charge to the jury was passed on by the Illinois courts and sustained by them over the objection that as so read it violated the Fourteenth Amendment. The fact that the parties did not dispute its construction makes the adjudication no less ripe for our review, as the *Stromberg* decision indicates. We can only take the statute as the state courts read it. From our point of view it is immaterial whether the state law question as to its meaning was controverted or accepted. The pinch of the statute is in its application. It is that question which the petitioner has brought here. To say therefore that the question on this phase of the case is whether the trial judge gave a wrong charge is wholly to misconceive the issue.

But it is said that throughout the appellate proceedings the Illinois courts assumed that the only conduct punishable and punished under the ordinance was conduct constituting "fighting words." That emphasizes, however, the importance of the rule of the *Stromberg case*. Petitioner was not convicted under a statute so narrowly construed. For all anyone knows he was convicted under the parts of the ordinance (as construed) which, for example, make it an offense merely to invite dispute or to bring about a condition of unrest. We cannot avoid that issue by saying that all Illinois did was to measure petitioner's conduct, not the ordinance, against the Constitution. Petitioner raised both points—that his speech was protected by the Constitution; that the inclusion of his speech within the ordinance was a violation of the Constitution. We would, therefore, strain at technicalities to conclude that the constitutionality of the ordinance as construed and applied to petitioner was not before the Illinois. courts. The record makes clear that petitioner at all times challenged the constitutionality of the ordinance as construed and applied to him.

Mr. Justice Jackson, dissenting: . . . I begin with the oft-forgotten principle which this case demonstrates, that freedom of speech exists only under law and not independently of it. What would Terminiello's theoretical freedom of speech have amounted to had he not been given active aid by the officers of the law? He could reach the hall only with their help, could talk only because they restrained the mob, and could make his getaway only under their protection. We would do well to recall the words of Chief Justice Hughes in *Cox* v. *New Hampshire* (312 U. S. 569, 574): "Civil liberties, as guaranteed by the Constitution, imply the existence of an organized society maintaining public order without which liberty itself would be lost in the excesses of unrestrained abuses. . . ."

This case demonstrates also that this Court's service to free speech is essentially negative and can consist only of reviewing actions by local magistrates. But if free speech is to be a practical reality, affirmative and immediate protection is required;

and it can come only from nonjudicial sources. It depends on local police, maintained by law-abiding taxpayers, who, regardless of their own feelings, risk themselves to maintain supremacy of law. Terminiello's theoretical right to speak free from interference would have no reality if Chicago should withdraw its officers to some other section of the city, or if the men assigned to the task should look the other way when the crowd threatens Terminiello. Can society be expected to keep these men at Terminiello's service if it has nothing to say of his behavior which may force them into dangerous action?

No one will disagree that the fundamental, permanent and overriding policy of police and courts should be to permit and encourage utmost freedom of utterance. It is the legal right of any American citizen to advocate peaceful adoption of fascism or communism, socialism or capitalism. He may go far in expressing sentiments whether pro-semitic or anti-semitic, pro-Negro or anti-Negro, pro-Catholic or anti-Catholic. He is legally free to argue for some anti-American system of government to supersede by constitutional methods the one we have. It is our philosophy that the course of government should be controlled by a consensus of the governed. This process of reaching intelligent popular decisions requires free discussion. Hence we should tolerate no law or custom of censorship or suppression.

But we must bear in mind also that no serious outbreak of mob violence, race rioting, lynching or public disorder is likely to get going without help of some speech-making to some mass of people. A street may be filled with men and women and the crowd still not be a mob. Unity of purpose, passion and hatred, which merges the many minds of a crowd into the mindlessness of a mob, almost invariably is supplied by speeches. It is naive, or worse, to teach that oratory with this object or effect is a service to liberty. No mob has ever protected any liberty, even its own, but if not put down it always winds up in an orgy of lawlessness which respects no liberties.

In considering abuse of freedom by provocative utterances it is necessary to observe that the law is more tolerant of discussion than are most individuals or communities. Law is so indifferent to subjects of talk that I think of none that it should close to discussion. Religious, social and political topics that in other times or countries have not been open to lawful debate may be freely discussed here.

Because a subject is legally arguable, however, does not mean that public sentiment will be patient of its advocacy at all times and in all manners. So it happens that, while peaceful advocacy of communism or fascism is tolerated by the law, both of these doctrines arouse passionate reactions. A great number of people do not agree that introduction to America of communism or fascism is even debatable. Hence many speeches, such as that of Terminiello, may be legally permissible but may nevertheless in some surroundings, be a menace to peace and order. When conditions show the speaker that this is the case, as it did here, there certainly comes a point beyond which he cannot indulge in provocations to violence without being answerable to society.

Determination of such an issue involves a heavy responsibility. Courts must beware lest they become mere organs of popular intolerance. Not every show of opposition can justify treating a speech as a breach of peace. Neither speakers nor courts are obliged always and in all circumstances to yield to prevailing opinion and feeling. As a people grow in capacity for civilization and liberty their tolerance will grow, and they will endure, if not welcome, discussion even on topics as to which they are committed. They regard convictions as tentative and know that time and events will make their own terms with theories, by whomever and by whatever majorities they are held, and many will be proved wrong. But on our way to this idealistic state of tolerance the police have to deal with men as they are. The crowd mind is never tolerant of any idea which does not conform to its herd opinion. It does not want a tolerant effort at meeting of minds. It does not know the futility of trying to mob an idea. Released from the sense of personal responsibility that would restrain even the worst individuals in it if alone and brave with the courage of numbers, both radical and reactionary mobs endanger liberty as well as order. The authorities must control them and they are entitled to place some checks upon those whose behavior or speech calls such mobs into being. When the right of society to freedom from probable violence should prevail over the right of an individual to defy opposing opinion, presents a problem that always tests wisdom and often calls for immediate and vigorous action to preserve public order and safety.

I do not think that the Constitution of the United States denies to the states and the municipalities power to solve that problem in the light of local conditions, at least so long as danger to public order is not invoked in bad faith, as a cover for censorship or suppression. The preamble declares domestic tranquility as well as liberty to be an object in founding a federal government and I do not think the forefathers were naive in believing both can be fostered by the law.

Certain practical reasons reinforce the legal view that cities and states should be sustained in the power to keep their streets from becoming the battleground for these hostile ideologies to the destruction and detriment of public order. There is no other power that can do it. Theirs are the only police that are on the spot. The Federal Government has no police force. The Federal Bureau of Investigation is, and should remain, not a police but an investigative service. To date the only federal agency for preserving and restoring order when local authority fails has been the army. And when the military steps in, the court takes a less liberal view of the rights of the individual and sustains most arbitrary exercises of military power. (See *Korematsu* v. *United States*, 323 U. S. 214.) Every failure of local authority to deal with riot problems results in a demand for the establishment of a federal police or intervention by federal authority. In my opinion, locally established and controlled police can never develop into the menace to general civil liberties that is inherent in a federal police.

The ways in which mob violence may be worked up are subtle and various. Rarely will a speaker directly urge a crowd to lay hands on a victim or class of victims. An effective and safer way is to incite mob action while pretending to deplore it, after the classic example of Antony, and this was not lost on Terminiello. And whether one may be the cause of mob violence by his own personification or advocacy of ideas which a crowd already fears and hates, is not solved merely by going through a transcript of the speech to pick out "fighting words." The most insulting words can be neutralized if the speaker will smile when he says them, but a belligerent personality and an aggressive manner may kindle a fight without use of words that in cold type shock us. True judgment will be aided by observation of the individual defendant, as was possible for this jury and trial court but impossible for us.

There are many appeals these days to liberty, often by those who are working for an opportunity to taunt democracy with its stupidity in furnishing them the weapons to destroy it as did Goebbels when he said: "When democracy granted democratic methods for us in times of opposition, this [Nazi seizure of power] was bound to happen in a democratic system. However, we National Socialists never asserted that we represented a democratic point of view, but we have declared openly that we used democratic methods only in order to gain the power and that, after assuming the power, we would deny to our adversaries without any consideration the means which were granted to us in times of [our] opposition." (1 *Nazi Conspiracy & Aggression* [GPO 1946] 202, Docs. 2500-PS, 2412-PS.)

Invocation of constitutional liberties as part of the strategy for overthrowing them presents a dilemma to a free people which may not be soluble by constitutional logic alone.

But I would not be understood as suggesting that the United States can or should meet this dilemma by suppression of free, open and public speaking on the part of any group or ideology. Suppression has never been a successful permanent policy; any surface serenity that it creates is a false security, while conspiratorial forces go underground. My confidence in American institutions and in the sound sense of the American people is such that if with a stroke of the pen I could silence every Fascist and Communist speaker, I would not do it. For I agree with Woodrow Wilson, who said:

I have always been among those who believed that the greatest freedom of speech was the greatest safety, because if a man is a fool, th best thing to do is to encourage him to advertise the fact by speaking. It cannot be so easily discovered if you allow him to remain silent and look wise, but if you let him speak, the secret is out and the world knows that he is a fool. So it is by the exposure of folly that it is defeated; not by the seclusion of folly, and in this free air of free speech men get into that sort of communication with one another which constitutes the basis of all common achievement.—Address at the Institute of France, Paris, May 10, 1919 (2 *Selected Literary and Political Papers and Addresses of Woodrow Wilson* [1926] 333.).

But if we maintain a general policy of free speaking, we must recognize that its inevitable consequence will be sporadic local outbreaks of violence, for it is the nature of men to be intolerant of attacks upon institutions, personalities and ideas for which they really care. In the long run, maintenance of free speech will be more endangered if the population can have no protection from the abuses which lead to violence. No liberty is made more secure by holding that its abuses are inseparable from its enjoyment. We must not forget that it is the free democratic communities that ask us to trust them to maintain peace with liberty and that the factions engaged in this battle are not interested permanently in either. What would it matter to Terminiello if the police batter up some Communists or, on the other hand, if the Communists batter up some policemen? Either result makes grist for his mill; either would help promote hysteria and the demand for strong-arm methods in dealing with his adversaries. And what, on the other hand, have the Communist agitators to lose from a battle with the police?

This Court has gone far toward accepting the doctrine that civil liberty means the removal of all restaints from these crowds and that all local attempts to maintain order are impairments of the liberty of the citizen. The choice is not between order and liberty. It is between liberty with order and anarchy without either. There is danger that, if the Court does not temper its doctrinaire logic with a little practical wisdom, it will convert the constitutional Bill of Rights into a suicide pact.

I would affirm the conviction. Mr. Justice Burton joins in this opinion.

PERSONAL TRIBUTE AND
REMINISCENCE

THE MEANING OF AMERICA [1]

HERBERT HOOVER [2]

Mr. Herbert Hoover, only living former president of the United States, gave this address at his birthplace, West Branch, Iowa, the afternoon of August 10, 1948. It was broadcast over the Mutual network and several local stations. The occasion was the celebration of Hoover's seventy-fourth birthday and of his homecoming.

About fifteen thousand, some of them his boyhood schoolmates, most of them neighborhood Iowans, joined in the all-day program. The gathering was non-political. Twenty-five bands, drum corps, and youth organizations paraded from the high school through the decorated streets to the reviewing stand in Hoover Park, near the restored two-room cottage where Hoover was born. A picnic dinner preceded the speech making.

Virgil Hancher, President of the State University of Iowa, gave the invocation, and Governor Robert Blue, the introduction.

The crowd and speaker had complete rapport. Cheers, applause, and laughter were hearty and frequent. Hoover, despite his advanced years, was probably at his peak in speaking effectiveness. His voice was firm, relaxed, and pleasantly conversational. His delivery harmonized with the reminiscent and personal character of his speech. He impressed with his warm understanding of the people before him and his humorous treatment of his humble boyhood. Critics called him "mellow." Although his discourse was without formal oratorical elements, its simple portrayal of his background, his developing appreciation of American principles, the successive experiences that "brought him every honor to which man could aspire" were deeply moving and genuinely eloquent. The address will rank among the more permanent of Hoover's platform contributions.

Ladies and Gentlemen, Governor Blue and members of your Committee: I am deeply grateful for your reception and the

[1] Reprinted through the courtesy of Mr. Hoover. The text was authenticated by LeRoy Cowperthwaite, Department of Speech, State University of Iowa, from the WSUI wire recording.

[2] For biographical note, see Appendix.

honor which you do to me today. I deeply appreciate the many thousands of kindly acts and kindly wishes which have marked this day. They come both from those of you who are present and from many parts of my country—which adds to my gratitude.

I am glad to have your invitation to come again to this Iowa village where I was born. Here I spent, as you know, the first ten years of my boyhood. My parents and grandparents came to this village in the covered wagon—pioneers in this community. They lie buried over the hill. They broke the prairie into homes of independent living. They worshipped God; they did their duty to their neighbors. They toiled to bring to their children greater comfort, better education and to open to them wider opportunities than had been theirs.

I am proud to have been born in Iowa. But, through the eyes of a ten-year-old boy it was a place of adventure and daily discoveries—the wonder of the growing crops, the excitements of the harvest, the journeys to the woods for nuts and hunting, the joys of snowy winters, the comfort of the family fireside, of good food and tender care. And out of the excessive energy of all small boys, the evenings were filled with accounts of defeat and victory over animate and inanimate things—so far as was permitted in a Quaker community.

Indelible in those recollections was a widowed mother, sitting with her needle, cheerfully supporting three children and at the same time ministering to her neighbors. And after that came life with Uncle Allan on his farm near this village, there, at that place, with the joys and sorrows which come to every small boy enroute to life's disciplines by way of farm chores. And among these chores was the unending making of provisions for the next winter. But in those primitive days, social security was had from the family cellar, not from the Federal Government. [*Laughter and applause*]

You may be surprised if I tell you that at an age somewhat under ten I began here my first national service. By my own efforts I furnished firecrackers required for the adequate celebration of the Independence of the United States on July 4th, 1882. To get those firecrackers, I entered into collective bargaining by which it was settled, not by me, [*Laughter*] that I should receive one cent per hundred for picking potato bugs in a field in sight of this stand. [*Laughter*] My impression then, and now is, that it was an oppressive wage rate. [*Laughter*]

Also, I took part in the political issues of the day by walking beside a Garfield torchlight procession in the presidential campaign of 1884. And by the village flags at half-mast, I learned of the assassination of Garfield, with some dim understanding that somewhere in the nation great men guarded its welfare.

One of the indelible impressions of memory was the original Quaker Meeting House. Those recollections chiefly revolve around the stiff repression of the explosive energies of a small boy sitting out the long silences. One time, however, the silence was broken by the shrill voice of Aunt Hannah. She was moved in meeting bitterly to denounce the modernistic tendencies of those times. She had very firm views on any form of recreation, which included singing in Sunday school. She closed with a peroration to the effect that if these tendencies persisted that edifice dedicated to God would some day become in fact a place of abomination—a "the-atre." And truly, the old meeting house in its decadent years, having made way for a better edifice, became a movie house, [*Laughter*] Now my view is that the abomination part of Aunt Hannah depends on the choice of the film.

And among these recollections was that of a great lady who first taught me in school and who remained my friend during her whole long useful life, Mrs. Mollie Carran. It was from her that I first heard something about the word American. Now many great writers and statesmen have attempted to express what we mean by that word. But there is an imponderable within it which reaches to the soul of our people and defies any measure.

America means more than a continent bounded by two oceans. It is more than pride of military power, or glory in war, or in victory. It means more than vast expanse of farms, of great factories or mines, or magnificent cities, or millions of automobiles and radios. It is more even than the traditions of the great tide westward from Europe which pioneered the conquest of this continent. It is more than our literature, our music, our poetry. For other nations have all these things also.

Maybe the intangible that we cannot describe within that word lies in the personal experience and the living of each of us rather than in phrases, however inspiring.

Perhaps without immodesty I can claim to have had some experience in what the word *American* means. I have lived many kinds of American life. After my boyhood in this Iowa village, I lived as the ward of a country doctor in Oregon. And I lived amongst those to whom hard work was the price of existence. The opportunities of America opened out to me in the public schools. They carried me to professional training in an American university. I began by working with my own hands for my daily bread. I have tasted of the despair of fruitless search for a job. I know the kindly encouragement of a humble boarding-house keeper. I know now that at that time there was an economic depression either coming or going, I don't know which. But nobody told me of it. So I didn't have the modern worry of what the Federal Government would do about it.

Also I have conducted the administration of great industries with their problems of their production and the well-being of their employees.

I have seen America in contrast with many nations and many races. My profession took me into many lands under many kinds of government. I have worked with their great spiritual leaders and their great statesmen. I have worked in governments of free men, of tyrannies, of Socialists and Communists. I have met with princes, kings, and despots and political desperados.

I have seen the squalor of Asia, the frozen class barriers of Europe. And I was not a tourist. I was associated in their working lives and their problems. I had to deal with their social systems and their governments. But outstanding everywhere to these great masses of people there was always a hallowed word —"America." To them it was the hope of the world.

And my every frequent homecoming has been a re-affirmation of the glory of America. Each time my soul was washed by the relief from grinding poverty of other nations, by the greater kindliness and frankness which comes from the acceptance of equality and the belief in wide-open opportunity to all who want to take advantage of the chance. And it is more than that.

America is a land of self-respect, and self-respect born alone of free men and free women.

In later years I participated on behalf of America in a great war. I saw the untold misery and revolution. I have seen liberty die and tyranny rise. I have seen human slavery again on the march.

I have been repeatedly placed by my countrymen where I need to deal with the hurricanes of social and economic destruction that have swept the world. I have seen bitter famine and the worst misery that the brutality of war can produce.

And I have had every honor to which any man could aspire. Now there is no place on the whole earth except here in America where all the sons of man could have this chance in life.

I recount all this in order that, in the old Quaker terms, I can give my own testimony.

That the meaning of our word "America" flows from one pure thought. The soul of our America is its freedom of mind and spirit in man. Here alone are the open windows through which pours the sunlight of the human spirit and here alone is human dignity not a dream, but an accomplishment—perhaps not perfect but more full than ever before in the history of the world.

Perhaps another etching of another meaning of this word America lies in this very community. It, as you know, was largely settled by Quakers over ninety years ago. And this small religious sect in England had declared that certain freedoms of man came from the Creator and not from the state. And they declared this a hundred and fifty years before it appears in the Declaration of Independence of the United States. They spent a great deal of time in British stocks and in jails for their first outburst of the faith in the dignity of the individual man.

And then they came in refuge to New England. But the Puritans cut off their ears by way of disapproval of their perhaps excessive religious individualism. And then came the great refuge which William Penn provided in Pennsylvania. From New England and Pennsylvania some of the ancestors of this community, before the Revolution, migrated first to Maryland, and after a generation they moved to the Piedmont in North Carolina. Then early in the last century when slavery began to encroach upon them, most of that community—five thousand of them—organized a concerted trek to Ohio and Indiana. This time they were seeking not freedom from religious persecution but freedom from the greatest stain in human liberty, that is, slavery. Again after a generation they hitched up their covered wagons and settled on these prairies here abouts.

Now everywhere along these treks there sprang up homes and farms. But more vital was the school and the meeting house with its deep roots in religious faith, its tolerance and its devotion to liberty of the individual. And in these people there was the will to serve their community and their country. Even this village was a station on the underground through which Negroes were aided to the freedom of Canada. Sons of this community were in the then Red Cross of the Civil War. And despite their peace-loving faith, many of their sons were enrolled in the Union Army to battle for free men.

That imbedded individualism, that reliance, that sense of service, and above all those moral and spiritual foundations were not confined to the Quakers. They were but one item in the mighty tide of these qualities of many larger religious bodies which make up the intangibles of our word "American."

And at the time our ancestors were proclaiming that the Creator had endowed mankind with rights of freedom as the child of God, with a free will, there was being proclaimed by Hegel and later by Karl Marx a satanic philosophy of agnosticism that the rights of man came from the state. The greatness of America today comes from the one philosophy, the despair and frustration of Europe from the other.

Now there are today fuzzy-minded people in our country who would compromise in this fundamental concept. They scoff at these tested qualities of men which, as I related to you, have come to this community. They never have understood and they never will understand what the word America means. They explain that these qualities were good while there was a continent to conquer, and a nation to build. They say that time has passed. Now no doubt the land frontier has passed. But the frontiers of science and new living are barely opening, in this world.

This new land with all its high promise cannot and will not be conquered except by men inspired from the same concepts of free spirit that settled this state of Iowa.

It is these moral and spiritual qualities in free men which fulfill the meaning and the dream of the word American.   And with them will come centuries of further greatness to our country.

Now to my boyhood friends and those thousands of you who have done me this great honor today, I again express my appreciation and my deep gratitude to you all.   Thank you.   [*Prolonged applause*]

TRIBUTE TO SENATOR BARKLEY
AND RESPONSE [3]

ARTHUR H. VANDENBERG, ALBEN W. BARKLEY [4]

Senator Arthur H. Vandenberg, President pro tempore of the Senate, called the Senate to order at twelve o'clock on January 3, 1949, for the purpose of introducing new members and organizing that body.

After the prayer by the Chaplain, the Reverend Peter Marshall, Senator Vandenberg proceeded with the administration of oath to the thirty-two Senators-elect.

Immediately after this ceremony, Vandenberg gave the brief address below. It and the reply are examples of typical Senate courtesy speeches of tribute and response. Behind the seeming levity lay deep respect of the two speakers for what each had accomplished as a political leader.

Vandenberg, as Chairman of the Senate Committee on Foreign Affairs during 1947-48, had been instrumental in carrying through a bipartisan foreign policy. It is doubtful whether the Truman proposals for dealing with the Russian "cold war" would have had Senate sanction without Vandenberg's aggressive support.[5]

Barkley had also displayed statesmanship of high order during the preceding years in the Senate. Moreover, his vigorous and effective speech-making in the campaign of 1948 and his triumph at the polls in the November election had strengthened his prestige and popularity both among the American citizenry and his fellow Senators.[6]

MR. VANDENBERG, President pro tempore: The Chair notes that the senior Senator from Kentucky rises and asks for recognition. Before the Chair recognizes the Senator from Kentucky he would like to assume that he has unanimous consent to say a, word to him upon this first occasion when he has appeared in

[3] This text is taken from *Congressional Record*. 81st Congress, 1st session. 95:1-2. January 3, 1949 (daily edition). By permission of Senator Vandenberg and Vice President Barkley.

[4] For biographical notes, see Appendix.

[5] For further comment on Vandenberg as a speaker, see *Representative American Speeches:* "Memorial Day Address," *1937-1939*, p39-44; "American Foreign Policy," *1944-1945*, p43-55; "United Nations Assembly," *1945-1946*, p45-9; "For Aid to Greece and Turkey," *1946-1947*, p51-6; "For the Appointment of Lilienthal," *1946-1947*, p122-33; "European Recovery Program," *1947-1948*, p24-47.

[6] For further comment on Barkley as a speaker, see *Representative American Speeches:* "Foreign Policies of Roosevelt," *1938-1939*, p53-9; "Against Roosevelt's Tax Veto," *1943-1944*, p188-99.

this Chamber since his recent election. [*Applause, Senators rising*]

Assuming the unanimous consent of the Senate, the Chair would like to offer two or three observations.

As a result of the recent accident, [*laughter*] the distinguished senior Senator from Kentucky will soon lose his right to stand upon this floor and be recognized. He will soon lose his right of free speech within these walls. He will soon lose his vote. In fact, his civil liberties are disintegrating faster than in any other instance the Chair recalls. [*Laughter*] But as a result of the same accident the senior Senator from Michigan is about to recognize the Senator from Kentucky, or any other Senator, for the last time. [*Laughter*]

It seems to the Chair that this makes the occasion something of an event for both the senior Senator from Kentucky and the senior Senator from Michigan. Therefore, the President pro tempore, with great emphasis on the Latin part of that title, would like to say to the Senator from Kentucky—and he knows he speaks for the entire body—that though he may lack the right of recognition on the floor, many other recognitions can never be taken from him.

There will always be the recognition of the fact that he is one of the great Senators of his time and generation. [*Applause*]

There will always be recognition of integrity without a blemish through more than three decades of public service beneath the dome of the Capitol of the Republic.

There will always be recognition of difficult achievements in successful leadership during critical times when his fidelity as a partisan was always matched by his faithfulness as a patriot and by his constant courtesy and good faith toward those of us in loyal opposition.

There will always be recognition of courage and eloquence. There will always be recognition of patience and humility. There will always be recognition of rare capacity for friendly fellowship. There will always be recognition of a great, human soul.

The Chair recognizes the next Vice President of the United States. [*Applause, Senators rising*]

MR. BARKLEY: Mr. President, the generosity of the Chair and of my colleagues here has almost made me forget the purpose for which I rose. That was to submit a formal resolution following the ascertainment of a quorum of the Senate. I will not submit that resolution, however, until I have very feebly expressed my deep appreciation not only of what the President pro tempore has said but of the response made by my colleagues here without regard to politics upon this occasion.

There was one thing about the remarks of the President pro tempore which disturbed me a little, and that was the evident pleasure, if not hilarity, with which he announced that he was retiring from the chair. Inasmuch as I am to enter upon what Vice President Marshall called a four-year period of silence when he took the oath of office as Vice President, I am somewhat disturbed about the pleasure with which the Chair retires from the position of President of the Senate.

I recognize the fact that by this transfer I shall lose a good many of my civil liberties; but I presume there are some liberties that the Chair may assume while occupying the chair that are equal to civil liberties—provided they are always civil. [*Laughter*]

I do not know how I shall adjust myself to the role of Presiding Officer. I have been here in what I call the "bull pen" for so many years that I fear that some day I may walk down from the rostrum, roll up my sleeves, and begin to engage in debate, to be called down by whoever happens to be in the chair at the time.

I thank the Chair and my colleagues for their generous demonstration. I am not sure whether that demonstration and that evidence of favor and good will is due to the fact that I am getting out of the Senate, or that I am going to preside over it. Whatever may have prompted it—and I accept it in good faith— I greatly appreciate the good will which the Chair has shown, and the cordiality and respect with which we have dealt with one another here in the legislative process during the years of my membership in the Senate.

The Senate of the United States comes in for its share of criticism and denunciation, and it comes in now and then for what I think is an overplay of contemptuous asseverations with respect to its processes; but after all, with all its failings and shortcomings—and they are outstanding in some respects—it yet remains the one great forum for the debate of legislation and for the working out of democratic process among the nations of the world. It will be a sad day in the history of this country if the United States Senate—or, for that matter, the House of Representatives—ceases to be the forum where men express their opinions and advocate whatever appeals to their judgment and their conscience in the process of making our nation a greater example of democracy and self-government.

I leave this seat with sentiments of deep regret. I leave it with a sense of appreciation, not only, but with a sense of humility. I realize how far short I may fall in the performance of my duty at the Presiding Office of this body. But with the cooperation and good will of Members on both sides, I hope I may discharge the duties acceptably to the Senate and to the country, and in fulfillment of our ideals of democracy.

Before I submit the resolution to which I have referred, I wish also to say a word in regard to the retiring Presiding Officer of the Senate of the United States. Because of the death of President Roosevelt and the assumption of the Presidency by the then Vice President, Mr. Truman, the Senator from Michigan became, to all intents and purposes, Vice President of the United States, in the sense that he is President of the Senate.

During my membership in this body and during my observation of it, no man has ever occupied that position with greater dignity, greater force, or greater understanding of the proprieties of leadership, not only in the Senate, but as the Presiding Officer of the Senate, than has the Senator from Michigan, who is about to retire. We have all enjoyed his performance of the function of Presiding Officer of the Senate. We have respected his views in regard to decisions. Though sometimes disagreeing with them, we have always known that his decisions and rulings came out of a deep consciousness of his obligation to the Senate and to the country.

While I cannot say in all candor that I am sorry that the Senator from Michigan is retiring from the position of President pro tempore, because in the very nature of things, politics being what it is, we must have another President pro tempore, I will say that if we had not won the election last November, and if there were not to be a Vice President of the United States—as there has not been for now nearly four years—and we had to have a Republican President pro tempore, I would rather the Senator from Michigan would preside over the Senate than any other man. [*Applause*]

PRESIDENTIAL CAMPAIGN

MADISON SQUARE GARDEN ADDRESS [1]

Thomas E. Dewey [2]

Thomas E. Dewey, Governor of New York, delivered this political address, his final platform appeal, at Madison Square Garden, New York City on Saturday evening, October 30, 1948. The speech was broadcast over the nation-wide network of the National Broadcasting Company from 9:30 to 10:00 E. S. T. and televised over the Eastern Network of the Columbia Broadcasting System.

The nineteen thousand Republican sympathizers, packing the hall three or four hours before Dewey's arrival, had listened to speeches by Thomas J. Curran, New York County Republican leader, Senator Irving M. Ives and others, and viewed a parade of stage and screen and radio personalities, including Gene Tunney, Tex McCrary, Rube Goldberg and Guy Kibbee. Some hundred thousand saw the Dewey entourage proceed from the Hotel Roosevelt to the Garden. After the evening address, the presidential candidate, on a small speaker's stand outside the Garden, talked to an overflow sidewalk audience of ten thousand.

The Madison Square audience greeted Dewey's platform arrival with a demonstration of more than six minutes. Continually the auditors interrupted the speaker with applause and at times with loud laughter.

The New York governor in three tours had traveled sixteen thousand miles and had delivered a hundred and seventy-five speeches. Although Dewey had large turn-outs, Truman, according to press reports, apparently secured larger and more sympathetic audiences.

Throughout the campaign the American audience in general was described as comparatively "apathetic" despite the energetic speechmaking of these two debaters. Perhaps many Republicans were complacent because the pollsters assured them of victory; perhaps the general prosperity and sense of security explained some indifferences; perhaps it was hard for the electorate to note sharp differences in the position of the two parties concerning major issues. The two candidates

---

[1] The text as recorded and transcribed by the New York *Times.* A text prepared for delivery was furnished through the courtesy of Paul E. Lockwood, Secretary to Governor Dewey.

[2] For biographical note, see Appendix.

[3] Dewey also traveled widely in the 1948 Republican primary and gave hundreds of speeches. *Representative American Speeches: 1947-48*, p144-67 for the Dewy-Stassen debate.

talked about different matters. A Dewey speech of September 20th, over two networks, received a Hooper rating of 12.7. A Dewey speech in 1944, over only one network, rated 18.4.[4] The election figures confirmed these reports of audience apathy. The total popular vote of 1948 despite the population increase, was 47,110,000 as compared with 47,974,000 in 1944 and 49,901,835 in 1940. In 1948 barely 50 per cent of those eligible voted.[5]

Dewey at Madison Square Garden summarized his Republican tenets. In prefatory remarks he reminded his visible and invisible audience that his strategy in his political drive had been to present his cause with a dignity "worthy of America."

His thesis was that of a unified America. He would ameliorate the lot of farmers; would support prices and extend rural electrification; concentrate on conservation of natural resources. Labor interests of every sort would have his benediction and close cooperation. Old age, the unemployed, and other units would have his political succor. Social security for all was likewise one of his basic goals. Civil rights, too, "our most cherished heritage," he would defend and extend. Finally, international peace and cooperation would ensue in a Republican regime. Such, in essence were his principles. They inspired him to full eloquence.

What was lacking? Although his oratory, especially in the closing paragraphs, was genuine, a kind of semantic abstractness pervaded all. To translate or interpret the phrases, the reader or hearer would need to revert to Dewey's speeches at Pittsburgh, or at Boston, or at Chicago, or at Oklahoma City. The specific equivalents of the generalizations had been previously expressed here and there (for example at Boston). But the American public in general, absorbed in their prosperous and routine concerns, were usually unable to distinguish these subtleties from the more specific utterances of "that Missouri salesman." The latter used the vernacular of the here-and-now.

The mystery of why Dewey the lawyer, the experienced, successful challenger of Stassen, the battling governor of the greatest state in the Union, moved so tardily in grappling effectively with his Democratic antagonist, is hard to explain. Granted that Taft and the Eightieth Congress were millstones and that Gallup misread the signs of the times, still Dewey might have punctured the pseudo-logic and exposed the soft core of plausibility accompanying some of the pleas of his rival.

What of the Dewey delivery? Both Dewey and Truman need to be evaluated with respect to their presentation to visible crowds and to the radio and television audiences. Dewey's reserve and dignity were reflected in his speaking personality. He was at his vocal best over the radio. His reading was fluent and sounded like extempore speaking. His tones conveyed confidence and his diction, cultivation and precision.

    [4] New York *Times*. Sunday, October 10, 1948. Section IV, p 1.
    [5] *United States News*. 20:13. November 12, 1948.

The very excellence of his inflections, vocal quality, pitch variety, pauses, and control of vocal intensity, however, diverted attention to his delivery. Often listeners felt that a studiousness was apparent, a concern for presentation, whereas the highest art demanded more complete absorption in the subject itself and in the audience. Effective communication is a two-way process.

Truman, by contrast, sometimes fumbled with his manuscript and failed to communicate his ideas. Later, when he resorted more frequently to notes, he strikingly improved in timing, emphasis, vocal informality and in genuine communicativeness.

Radio experts, although crediting Dewey with an unusually good radio voice, attributed no small part of the November results to Truman's improvement in radio effectiveness. However the relative vocal skills of these two performers may be estimated, students of speech agree that the radio was a powerful agency in the 1948 campaign and that the microphone, much more than the hundreds of "whistle stops," influenced millions of voter-listeners to make up their minds during the weeks before November second.[6]

It is great to be home again and you have given me a perfectly wonderful homecoming. It is all the more wonderful because it is a homecoming on the eve of victory.

I am deeply moved by your welcome—the more deeply because I know this welcome is not meant just for me or just for the Republican Party. You are cheering tonight for the America that is on the way.

I can report to you tonight that all over this magnificent land of ours, there is a rising tide of confidence and hope. On next Tuesday the American people will say with their votes what they already feel in their hearts. You are cheering tonight for a great people who are resolved to get a government they can cheer about.

The people of the United States know there is nothing wrong with our government that good government will not cure. Our people know the kind of America they want. They want an advancing America in a world at peace. They want an America in which we can have both social progress and individual freedom —an America with security and opportunity for all. That is the America they will vote for on next Tuesday. That is why next

[6] See *Quarterly Journal of Speech.* 34:432-8. December 1948. "Radio in the 1948 campaign." Harrison B. Summers.

Tuesday's victory will be a victory for all our people and for the cause of peace and freedom in the world.

In this time of grave crisis in the world, I am very proud tonight that our Republican Party has waged this campaign, not just for our party's good, but above everything else, for the good of our country.

I am happy to have waged this campaign in partnership with a great American, the grand Governor of California, the next Vice President of the United States, Earl Warren.

At the start of this campaign, Governor Warren and I spent many hours together discussing our plans. From the very first we agreed that something more important was at stake in this campaign than merely winning an election. We agreed that this was too grave a time for politics as usual, for political circuses and sideshows; that it was too grave a time for cheap wise-cracking; that it was too grave a time for ranting, boasting partisanship. We agreed that in this grave time we would conduct a campaign worthy of America. I am very happy that we can look back over the weeks of our campaigning and say: "This has been good for our country." I am proud that we can look ahead to our victory and say: "America won."

Tomorrow night is Hallowe'en, a night traditionally given over by our children to ghost stories, hobgobblins, and witches on broomsticks. I mention the date because since this campaign began, some people have been trying to give the impression that every night is Hallowe'en. Grown men have been going around our country threatening: "Vote our way, or the Goblins will get you."

We have been hearing blood-curdling stories about "mossbacks," "bloodsuckers," "men with calculating machines where their hearts ought to be," and one shadowy ogre after another.

Members of Congress, elected by the people, have had special Hallowe'en treatments by these tellers of tall tales. They are described as "predatory animals." Each has a "mossback." They do their dreadful work with "meat axes, butcher knives and sabers," and what do these monsters eat?—Why, "Red Herring," of course. And do you know what? When the Republicans win this election—and this tops them all—when the Republicans win, it is charged, "They will tear you apart." But our people have not been fooled or frightened. Hallowe'en will be over tomorrow night, but next Tuesday the people of America are really going to bring this nightmare to an end.

Now, why do you suppose grown men would ever have used such desperate tactics in a free election anyway?

The reason is that the Democratic Party is today a splintered and divided party. Its own house is divided and at the point of collapse. Its right wing doesn't know what its left is doing—or wishes it didn't—and what's left of it is exceedingly unhappy about both wings. Its leadership presents to all the world a picture of what seems to be a wobbling, indecisive, and divided America. By its daily shifts in policy our friends at the Council tables for peace are left stunned and the work for peace is paralyzed.

In this grave hour, a party that cannot keep the peace within itself cannot be entrusted with the solemn task of uniting our country or of keeping peace in the world. This administration failed with a Democratic Congress. It failed with a Republican Congress. Now it wants a chance to fail again. Here is an administration that is actually campaigning against the traditional American ideals of unity and competence. It ridicules the idea of teamwork. It has been divided against itself for so long that it has forgotten the meaning of unity, and it never did know the meaning of teamwork or competence.

The time has come to bring these tragedies to an end. For the sake of the people of our country and the peace of the world, we must have better government. We can and we will get a competent, warm-hearted stable government for our country.

Tonight I invite every citizen—wherever he lives, however he works for a living, whatever his party—Republican, Democrat and independent alike—to join with us in this cause. I am grateful to the millions of sincere Democrats and independents who are for this victory. It is everybody's cause, for it means a better, happier future for every American.

As a people you and I have made great progress during this campaign. We have rediscovered our belief in the old-fashioned American idea of teamwork. We have rediscovered the great fundamental that when Americans are united on a team it is unbeatable. We are again discovering the solemn truth that every one of us is important to every other one of us and each of us is precious in the eyes of God. We are beginning to believe again in the reality of the American dream— and in the material and spiritual capacities of our people to make that dream come true.

As a people, we have taken stock of what is required of us for this great enterprise and our courage and faith have been renewed by what we have found. Because of the skill and industry of our farmers, our land is producing bountifully for our health and strength and for the men, women and children in the world's free, peace-loving nations. All over our country we have seen the great job our farmers are doing to conserve and increase the fertility of our nation's soil. We are determined to have a government that knows how to help them do a still better soil conservation job—and our farmers know that kind of government is on the way.

In the cities and towns of our country our people are coming to understand that the prosperity of the American farmer is essential to the prosperity of all the rest of us. It was the present Republican Congress which passed the first long-range price support program and the largest rural electrification program in our history. We will continue and strengthen those programs. More than ever before our country and the world are depending on America's farmers. Beginning next January 20, America's farmers will have an administration they know they can depend on.

All over the nation we need a new and vital approach to the conservation and better use of our natural resources—our forests and grazing lands, our mines—and the water resources of our great river systems. It is our natural resources combined with American ingenuity and skill and industry that have made our way of living the envy of all the world. Good government will help our people to conserve these resources and put them to wider and better use for the good of all of us and for the increased strength of the nation. Your next national administration will enlist Americans to do that job who are able to do it well, who will stick to their job, day in and day out, and see that we get it done.

We know that labor is a cornerstone of America's strength and that what is good for labor is good for everyone. In this free land, as in no other land, labor is free; free to organize, to bargain collectively, to strike; free to choose jobs and to change jobs; free to speak up and to talk back—and free, may I add, to go to the polls next Tuesday and vote in secret according to no dictates save the dictates of conscience.

Labor's freedoms were won through long decades of struggle. They are part of our American heritage. They will be zealously guarded and extended. American labor is going forward with a forward-moving America and with an administration in Washington which will be not merely its fair-weather friend, but its all-weather friend.

Of all the vast resources of our great country, the most precious of all is its people. The increasing security and well-being of our people are a first objective of government. Our nation has moved permanently away from the era of dog-eat-dog when our people had little or no protection against the bitter hazards of unemployment or disability or old age. We are going forward to a greater security for all our people which will make all America more secure. There will be such a release of initiative and productive power that the defeatists and the prophets of boom and bust will be utterly and completely discredited. A happier, more productive America will be one of the answers of our free people to the enemies of freedom.

The greatness of our country is not an accident. It is the achievement of millions of men and women who came to the shores of this new world with new hope in their hearts and a great light in their eyes. They were inspired to live up to those hopes and to help their country to live up to their dreams. Our fathers came to these shores speaking many languages—but the unspoken language of freedom was in their hearts. They were poor in many material things. But they were rich in the things of the spirit—in what they aspired for and in the good life they were going to make for their children.

That love of freedom has blessed our land and made it great. We shall now go forward to keep our freedom in a world where intolerance and strife and godless materialism are on the march. As a nation we shall again make human liberty our intense, devoted, active concern. Here at home we will carry on the fight against injustice and discrimination, the fight for the civil liberties of all our people in all our land.

These things we can do. With our faith in ourselves renewed, with competence and devotion restored to our government, with unity and strength of purpose among us there is nothing as a people we cannot do. There is nothing we cannot do, provided only that we have peace.

All of us—every one of us on every farm and ranch, in every village and town and city in this land—want one thing above all others—a world at peace. We want our sons and daughters to be able to plan their futures and live their lives without this overshadowing threat of another war. That is the cause that lies closest to our hearts tonight. That is the cause, above all other causes, to which your next national administration will be dedicated.

We will wage the peace patiently and firmly, with intense labor and a new devotion. We will enlist for this momentous task Americans of the highest order of competence. We will follow strong, clear policies. The world will, once again, know where we stand and it will be the same every day. We shall be all out on the side of human freedom. We will work for peace through the United Nations and by every honorable means wherever the peace is threatened. We will wage the peace in solidarity of purpose with every other free people—and we will wage it without hatred of any people. We will wage the peace knowing that by the verdict of history and in the eyes of God, justice and freedom and human decency have always been and will always be the right cause.

Tonight we are called, not to pride and boasting, but to humility. In this momentous time our country is called to renew its faith so that the world can begin to have hope again; to renew its strength so that the world can begin to be of good courage again; to renew its vision so that the world can begin

to move forward again out of this present darkness toward the
bright light of lasting peace.

This is the eve of victory. Let us use our victory, not for
ourselves—but for an America that is greater than ourselves.
Let us humbly pray that our children and their children will
look back on this election of 1948 and say, with thankful hearts:
"That was good for our country."

MADISON SQUARE GARDEN ADDRESS [7]

HARRY S. TRUMAN [8]

President Harry S. Truman gave this political campaign speech at Madison Square Garden, New York City, on Thursday, October 28, 1948. Twelve thousand gathered there under the auspices of the Liberal Party, a coalition of New Deal and other Democrats, and of "independents"—mostly organized labor groups. The address climaxed the first of his two-day election eve campaign in Greater New York City.

Preceding his evening rally, the President toured some nine miles of streets, in view of hundreds of thousands of late afternoon and evening throngs. This political demonstration was accompanied by ticker tape, confetti, red fire, and cheers. The President paused long enough in his tour to speak briefly to three home-bound crowds. The schedule augured well for strong support on Tuesday.

Truman concluded his New York drive and wind-up of his Eastern campaign with an address at the Academy of Music, Brooklyn, the next evening, Friday, October 29. He ended his 1948 speech-making with an extempore talk at St. Louis on October 30, and an election eve broadcast from Independence, Missouri. In all he made seven separate campaign trips. After Labor Day he covered twenty-two thousand miles, and gave two hundred and seventy-five speeches, many at "whistle stops," and to some six million auditors. In a single day, for example, he delivered sixteen talks. The average was ten a day. "Truman spoke to his fellow Americans in the most intensive platform activity the country has ever seen—either before or since radio came into popular use." [9]

At Madison Square Garden the speaker recapitulated the issues he had stressed since his acceptance speech in the early morning hours of July 15th. His propositions included: (1) The Republicans have failed in their futile opposition to the New Deal program, economic, social, and military, since 1932. (2) The Republicans refuse to go along with the proposals to elevate the hourly minimum wage to seventy-five cents; in the widening of social security programs; in the endorsement of an all-out health program and extensive federal aid to education; in the repeal of the Taft-Hartley labor law; in any constructive solution

[7] The text of this speech "as actually delivered" was furnished by Charles G. Ross, Secretary to the President.

[8] For biographical note, see Appendix.

[9] *Quarterly Journal of Speech.* 34:424. December 1948. "Truman—A Winning Speaker." Jennings Randolph.

of the problem of prices; in supporting a low-cost housing program. Although the President at Madison Square Garden pleaded for a strong Israel in conformity with the boundaries set by the first United Nations plan, both candidates hardly made international policies a major issue in the campaign.

This New York City address was in the President's typical campaign vein and language, a style Truman had gradually evolved during his hundreds of appearances throughout September and October. He was informal, colloquial, concrete, sarcastic, humorous, individual (like Harry Truman) and decisively aggressive. He was always alert to his audience. He praised his friends but mostly castigated his political foes. Typical were his expressions, such as "Dewey, a 'me too man'," "Hoovervilles," "ragged individualism," "awful mess," "stuffing pay envelopes with propaganda," "Republican moaning and groaning," "second hand candidate," "do-nothing 80th Congress," "the GOP stands for 'Grand Old Platitudes.'"

Did Truman compose his speeches? Obviously he had little time to carve out the hundreds of campaign talks. Charles Ross reports that Truman's corps of writers and speech advisers included Clark M. Clifford, Charles S. Murphy, George Elsey, Philleo Nash. Ross himself undoubtedly had a large share in the composition. Judge Samuel Rosenman was known to have had a hand in the New York City speeches. Certainly many of the back platform extemporaneous talks were the President's own; so were some of the longer addresses (e.g., the St. Louis speech "as actually given").[10]

Certainly the text of the Madison Square talk and the others reflect the speaker's modes of thinking and language. Much journalistic heightening and organizational movement are evident, reflecting creative skill other than Truman's. The aids and speech-composers at least knew the personality of their leader and in collaboration with him produced discourses that bore a clear Truman stamp.

What of the delivery? The saving grace of Truman's delivery was his platform ease, his insistence on absolute naturalness and avoidance of any vocal pretentiousness or artificiality. His personality, his earnestness, physical and emotional vigor, his sensitiveness to his audiences and his continual rapport with them, more than any graces of voice or bodily action, account for most of his platform effectiveness. His obvious vocal limitations, a monotony of pitch and of vocal intensity, his uneven and uncultivated articulation and vocalization, with the kindred limitations of language and thinking will continue to limit him to a secondary group of platform leaders in American history. He was without question an outstanding speaker in the 1948 campaign. This appraisal and conclusion are a significant commentary on the mediocre character of American campaign speaking in 1948.

[10] *Collier's*. 122:15. December 25, 1948. "How Truman Did It." Charles G. Ross.

What of the results of Truman's campaign oratory? The Truman victory in November 1948 astounded pollsters, experts, journalists, even many a loyal and expert Democratic diagnostician. The election was the closest in thirty-two years, and the total vote was the smallest since 1932—23,386,000 for Truman (304 electoral votes), 21,368,000 for Dewey (189 electoral votes), and a few more than a million for Wallace. The Eighty-First Congress was composed of 263 Democrats and 171 Republicans in the House; of 54 Democrats and 42 Republican Senators in the Senate.

The results were due partly to (1) the failure of Wallace to poll more than a million votes, (2) the strong labor support of Truman, (3) the residue of New Deal sentiment, (4) the considerable farm support, (5) the general prosperity, (6) the failure of Republican campaign strategy to estimate more accurately the weakness of the Thurmond and Wallace votes as factors, and (7) the speech-making aggressiveness of Truman that convinced many voters that their best advantage lay in supporting him.

Thank you very much. Thank you. It is certainly good to be here tonight. You know, I was here four years ago on the same errand. It's always a pleasure to come to this great city—especially when you have so many friends.

But there is a special reason why I am glad to be here tonight. New York is a mighty source of strength in the battle we are waging to preserve liberal government in the United States. It is the birthplace of many liberal and progressive programs which have restored the strength of the nation during the last sixteen years. It is the state of those true democrats and great Americans, Al Smith, Bob Wagner, Herbert Lehman—and above all, Franklin Roosevelt. It was here in this state that these men did so much to give new life and new meaning to the principles of democracy. And when I say "democracy," I mean democracy as we understand it in this country. Because of their great work our country, and the entire world, is a better place in which to live.

We have come here tonight to this great gathering under the banner of the Liberal Party—a party which has done so much for liberal causes. And I consider it an honor to be here with the Liberal Party under that banner.

We have come here tonight with one mind and one purpose. We have come to pledge once more our faith in liberal government, and to place in firm control of our national affairs those who believe with all their hearts in the principles of Franklin D. Roosevelt.

Now, I have a confession to make to you here tonight. For the last two or three weeks I've had a queer feeling that I'm being followed, that someone is following me. I felt it so strongly that I went into consultation with the White House physician. And I told him that I kept having this feeling, that everywhere I go there's somebody following behind me. The White House physician told me not to worry. He said: "You keep right on your way. There is one place where that fellow is not going to follow you—and that's in the White House."

I think the Doctor's right. I'm going to be there, working for the people, for four more years because you believe that I'm trying to do the right thing.

Now, there are some other places besides the White House where this gentleman won't follow me. He won't follow me if I go into the record of the Democratic and Republican Parties.

The Republican candidate can follow me all the way from Los Angeles to Madison Square Garden, but the Republican record makes it certain that he will still be trailing along behind when the votes are counted. He is doing all he can to make you forget that record. He doesn't dare talk about it. I have never in my life been in a campaign where the opposition refused absolutely to discuss the issues of the campaign. I can't understand that sort of an approach. But after I had analyzed the situation I came to the conclusion that the record of the Republican Party is much too bad to talk about. The Republican candidate is trying to run on the record of the Democratic Party—of Franklin Roosevelt and myself. He's a "me too" man.

Let's take a look at the record and see why he can't talk about the record of the Republican Party. Let's go back a few years. In 1928 the Republicans elected a well-known efficiency engineer named Herbert Hoover, and they promised us everything. They told us if we wanted prosperity we must vote for Hoover. Well, the people fell for it. And I think this new candidate—well, he's not a new candidate—I think this second-hand candidate thinks the same way. You know what a bitter experience you had after that.

Many of you here tonight remember 1932. Over in Central Park men and women were living in little groups of shacks made of cardboard and old boxes. They were known as "Hoovervilles." Out here on Eighth Avenue veterans were selling apples. Ragged individualism, I suppose that's what you would call it. Farm foreclosures, home-owners' evictions, starvation wages, labor unions disrupted by company spies and thugs—that was the Republican record when they last had control of the Government. And, you know, there is a peculiar thing about this campaign. I have never heard of a single Republican candidate for office point with pride to any Republican administration or any Republican President.

Now, they made an awful mess of things when they had control back there when they were elected in 1928. And in 1932 we turned them out. The vigorous action which saved the Nation and restored our faith came with the Democrats, with the New Deal, and with Franklin Roosevelt.

We saved the banks. Now, in the last three years there hasn't been a single bank failure in the United States.

We saved industry. Now, industry last year and this year have made the biggest profits they ever made in the history of the country—17 billions last year, and nearly 20 billions this year. That's profit after taxes.

We saved the insurance companies. We saved the railways.

At that point the Republicans said we had done enough. But we went right on saving this great Nation of ours. We saved the people—the farmers, the workers, the unemployed, the old people who had lost their savings, and the young people who had never had a chance. And while we were at it, we saved the United States of America. We replanted the forests, we began soil conservation, we built great dams, we developed whole river valleys. We built roads and bridges, school houses and court houses. We built sidewalks and sewers, parks, and playgrounds, and low-rent housing—and quite a few battleships, too.

And all the time, the Republicans kept moaning that we were going too far. I was in the Senate during those years, and I heard them moaning. And the Congressional Record is the best evidence of the policies that the Republicans wanted to pursue, but they couldn't do it. They said we were undermining our own moral fiber—we were destroying individual initiative—that Roosevelt was a dictator—that we were opposed to free enterprise. Now, as early as 1936 they began saying that we were Communistic, and socialistic, red, or radical—because we cared for the people and the people knew it, and liked it. They tried to scare labor in 1936—you all remember this—by stuffing pay envelopes with propaganda against social security. That didn't work. They tried a new line of propaganda in 1940, and again it didn't work. The people know better. They broke with tradition and chose Roosevelt for a third term.

World War II had come and the country was in danger. But that meant nothing to Republican leadership. They came within a single vote in the Congress of the United States of disbanding our Army three months before Pearl Harbor—and they spent thousands of dollars and time, without stint, trying to prove that Pearl Harbor was brought about by one of the greatest Presidents who ever sat in the White House—and it's all turned out to be a pack of lies! They hindered and delayed our efforts to rearm the Nation. Nobody knows more about that than I do, for I was there watching them.

And all the time they kept moaning and groaning that the New Deal had weakened America. Weakened America—think of that! Now, Tojo and Hitler knew better than that. They know the answer to that one, even if the Republicans don't.

But the Republicans kept on trying to stop us, trying to stop the people and trying to kill the New Deal.

In 1944 the Republicans tried to talk their way into power again. They nominated a man who was violently opposed to the New Deal. In fact, he wrote a book about us. They nominated the same man they nominated this year—that's the reason I said he was a secondhand candidate. He was saying the same things in 1944 that he is saying today. He was attacking Franklin Roosevelt's administration then, and he is attacking my administration now. He says that because I want to talk about those things and because I want to talk about the issues that I'm just an ordinary political mud-slinger. When I go out to the people of the United States, in every corner of the United States, in nearly every State of the Union, and tell them what the facts are—then I'm a mud-slinger. He can't stand the facts—that's what the trouble is.

Time and again in 1944 he told the voters that what we need is "strength and unity." He promised to displace—and I quote—"A tired, exhausted, quarreling and bickering administration with a fresh and vigorous administration." Now, doesn't that sound familiar to you? And he asked, and I quote again: "Is the New Deal, the tired and quarrelsome New Deal, all America has to offer? "Must we go back," he asked—"Must we go back to leaf-raking and doles?" Well, you people stuck by the New Deal in 1944, and we haven't had to go back to leaf-raking or the doles, or anything else of that kind. And the reason we haven't had to go back to Hooverville and bread lines and soup kitchens is because the Democratic policies of the New Deal are correct and right, and they're for all the people and not just for the privileged few.

I must say, though, that some of you are partly to blame for this, because you didn't vote in 1946: That Republican do-nothing 80th Congress did all it could to start us back down that dismal road.

Here's another one. At Baltimore just before the 1944 election the Republican candidate said: "We must have a President who can and will work with Congress." He said he "would like to start the largest house-cleaning Washington ever had." That sounds familiar, too, doesn't it? Now he is playing the same old record again, and the record is stuck in the same old groove. What a wonderful thing it was for the people of this United States that they didn't have a President who would go along with that good-for-nothing 80th Congress! Now, he was speaking of the war-time administration of one of the greatest men in history, who was leading a united people to victory in the greatest war of all time. Roosevelt believed in the people, and the people believed in Roosevelt—and so did I. Even with millions of men overseas and away from their homes the Roosevelt ticket won in 1944. Let me put it differently: The Republicans lost and the people won again in 1944.

You know what happened then. We won the war in the most complete military victory ever recorded in history. And since the war we have enjoyed the greatest peace-time prosperity in our history.

My friends, that's the record. And as Al Smith said, "If you look at the record, you can't go wrong." The record of Republican failure and Democratic success—that's why the Republican candidate won't follow me when I talk about the record.

There's another place also where he won't follow me. He won't follow me in discussing the issues of this campaign.

He can follow me into Framingham, Massachusetts, but he won't follow me in raising the minimum wage to at least 75 cents an hour. He said in this campaign that he is for a minimum wage—and I think the smaller the minimum the better it suits him.

He can follow me into Cleveland, but he won't follow me and broaden the coverage of our social security insurance laws and increase their benefits by 50 per cent. You know, an old couple now only get $40 a month, and that's mighty little—just like that minimum wage—$16 a week. I've said time and again around this country that I wish the Republican Congressmen would have to live in Washington for a while on $16 a week or $40 a month. I think they would change their minds just a little bit.

He can follow me into Chicago, but he won't follow me in demanding that Congress pass laws for health insurance and medical care. You know, it's a shame and a disgrace that a Country as rich and as important as this great Country is today—the leader of all the world—is not able to give the people in the middle the proper kind of medical care. I've asked for health insurance because health insurance is the answer to a healthy Nation—and some day we're going to get it.

He can follow me into Boston, but he won't follow me in calling for Federal aid to education so that teachers can get a living wage, and so that modern schools can be built, and so that our children can get a decent education. That's another disgrace on this great Country. And our Republican opponent has said that the teachers' lobby—he called it "The Teachers' Organization"; he's trying to work against the teachers' lobby— he says it's the most vicious thing in this Country. Vicious because the teachers want to get a living wage and because they want to get decent housing for our school children! Now, we give money to the States to build roads. Why can't we also give money to the States from the Federal Government to build school houses and pay teachers? I think it's much more important to see that the children that ride in the buses over those roads get the proper kind of schooling and the proper sort of teachers than it is to build the roads, myself. He doesn't go along with me on that.

He can follow me to Pittsfield and Providence, but when he gets there they needn't expect him to give them any help on low-cost housing. You know, low-cost houses have been before the Congress for three years. It passed the Senate twice. First it was the Wagner-Ellender-Taft bill. That was killed. And then they introduced a new bill in the 80th Congress and they called it the Taft-Ellender-Wagner bill. And when it came up for consideration the Republican leadership in the House of Representatives wouldn't even let it in, and the Members of Congress in the Lower House couldn't even vote on it; and when it came back for reconsideration in the Senate Mr. Taft ran out on his own bill. I don't understand that.

He can follow me into New York City—and I wouldn't be surprised if he followed me right here into Madison Square Garden—but he won't follow me in demanding the repeal of the Taft-Hartley Law. You can be sure of that. He can follow me right up here on this platform next Saturday night, but he won't follow me in calling for a law to control high prices You can be sure of that.

On all these issues, when it comes to doing something for the people, the Republican candidate won't follow me—you

can be sure of that. Sometimes it looks as if he is almost per-
suaded to follow me on some of these questions, but that's as
far as he goes, and that, ladies and gentlemen, is as far as he's
going to go. Because every time the Republican candidate looks
at the program of the Democratic Party, he says, "Me too,"
and his party's record says, "Nothing doing." And his party's
record speaks louder than he does. You know, he is trying to
persuade the people at large in the Country that the elephant's
got the new look, but it's just the same old elephant—you can
be sure of that.

He could follow me all over the country in his campaign
special, but he couldn't get his party to follow me and support
a decent law for displaced persons.

Now, he couldn't get that old elephant to behave before
election time, and I wonder how in the world he's going to get
it to behave after election time with that same old leadership
in the Congress. He can't do it.

Now, let me say in all seriousness that I am glad the
Republican candidate has followed me around over the Country,
because it has shown the people how little he has to offer them.
And the American people are not going to be fooled. They want
to hear something more than platitudes. You know, "GOP"
now stands for "Grand Old Platitudes."

The Republican candidate can follow me to every city, town,
and village in this Country. But so long as he is afraid to tell
where he stands on the issues he will lose more votes than he
gains. Some of those Republican papers now are getting a little
scared. They agree I might win. Don't you worry about that—
I will win! A Democratic victory is on the way and he is doing
all he can to help us win it, and I'm glad of that.

I wish to speak now upon a subject that has been of great
interest to me as your President. It is the subject of Israel.
Now, this is a most important subject and must not be resolved
as a matter of politics during a political campaign. I have
refused, consistently to play politics with that question. I have
refused, first, because it is my responsibility to see that our
policy in Israel fits in with our foreign policy throughout the
world; second, it is my desire to help build in Palestine a strong,

prosperous, free, and independent democratic State. It must be large enough, free enough, and strong enough to make its people self-supporting and secure.

As President of the United States, back in 1945, I was the first to call for the immediate opening of Palestine to immigration to the extent of at least 100,000 persons. The United States, under my administration, led the way in November, 1947, and was responsible for the resolution of the United Nations setting up Israel, not only as a homeland, but as a free and independent political State. The United States was the first to give full and complete recognition to the new State of Israel in April, 1948, and recognition to its provisional government.

I have never changed my position on Palestine or Israel. As I have previously announced, I have stood—and still stand—on the present Democratic platform of 1948. The platform of 1944 had provisions in it under which I have been trying to act. The platform of 1948 reiterates those positions and goes a little further—and I am glad it did go a little further. What we need now is to help the people of Israel—and they have proved themselves worthy of the best traditions of hardy pioneers. They have created out of the barren desert a modern and efficient State, with the highest standards of western civilization. They have demonstrated that Israel deserves to take its place in the family of nations.

That is our objective. We shall work toward it, but we will not work toward it in a partisan and political way. I am confident that that objective will be reached. I know that no American citizen, of whatever race or religion, would want us to deal with the question of Palestine on any other basis than the welfare of all Americans of every race and faith.

That is the spirit in which all liberals face the issues of this campaign. We are concerned with justice, and we are deeply concerned with human rights—here in America as well as in the rest of the world.

I am happy to say to you tonight that the spirit of liberalism is going to triumph at the polls on November 2nd, just as sure as you are sitting in this hall.

The forces of reaction gained a beachhead in 1946 when they elected a Republican Congress. And this year they have redoubled their efforts to take over control of your Government. And it is your Government when you exercise the right to vote. And when you don't exercise the right to vote you can't complain when such things as the 80th Congress come along and commence doing things to you.

I have never lost faith in the people. I knew that when the issues were laid before them they would arise to preserve their liberties. I have not been disappointed. All over the country the people have become aroused. Democracy is on the march, and it's on the march to victory!

I have only one request to make of you: vote on Election Day. Vote for yourselves. You don't have to vote for me. Vote in your own interests. And when you do that, you can only vote one way—vote for the welfare of the Country, vote for the welfare of the world, and vote for your own welfare by voting the Democratic ticket straight on November 2nd.

PROGRESSIVE PARTY COMMITMENTS [11]

HENRY A. WALLACE [12]

Henry A. Wallace, Progressive Party candidate for President of the United States, gave this acceptance speech at Shibe Park, Philadelphia, Pennsylvania, on Saturday evening, July 24, 1948. A crowd of twenty-five thousand paid admission to hear the address.

The Progressive movement, an off-shoot of left wing criticism of the policies of the Truman administration, arose when Wallace split with Truman on the Russian issue. On September 20, 1946, at the President's request, Mr. Wallace resigned as Secretary of Commerce. [13]

On December 29, 1947, addressing a gathering of the Progressive Citizens of America in Chicago, Wallace announced his candidacy for the presidency. [14] This group developed a national organization to support him. Wallace himself spoke throughout the nation and raised considerable money for the campaign.

The Philadelphia convention opened on July 22 with two hundred delegates from forty-eight states. Much parading, singing, and other demonstration dominated the occasion. The platform was strongly leftist and, according to the press, suggested the Communist party line. The delegates adopted the Progressive Party name and by acclamation nominated Wallace for the presidency and Senator Glen H. Taylor, of Idaho, as his running mate.

At Shibe Park, Wallace was at his best as a speaker. With deep sincerity and emotional heightening he denounced the old parties and identified his progressive proposals with his individual position and leadership. He was the champion of peace with Russia, of a liberal program for dealing with agriculture, housing, social security, health, economic planning, high living costs, civil rights, and Israel.

As of July 1948, the Progressives estimated that upwards of ten million would support their ticket. Impartial observers guessed that four or five million might do so. On that basis the Republicans apparently based much of their campaign strategy. It was assumed that enough minority groups, including labor, would abandon the Democratic party in Illinois, Ohio, New York, and Pennsylvania to insure Dewey's victory.

[11] Text furnished by the National Wallace for President Committee, New York City, through the courtesy of C. B. Baldwin, Campaign Manager.

[12] For biographical note, see Appendix.

[13] See Introductory note and text, Henry A. Wallace, "Is American Foreign Policy Leading to War?" *Representative American Speeches: 1946-1947*, p33-42.

[14] See Henry A. Wallace, "I Shall Run in 1948," *Representative American Speeches: 1947-1948*, p137-43.

Despite the energetic crusade of Wallace and his fellow speakers, the considerable financial support at the rallies, and the revival fervor of the audiences, his appeal steadily lessened. To what extent the Wallacites were controlled by and committed to the Communist Party line later historians will determine. Some voters, in any case, believed that the Wallace movement was identified with communistic leadership. In the November election the Wallace vote totalled about a million.

Four years and four days ago, as Vice President of the United States and head of the Iowa delegation to the Democratic Convention, I rose to second the nomination of Franklin Roosevelt, and said:

The future belongs to those who go down the line unswervingly for the liberal principles of both political democracy and economic democracy regardless of race, color, or religion. . . . Roosevelt can and will lead the United States, in cooperation with the rest of the world, toward that type of peace which will prevent World War III.

That was four years ago. Do you remember that summer of casualty lists, and the wreckage still smoldering on the beaches of Normandy? A time of dying and destruction . . . and yet, something more.

For in that time, you remember, every one of us held a dream. At the lathe, in the fields in early morning, at the kitchen window, sweating out a barrage in the line, every one of us dreamed of a time when the sound of peace would come back to the land, and there would be no more fear, and men would begin to build again.

And in that dark time, you remember, Franklin Roosevelt looked beyond the horizon and gave us a vision of peace, an Economic Bill of Rights; the right to work, for every man willing; the right of every family to a decent home; the right to protection from the fears of old age and sickness; the right to a good education; all the rights which spell security for every man, woman, and child, from the cradle to the grave.

It was the dream that all of us had, and Roosevelt put it into words, and we loved him for it. Two years later the war was over, and Franklin Roosevelt was dead. And what followed was the great betrayal. Instead of the dream, we have inherited disillusion. Instead of the promised years of harvest, the years of the locust are upon us. In Hyde Park they buried our President—and in Washington they buried our dreams.

One day after Roosevelt died, Harry Truman entered the White House. And forty-six days later, Herbert Hoover was there. It was a time of comings and goings. Into the government came the ghosts of the Great Depression, the banking house boys and the oilwell diplomats.

In marched the Generals—and out went the men who had built the TVA and the Grand Coulee, the men who had planned social security and built federal housing, the men who had dug the farmer out of the Dust Bowl, and the workman out of the sweatshop. A time of comings and goings . . . the shadows of the past coming in fast—and the lights going out slowly—the exodus of the torchbearers of the New Deal.

I was still in the Cabinet—hoping that we might yet return, somehow, to the course Franklin Roosevelt had charted for the nation in peace. And in that great hope, two years ago this month, I wrote to the President.

I warned him that we had fallen upon cynical counsel, that the bankers and the brokers and the big brass had launched us upon a dangerous policy—the "get tough policy."

I said then that our postwar actions have not yet been adjusted to the lessons gained from experience of Allied cooperation during the war and the facts of the Atomic Age.

I said that it would be fruitless to seek solutions for specific problems without establishing an atmosphere of mutual trust and confidence—and I warned that our "get tough" policy would only produce a "get tougher" policy. That warning was before the crises in Greece, in Italy, in Palestine, in Czechoslovakia. That warning was two years ago—two years before Berlin.

You have read your papers. In the two years since the people who planned for living were eased out of Washington, and the ghosts who plan for destruction were invited in—in those two short years during which the Department of State has been subtly annexed to the Pentagon, and the hand of the military has come to guide the pen of the diplomat—we have ricocheted from crisis to crisis. The "get tough policy" has spawned its inevitable breed—the "get tougher policy."

And what harvest do we have of all our hoping, what fruits of the hard-won victory? Not peace—but the sword; not an Economic Bill of Rights—but a mounting bill of wrongs. Not life—but tens of thousands of deaths, on unnecessary battlefields in Greece—in Palestine—in China. One world, yes—frozen in one fear.

The world's eyes today focus upon the burning spot of the cold war—Berlin. Berlin need not have happened. Berlin did not happen. Berlin was caused.

When we were set out on the road of the "get tough" policy, I warned that its end was inevitable. Berlin is becoming that end.

There is no reason why the peace of a world should hang on the actions of a handful of military men stationed in Germany! In all earnestness, I assure you that if I were President, there would be no crisis in Berlin today. I assure you that without sacrificing a single American principle or public interest, we would have found agreement long before now with the Soviet government, and with our other wartime allies. Long before now we could have embarked upon a policy for Germany upon which a sound foundation could be built for peace throughout Europe.

It is not by accident that Germany has become, once again, the heart of a crisis. Germany will be the core of every world crisis until we have come to an agreement with the Soviet Union. We have been maneuvered into a policy whose specific purpose has been this, and only this: to revive the power of the industrialists and cartelists who heiled Hitler and financed his fascism, and who were the wellspring of his war chest.

In the Western Zone of Germany today, we are told, there is enjoyed "peace with justice." This so-called just peace is not just. It is a peace which rebuilds the war-making potential of German industry in the Western Zone.

This justice is being dispensed by local judges, of whom 70 per cent are former Nazi officials. German war industry is on the rise again—and its managers are the same Krupp and I. G.

Farben men who made Germany into Hitlerland. There is no peace, no justice—for either Allies or former enemies in our German policy. It is a child born of lust for power and profit. With a Germany groomed and muscled as the easternmost outpost of another war, we cannot make a peace. Nor can the world which watches helplessly.

I repeat. If I were President, there would be no crisis in Berlin. Do you remember when—only two months ago—our Ambassador to Moscow sent a note to the Kremlin? It was a note which seemed to be an invitation to sit around the table of reason—an invitation to talk over the problems which have created this continued state of crisis? Do you remember how the Russians responded with what seemed like real eagerness? You remember that day. It was as if somebody had suddenly declared peace. Sit down and talk it over, we said—that's the way. But what happened? Within twenty-four hours, our administration, having consulted its carbon-copy opposite party, slammed the door it had itself swung open.

On that day, I addressed an open letter to Premier Stalin. I detailed a program which would have safeguarded the interests of both nations and preserved the peace. Ten days later, when Stalin responded to that open letter, the "get tough" boys slammed the door again. Since that time, there have been no more approaches—except toward conflict. There are two sides to every curtain. And so, Germany still festers at the heart of all peace-making—yet, by closing the door to peace talks with Russian leaders, nothing remains but the fruitless discussions of minor officials in Berlin.

I say the peace of the world is far too fragile to be shuttled back and forth through a narrow air corridor in freighter planes. I say the lives of our children, and our children's parents, are far too precious to be left to the tempers of second lieutenants at road barriers where zone meets zone—or to the generals who are quoted calmly as favoring a "show of strength."

I say that if reasonable men, men without special interests, peace-loving men—if Franklin Roosevelt were in Washington today—there would be no crisis in Berlin. Long before this, the leaders of both nations would have rooted out the causes for conflict.

We hear it said that we should have a showdown at Berlin. But what is the showdown about? What is the American public interest which will be served by a showdown? There may be some private interests—some interests of Dillon, Read and international bankers. But there is no public interest. Dillon, Read's distinguished alumni, Secretary Forrestal and General Draper and Dewey's Wall Street lawyer, John F. Dulles, are major advisors on this issue, but I have yet to meet the American in shop or field or college or independent business who wants to give up his life to defend Dillon, Read.

I think we should look coldly at some of the facts which confront us if the cold war developed into a hot war: There is not a single nation on the European continent prepared to put an army into the field to defend Anglo-Saxon, that is, British and American policies.

We can buy generals with dollars, but we can't buy wartime armies. These generals won't die in battle. Soldiers would. We can support—and we are supporting—armies during this time of cold war, but we can't purchase suicide. We can buy governments, but we can't buy people.

It is said that we must have a showdown or lose prestige. Truman may lose prestige. Dulles may lose prestige. But the American people won't lose prestige by demanding fundamental discussions looking to peace. Our prestige in Germany went sinking when we divided Germany and established the western sector as an American and British Puerto Rico—as a colony. When we did that we gave up Berlin politically and we can't lose anything by giving it up militarily in a search for peace.

We who are met here tonight—who are met here at a time of crisis—are talking to the people of the United States and the world on behalf of the everlasting principles of the founding fathers of our country.

We who are gathered here tonight recall the crisis of a hundred and fifty years ago when Thomas Jefferson was attacked here in the City of Philadelphia—attacked because he spoke courageously for the peaceful settlement of alleged

differences between the United States and France. It was a time
of terror unsurpassed till now. Thomas Jefferson was slandered
as the tool of French Revolutionaries bought with French gold.

One hundred and fifty years ago Thomas Jefferson took leadership in forming a new party—a successful new party which
overcame the odds of a hostile press, of wealth and vested
interests arrayed against it, and of a government which sought
to undermine the new movement by jailing its leaders.

The party Jefferson founded a hundred and fifty years ago
was buried here in Philadelphia last week. It could not survive
the Pawleys, the Hagues, the Crumps, the racists and bigots, the
generals, the admirals, the Wall Street alumni. A party founded
by a Jefferson died in the arms of a Truman.

But the spirit which animated that party in the days of
Jefferson has been captured anew. It has been captured by
those who have met here this week-end with a firm resolve to
keep our tradition of freedom that we may fulfill the promises
of an abundant, peaceful life for all men.

Four score and seven years ago, the successful candidate of
another new party took office in Washington. Lincoln, with the
Emancipation Proclamation, fulfilled the promise of the new
party which he led to victory. He headed a government of the
people, by the people, and for the people. In the generations
which followed his party became a party of the corporations,
by the corporations, and for the corporations. The party of a
Lincoln has been reduced to the party of a Dewey.

But we here tonight—we of the Progressive Party—we here
dedicate ourselves to the complete fulfillment of Lincoln's
promise; we consecrate ourselves to a second emancipation; an
emancipation that will achieve for the Negro and all Americans
of every race, creed, and national origin a full, free, and complete citizenship everywhere in these United States.

We ally ourselves against those who turn to nightmares the
peoples' dreams of peace and equality.

We ally ourselves to stand against the kings of privilege
who own the old parties—the corrupted parties, the parties
whose founders rebelled in times past, even as we do today,

against those whose private greed jeopardizes the general welfare.

We stand against their cold war and their red smear, under cover of which they steal our resources, strike terror into our hearts, and attempt to control our thoughts and dominate the life of man everywhere in the world.

We stand together to stop the disasters—economic, political, and military which their policies must breed.

Only those who take the spirit of Jefferson and Lincoln and apply it to the present world situation can bring the peace and security which will end fear and unleash creative force beyond the power of man to imagine.

It was in the spirit of Jefferson and Lincoln that Roosevelt challenged the money changers in his first Inaugural Address fifteen years ago. It was in the spirit of Jefferson and Lincoln that he told the Wall Street crowd in 1940 that they had met their master. In the spirit of Jefferson and Lincoln he outlined the Four Freedoms and the Economic Bill of Rights.

It was in the spirit of Jefferson and Lincoln that he addressed that great Senator, George Norris, and said: "I go along with you because it is my honest belief that you follow in their footsteps—radical like Jefferson, idealist like Lincoln, wild like Theodore Roosevelt, theorist like Wilson—dare to be all of these as you have in bygone years."

Franklin Roosevelt did not fear; he reveled in the names hurled by those who feared the shape of his vision. We of the new party—the Progressive Party—shall cherish the adjectives and mound of hate thrown at us. They are a measure of the fear in the temples of the money changers and the clubs of the military. The base metal of vituperation cannot withstand the attack of truth.

We of the Progressive Party must—and will—carry on where Roosevelt and Norris, and LaGuardia left off. They preserved for us all that was most precious, the old-fashioned Americanism that was built for us by Jefferson, Jackson, Lincoln, Theodore Roosevelt, and Woodrow Wilson.

There are some who say they agree with our objectives, but we are ahead of our times. But we are the land of pioneers and trail blazers. Though we have reached the end of the old trails to the West; a new wilderness rises before us. The wilderness of poverty and sickness and fear. Once again America has need of frontiersmen. A new frontier awaits us—no longer west to the Pacific—but forward across the wilderness of poverty, and sickness, and fear. We move, as the Pilgrim ships moved, as the Conestoga wagons moved, not ahead of our time, but in the very tide. And always before us, the bright star, the dream of the promised land, of what this nation might be.

But the American dream is no Utopian vision. We do not plan rocket ships for week-end trips to Mars. The dream is the hard and simple truth of what can be done. In one fleet of heavy bombers lies wealth and skill that could have saved Vanport from the flood waters, that could have taken a million veterans out of trailer camps and chicken coops. We can build new schools to rescue our children from the firetraps where they now crowd two at a desk. We can end the murderous tyranny of sickness and disease. The dream is nothing but the facts. The facts are that we spend $20 billion a year for cold war. The facts are that World Health authorities, given one tenth of this sum, could in one year with $2 billion—wipe from the face of the earth tuberculosis, typhoid, malaria, and cholera!

The cold war has already brought death to millions of Americans. Look at your friends. Read the papers. Here are casualty lists. Millions—sick of cancer, tuberculosis, of pellagra, of heart disease and polio. We can prevent and cure not only these diseases but a vast host of others by devoting our science as enthusiastically to peace as to war.

A nation that is shaped for life, not death, can save these lives—your lives, the lives of your families. Together we must rise up and write an end to the casualty lists of the cold war. This is the American way—to conquer the forces of nature—not our fellowmen.

Within the past month other men, candidates of the graveyard parties, have stood in this city, have flexed their muscles, and have declared their intention to continue the cold war whose heaviest tolls have been taken here at home. Both have said that "partisan politics must stop at the water's edge." They have declared their agreement. It is an agreement which would doom the nation and the world.

It is the policies which operate beyond the water's edge; the policies which demand heavy arms, and draft acts, and the waste of resources and skills in producing for disaster—it is those policies which determine the real wages for American workers, prices for American consumers, and the life-span of all the people of the world.

Yes, other candidates have stood before the American people to declare that they have made no commitments to obtain their nominations. But they have committed themselves; they have committed themselves to the policies of the Big Brass and Big Gold; to the policies of militarization and imperialism; to the policies which cast a shroud over the life-giving, life-saving course Franklin Roosevelt had charted for this post war world.

I tell you frankly that in obtaining the nomination of the Progressive Party—a nomination I accept with pride—I have made commitments. I have made them in every section of this land. I have made them in great halls and sports arenas, in huge open-air meetings and in small gatherings. I have made commitments in the basement of a Negro church and in union halls and on picket lines. I have made commitments. I have made them freely. I shall abide by them. I repeat them with pride:

I am committed to the policy of placing human rights above property rights.

I am committed to using the power of our democracy to control rigorously and, wherever necessary, to remove from private to public hands, the power of huge corporate monopolies and international big business.

I am committed to peaceful negotiations with the Soviet Government. I am committed to do everything I can through the New Party to save the lives of those who are now to be drafted through the establishment of peace without sacrificing any American principle or public interest.

I am committed to appointing to positions in the cabinet and administration men whose training and private interests cannot conflict with their public responsibilities.

I am committed to building and strengthening the United Nations as an instrument which can peacefully resolve differences between nations.

I am committed to using the power and prestige of the United States to help the peoples of the world, not their exploiters and rulers; to help the suffering, frustrated people in the colonial areas of the world even as we help older civilizations which have felt the full destructive force of war.

I am committed to planning as carefully and thoroughly for production for peace as the militarists and bankers plan and plot for war. For many of today's 60 million jobs are cold war jobs, unstable jobs, suicide jobs. I am committed to making 60 million—and more—jobs of producing for peace—housebuilding jobs, school building jobs, the jobs of building dams and power plants and highways and clinics.

I am committed to a program of progressive capitalism— a program which will protect from the tentacles of monopolists the initiative and creative and productive powers of truly independent enterprise.

I am committed to fighting, with everything I have, the ugly practice of stifling with Taft-Hartley injunctions and the power of government the free trade union organizations of our workers. I am committed to rooting out the causes of industrial conflict and anti-labor practices; to returning us to the basic principles of the National Labor Relations Act and to strengthening the democratic organizations which give our workers safeguards against economic and political injustice.

I am pledged to fight the murderers who block, impede, and stifle legislation and appropriations which would eliminate segregation and provide health and education facilities to bridge the gap of ten years life expectancy between a Negro child and a white child born this day.

I am pledged to licking inflation by stopping the cold war, the ruthless profiteering of monopolies, and the waste of resources which could give us an abundance of the goods of peace.

I am committed to helping lift the heavy hand of fear from our elder citizens, whose minds and bodies have served to build this America and whose reward must be the economic security which will enable them to spend their days with the peace of mind that comes from work well done and appreciated. And I am committed to those programs—principally the program for peace—which will lift from our young people the dread of war and drafts and unemployed and which will replace these fears with hope born of security and the equal opportunity to develop fully their individual talents and careers.

I am committed—as I have been my whole life through—to advancing those programs for agriculture which will increase the productivity of our land and better the lives of our farmers and their families.

I am committed to stopping the creation of fear; to using all my powers to prevent the fear-makers from clogging the minds of the people with the "red issue." The American people want and deserve fewer red issues and more red meat. Millions know and millions more must see that it is not the Kremlin, not the Communists who have sent milk to twenty-four cents a quart and meat to a dollar thirty a pound; that it is the red issue not the reds who did this to us.

Yes, I am committed and I am confident the New Party will commit itself to the principle of using our democratic process to the end that all men may enjoy the benefits made possible by modern science.

And I am committed to and do renounce the support of those who practice hate and preach prejudice; of those who would limit the civil rights of others; of those who would restrict the use of the ballot; of those who advocate force and violence; and I am committed to accept and do accept the support of those who favor the program for peace I have outlined here; the support of all those who truly believe in democracy.

ELECTION OF TRUMAN [15]

LOWELL THOMAS [16]

Lowell Thomas gave this radio commentary on Wednesday, November 3, 1948. As the script indicates, reporting immediately after the presidential election results were announced, he was called upon without much warning to interpret the surprising outcome of the campaign.

Thomas has been a radio news commentator for the National Broadcasting Company since 1930; and since 1935 commentator for the Century-Fox Movietone series. He speaks five times a week to an audience of several millions. In addition, he has lectured in "almost every town of over five thousand population in the United States and Canada."

His radio broadcasts are usually objective with none of the crusading practices of Fulton Lewis, Jr., or Drew Pearson. Thomas' radio voice is friendly, vigorous, "typically American" with little regional accent. His father, a scholarly physician, taught young Thomas to speak clearly and correctly. These speaking habits were further developed during Thomas' college and university speech training and experiences. He received a degree at Denver University, studied at the Kent College of Law and later joined the faculty, and studied at Princeton and taught public speaking there. He was a school and college public speaker and debater and later was elected national president of Tau Kappa Alpha, honorary forensic society for intercollegiate debaters and orators.

Of his public speaking, he has written: "I could write volumes on the subject of my public speaking adventures. My friends seem to think I have had more than my share of fun—jaunts around the world, expeditions to far countries, association with many of the world's leaders and glamorous figures, and so on. Well, I owe it almost entirely to public speaking.

"As I look back at it now, if given the chance to do it all over again, and if obliged to choose between four years in college and two years of straight public speaking, I would take the latter, because under the proper direction it could include most of what one gets from a four-year Liberal Arts course, and then some.

"I can think of nothing that is more likely to add to your stature than well-rounded training in public speaking, combined with plenty of practical experience." [17]

---

[15] Text and permission for reprinting supplied through the courtesy of Mr. Thomas and his secretary, Miss Ann St. Peter.

[16] For biographical notes, see Appendix.

[17] *The Speaker* of Tau Kappa Alpha, 23 No4, May 1939.

Our nation today may well salute the greatest political gladiator in American presidential history. The classic formula is this —to go in against great odds, wage a single-handed battle, keep on fighting when everybody else thinks it is hopeless, never yield an inch and then win out in the end. Which classic formula pretty much tells the story of President Truman in the election.

Memory is fresh, the news having told us day after day in copious detail—how Truman went out into the arena, and made it a personal hand-to-hand struggle. That is, he hit the trail across the country and back again, and then some more, talking to big crowds, little crowds, campaigning in great cities and at the whistle stops—belligerent, scrappy, scathing, attacking, always attacking, hurling bitter phrases, angry retorts, flinging every charge in the political dictionary against the Republicans. He never let up, stumping the country in the knockdown dragout tactics, familiar in the older tradition of American politics.

So what standards of comparison have we? In the middle of the last century this country had that wild and woolly, log cabin and hard cider presidential campaign, still remembered by the slogan—Tippecanoe and Tyler, too. But that electioneering uproar was staged, not by the candidate, but by the party—the aged candidate, William Henry Harrison, playing but little part in the noisy ructions.

Then for a great political gladiator of my youth, we go on to William Jennings Bryan, so famous for his many mighty efforts to be elected President. He campaigned across the country in resounding political warfare—but he never won.

Another paladin of presidential campaigning was Theodore Roosevelt, belligerent, scrappy, fighting it out with few holds barred. But the odds were in his favor—when he carried the country against Bryan. Later, with the odds against him in 1912, he performed prodigies of electioneering, doing battle for the Lord at Armageddon—but he lost.

So take what we have just seen—President Truman, hardly wanted by his party. Democrats in a two-way split, Dixiecrat and Wallace. Lukewarm support from his own political machine. So Harry Truman did it all by himself. That phrase may be a bit extreme, but it pretty well paints the picture of his apparently hopeless campaign—scrapping and punching his way to a narrow victory—the greatest upset in American political history.

The Dewey campaign was the complete contrast. The New York Governor traveled just as far and wide as the President, the same kind of itinerary, big speeches in big towns, rear platform appearances in little towns. But Dewey deliberately refrained from any suggestion of brass-knuckle campaigning. Both he and Governor Warren kept their end of the argument on a high level of conciliation, good feeling, and national harmony.

Early this morning, at Dewey headquarters, it was remarked that the Governor was running so far behind expectations— because he refused to get into a fight with his antagonist— would not close in for the rough and tumble of political in-fighting. It was remarked that Dewey could have done it, the old-time District Attorney drawing bills of indictment, and staging a savage prosecution of the Truman administration. Such today was the view of Dewey friends—after they began to recover from their first astonishment over the election returns.

Looking back on it all, it would seem to me that Governor Dewey was the Number One victim of the polls and the experts. Nearly all of us were deluded by those figures all the public opinion polls put forth—showing an easy Dewey sweep. The political experts agreeing so unanimously.

I, myself, made no prediction on this program. I never do. I leave prophesying to others and merely pass along the opinions of others. Which, I suppose, was a lucky thing. But I'd better not say too much about that, because if I had made a forecast, I'd have been as far wrong as all the rest. For I would have definitely and positively predicted the election of Dewey.

Well, we were all fooled. So consider the position of the New York Governor—as the Number One victim of the polls and experts. In the face of the universal verdict, he could only be convinced that victory was sure. So therefore he felt he could keep his political argument on a lofty plane and avoid anger and enmity, feuds and rancors—such as might not be good for a Dewey administration. In a scrap you don't take off your own coat and tie if it looks as though your opponent is in a state of collapse, and even the Democratic leaders had predicted easy victory for Dewey.

By a dignified campaign the two Governors also could escape commitments, the campaign promises, the specific pledges in detail—which so often plague a President after he takes office. Hence the elevated, abstract tone of the Dewey campaign —competing with the tough, hard-hitting tactics of Truman.

Today I heard an elevator man give his comment. He was angry. He had voted for Governor Dewey, and said in tones of wrath: "He talked too high. He didn't talk to the little people." Perhaps that may be a revealing tip—Dewey talking over the heads of the little people, while Truman was right among them, blasting away in the language of the common man. Which, by the way, is an excellent language to talk.

Dewey, himself, did wage a grass roots campaign in the Oregon primary—when he had that knockdown, dragout tussle with Harold Stassen, in the contest for the nomination. In Oregon, Dewey knew he had a do-or-die battle on his hands. He was battling against odds, and he did a stump-speaking job right down to earth—with all the simplicities of everyday speech. But once he had the GOP nomination, then the national campaign didn't look as though there'd really be a battle at all. So he presented us with broad policy rather than attempt to demolish an opponent.

One of Governor Dewey's close friends, Lynn Sumner, told me today of a couple of farmers, solid substantial men of the soil, who went to the polls yesterday. They were asked who were they going to vote for. The two farmers answered, "Truman." They were asked why. To which they replied: "Things are fine for farmers—so why vote for a change?"

That may explain a good deal about one of the surprises of those election returns last night. It was not astonishing for President Truman to carry the Labor vote; but when he carried the great farm states of the Middle West, Wisconsin, Ohio, Iowa, that was a tremendous surprise.

I imagine that when the figures are analyzed they will show that the chief element in the Dewey defeat was the

Republican failure to sweep the farm vote, traditionally Republican, in the states he had to have to win. To which the answer may be that agricultural prices being what they are, the farmer was in no mood of discontent with the administration in Washington. The question echoing from the land of tall corn—why vote for a change?

SCIENCE

SOCIAL RESPONSIBILITY OF SCIENCE [1]

HARRISON S. BROWN [2]

Dr. Harrison Scott Brown gave this address at the first session of the *Herald Tribune* High School Forum, held at the Waldorf-Astoria Hotel, New York City, on Saturday, March 5, 1949. The session was broadcast by the Columbia and American Broadcasting systems, and by the Du Pont Television.

On the same program were Paul G. Hoffman, economic cooperation administrator, who talked on "Youth and the European Recovery Program"; Dr. Richard L. Meier, on "Science and Freedom from Want"; and Sir Oliver Franks, British Ambassador to the United States, on "Progress to Recovery in Western Europe."

Dr. Brown has achieved outstanding results as a scientist. With degrees from the University of California and Johns Hopkins, he served in 1943 as assistant in the plutonium project at the University of Chicago, and later was assistant director of chemistry at the Clinton Laboratories, Oak Ridge, Tennessee, where the atom bomb was developed. After 1946 he joined the University of Chicago's Institute of Nuclear Studies.

Dr. Brown's scientific specialties have been "thermal diffusion of gases, mass spectroscopy, and nuclear chemistry." He has done pioneer research in the origin and chemical analysis of meteors. His research report on the theory that all meteorites in the solar system came from the explosion of a single planet, X, won him a $1,000 prize from the American Association for the Advancement of Science, in 1948.

Dr. Brown, as lecturer and public speaker, has been able to interpret scientific problems and discoveries clearly and simply for the layman. His address, for example, at a National Conference of the Speech Association of America in 1946, outlining some problems of atomic energy and national defense, was one of the high lights of a three-day convention. On the platform he is dynamic, active in vocal projection and bodily movement, and on occasion is strongly persuasive.

Because of the limited time allowed for his presentation at this *Herald Tribune* Forum, he enlarged on the problem of science in rela-

[1] Text is from the New York *Herald Tribune.* Monday, March 7, 1949. Permission for this reprint granted through the courtesy of the *New York Herald Tribune* and of Dr. Harrison Brown.

[2] For biographical note, see Appendix.

tion to "social lag," but failed to expand sufficiently his three-fold program for carrying out the social responsibility of science. Although the structure of his discourse is thus not well balanced, the speech is nevertheless an excellent illustration of successful adjustment of complicated ideas to a high school audience. It secured most favorable response from the hundreds of listeners.

Whenever I am asked to speak before a group of young men and women, my thoughts drift back to the days when I was graduated from high school and a prominent business man in my home town spoke at our commencement. "The world is in a sorry plight," he told us. "It is up to you—the citizens of tomorrow—to mold the world into a globe fit for human habitation. It is up to you to abolish war and to see to it that the necessities of life are made available to all mankind."

Such graduation speeches were given that year throughout the United States and throughout the world, and for all I know they are still being given.

But what happens when the high school graduate goes out into the world and attempts to change things for the better? He suddenly finds himself called "naive," "rash," "inexperienced." He learns that the oldsters really don't want the youngsters to remake the world after all. The soreness of the tops of many young heads (resulting from much battering against stone walls) testifies amply to the resistance that confronts them.

Yet if we look back a few years we find that the majority of the soldiers who fought and died in the last war were in their early twenties and younger. The majority of the scientists who contributed actively toward the development of the atomic bomb were in their twenties. Youngsters, we are told, are old enough to fight and die; they are old enough to help figure out how to make atomic bombs—but they are too young to have anything to say about what to do about the frightening problems that face the modern world and threaten to destroy it.

In speaking today about the social responsibilities of science, I will speak of things which are relatively easy for young people, but difficult for older persons, to understand. This is because young people possess a quality that in general diminishes with years: the quality of imagination. Imagination is a quality which is an integral part of science, and naturally endowed to young people. It is a quality which sadly enough evaporates with advancing age, yet it is a quality which our unhappy world needs in abundance at the present time.

For the last three centuries the findings of science have had marked impact upon society, but people on the whole have not understood just how our world has been affected, nor have they cared. From the time of Newton men began to realize that through technology, which is based upon the findings of science, substantial comforts and profits could be gained. From the time of Pasteur men began to realize that through the application of science to medicine they might be able to live longer.

From the time of Leonardo da Vinci, men appreciated that science could materially aid in winning wars. As years went by a technological materialism was developed; demands for new technical knowledge became greater and greater; more and more men became scientists and technologists. The scientist came to be looked upon as the creator of a new and abundant life. To make substantial profits, to work less, to live longer, to win wars—what more could the people of a nation desire? In the valor of its ignorance humanity accepted science and technology as its benefactors seldom questioning, seldom asking where it was leading.

And where has it led? To a large part of the world it has brought unprecedented comfort. To an even larger part of the world it has brought unprecedented agony.

To the world of the future (the world in which you young people must live) technological expansion may bring total catastrophe, or it may aid in the moulding of a balanced world in which men may have the opportunity to live in reasonable harmony with their environment and with each other. The end result will depend upon the wisdom and imagination with which we plan for the future—upon the wisdom and imagination with which we integrate our scientific and technical knowledge from other fields of human endeavor, into a pattern for a peaceful and stable world.

Let's look at the record. It is not a happy one! Science and technology have placed in the hands of the rulers of nations tools of coercion and persuasion of unprecedented effectiveness. Modern implements of war make it possible for small groups of men to enforce their rule over large groups of people. In modern totalitarian states, the weapons in the hands of rulers make impossible successful popular revolts.

In the past, uprisings against despotism by masses of people armed only with crude weapons were possible. Today, applied science makes despotism invulnerable to internal overthrow by violent means.

Improvements in transportation and communications have increased the effectiveness of police action. Revolutionary methods of mass communication, rotary presses, radio and motion pictures provide powerful tools for persuasion. Today, when propaganda can be spread to millions of people when the governed can be unknowingly fed with untruths and kept in ignorance of the truth by government control of communications outlets, the people become powerless.

It would be pleasant to believe that by creating new techniques in transportation and communication, thus making the world effectively smaller, some sort of a dent might have been made in minimizing the concept of intense nationalism. But the reverse has been true. The creation of vast industrial nations, competing with one another, and the creation of centralized national authorities of ever-increasing power have more than overbalanced the effect upon nationalism of increasing communication and education.

History has taught us that intense nationalism sooner or later results in wars between nations. Today wars are, more than ever before, wars of competing technologies. The first half of the twentieth century will go down in history as the period within which technological developments took place which converted destruction from a difficult operation into a fantastically easy one. But as yet, we have seen only the crude beginnings of what can be done, should circumstances dictate.

Now that nations, each in the interest of its own military security, have mobilized science, we can expect developments in the technology of war to proceed at an accelerated pace.

Even our good intentions have brought trouble. The spread of sanitation measures and the control of disease to ever-increasing bodies of humanity has created the problem of overpopulation. With the population check of disease removed, we are now confronted with the gigantic task of finding ways to feed people and to keep populations in check.

Increased populations and wars have, in turn, placed tremendous drains upon our natural resources, upon our power reserve, upon our arable land.

Indeed, it is not a pretty picture that confronts us. It has caused many persons to say that perhaps, like the dinosaur, mankind is doomed to extinction.

But fortunately our position is somewhat different from that of the dinosaur, whose size, which once permitted him to survive, destroyed him when his environment changed. The dinosaur did not create the environment that destroyed him. Man, through his thoughtless misuse of science, has created his. The dinosaur had no control over his environment. Man, if he wishes and if he is willing to apply science and technology properly, may have control over his.

Science and technology offer man important tools that may enable him better to control his environment and as a result enable him to control his destiny. Man must learn how to use those tools properly and he must apply his imagination to the task of devising the social and political institutions that will permit him to utilize the tools with maximum effectiveness.

As we have not thought sufficiently far into the future, the net result of our haphazard and unplanned use of science and technology has been disastrous to society. We should now, realizing the danger that confronts us, study the future, plan accordingly and utilize those aspects of science that can aid us in moulding a more hopeful destiny than that which now confronts us.

The first social responsibility of science is to shout from the housetops whenever it sees science and technology being used in the dangerous ways in which they have been used in the past.

The second responsibility is to develop wherever possible constructive solutions to the political problems that now confront mankind: the production of food, clothing and shelter.

A third, and in many respects an even more important responsibility exists, and that is to disseminate far and wide an attitude that I like to call the "scientific attitude."

The scientific attitude is at once a way of thought, a way of conduct and a way of life. It is an attitude that has been found essential for constructive scientific progress—an attitude which, if it were to be more widely disseminated, accepted, appreciated and used, would go a long way toward helping mankind resolve the many dilemmas that now confront it. A scientific attitude has many component parts, the most important of which are straightforward and easy to understand:

The scientist must avoid dogmatism. He must always insist upon valid argument. He must proceed cautiously, yet he must be ready for change. He must insist upon the truth. He cannot permit national fetishisms to influence his judgment. And above all, he must insist upon complete, undistorted and uncompromising freedom of speech.

The assimilation of a scientific attitude will enable all of you to build the kind of world you want to live in—a world free of fear, free of war and free of want.

BUSINESS AND LABOR

WHICH WAY AMERICA? [1]

RUTH ALEXANDER [2]

Dr. Ruth Alexander gave this address before the Northeastern Retail Lumberman's Association, New York City, on January 26, 1949. The speech is typical of her economic philosophy, her brisk journalistic style, and her skill as lecturer.

Dr. Alexander has been described as a Tory, Bourbon, Constitutionalist. A graduate of Northwestern in political science, and with a Ph.D. in economics, she has committed herself to staunch defense of the American capitalistic system. Early and late, on the platform, and through her syndicated column in the New York *Mirror* and a number of other dailies, and as an editor of *Finance,* she has crusaded for free enterprise.

The speech here reprinted is strongly emotional. For economic analysis that would admittedly be pretty dull, she has substituted unqualified denunciation of socialism and, by the method of residues, she has strongly established capitalism. One might logically ask, is there no middle ground to be practically recognized between unadulterated private enterprise and out-and-out government ownership and operation of the system of production, distribution, and consumption? What of private enterprise with government regulation and, in cases, even of government operation?

The language is fervid, colloquial, oral, and even dramatic. Her delivery, too, is lively, with pleasant vocal nuances, alternating with strong climaxes, and all reinforced by effective bodily interpretation.

Dr. Alexander, a lecturer since 1935, has been in wide demand. She has lectured on such subjects as "Education for freedom," "What does capitalism mean?" "Spiritual meaning of democracy," and "Shall man or the state survive?" She was a frequent speaker on the "Wake Up America" program and was the first woman to address the National Association of Manufacturers at their annual convention in New York.

Which way America?

Don't let the title fool you. It's not in the nature of a prediction—any man's folly. It won't tell you which way the

[1] Text and permission to reprint supplied through the courtesy of Dr. Alexander. Reprinted from *Vital Speeches of the Day.* 15:301-3. March 1, 1949.
[2] For biographical note, see Appendix.

international wind blows—any man's guess. It will tell you which way the flag at home—namely, where we stand; where we're headed; who pointed our nose in that direction and what we can do about it.

In other words, the content of this talk is an analysis of present trends—and inquiry into their origins and objectives. The purpose of this talk is to persuade businessmen to thow off their occupational timidity and speak up for themselves.

What have you got to lose?

Your good name has been taken from you. Your incomes have been pilfered and are on the way to confiscation. Your shelter is often on a thirty-day basis. Your children have been indoctrinated with communism in the name of a "liberal" education. And now your wives are to face the hazards of childbirth under doctors who are politically certified.

What are you waiting for?

I think I know. I think you are waiting for the answer to the $64 question—"But what can I do about it?"

You'd be surprised. You can do a great deal. You got yourselves into the dog house because you "scare easy." You can get yourselves out by refusing to scare at all.

Certainly there is no use talking about it if we don't intend to do anything about it. And if we can't—or won't—do anything about it now we might as well call it a day for the grand old USA, lie down, roll over, and purr at the feet of those who fake "love for humanity" in order to get power over humanity.

First, where do we stand?

By the terms of the President's messages, fulfilling his campaign promises with unprecedented fidelity, we have assumed the mantle of socialism. For fifteen years we hung by our eyelashes over the precipice of the police state. We are no longer on the brink. We are within the borders. A planned economy is inconceivable without Gestapo eyes and ears and jails to insure fulfillment of the plan—which, however wise, can never be unanimous.

I had hoped that the end result of the second war to spread Democracy would be as advertised. I thought that this time our shots for freedom might go home. But again they went wild. We set out to Americanize Europe. Instead, we Europeanized America. We set out to reverse the Socialist "trend of the times." Instead, we climbed on the band wagon. We set out to lead a "liberated" world away from a planned economy. Instead, we embraced it ourselves.

Of course it doesn't make sense. But there it is.

For better or worse, now—but not necessarily forever—the President's program makes us an integral part of the Socialist world. Our attitude toward property, privacy, and personality is based on the universal orthodox Socialist concept of the relationship between the individual and the state. Namely, the dominance of the state—defined as a living tissue, a pseudo-biological organism—over its subordinate and component parts, the individual citizens.

I am talking to you as producers—the most important group in our nation. I want to tell you something about your competitor—the state as producer. You may think you're in competition with one another, but the great menace to you all is the monopoly state. Let me read you my column for the New York *Mirror* of Sunday, January 30 [1949], on this subject and then you won't have to get it! (Just be sure you get all other Sundays to come!)

Last Sunday I said it made no difference who owns the instruments of production as long as the product or "national dividend" is large and is consumed by the people.

I want to elaborate that today.

It makes no difference whether one, a few, or many own our tools as long as they are in private hands. When they are owned or operated by the state that is something else again, and it makes all the difference in the world.

In any society the state is merely the name used to describe a group of men in power—for the time being or life, as the case may be.

These men, the state, do not make their living by creating and exchanging goods and services in the market place.

They are not "in trade," as the British snobs used to say. They are in politics. They are not producers. They are parasites who live off the productive efforts of the citizen taxpayers.

There is nothing wrong about that unless government becomes so swollen with bureaus, and their administrators, "bureaucrats," that the taxpayers are bled white.

In any case, the state produces nothing. Everything it has it gets. Everything it gives away it first must take away.

If the state decides to give Mr. Voteright Smith free room and board, free education, hospitalization, etc., etc., it must first take away the money to pay for these services from Mr. Taxpayer Jones. THERE IS NOTHING FREE.

When the state owns or operates industry it can afford to operate it at a loss. It has access to unlimited tax money with which it can subsidize its losses.

But private industry cannot operate at a loss for long. Unless it can keep its cost of production low enough to make an annual profit it must shut up shop.

Which do you think will operate more efficiently—the state which has no incentive to make a profit or private industry to which profit is a matter of life and death?

And which will result in the largest product, the greatest national dividend, the biggest piece of pie to be cut by us all? Efficiently operated industry, looking for a greater and greater reward, or inefficiently operated industry, indifferent alike to profit or loss? You don't need me to answer that. Just use your own common sense.

That's the story for January 30. I wish I could write every day instead of every Sunday. As a matter of fact, I do write every day! It takes me six days to compress an economic earthquake into five-hundred words and on the seventh I rest— just like the Bible says.

According to the President's proposals, which I assume will become laws, property, defined as producers' goods, is to be publicly owned and/or operated in key industries. Privacy— defined as the right of the individual to buy or sell; to labor or loaf; to sped or save—at his discretion—is to fall by the axe of the tax collector. Personally, defined as valuable variations in opinions, in choice of livelihood, education or association, is to be standardized by over-all conformation to the plan.

The outlook is grim. But there's always another chance. What are twenty years to history?

As of today, however, we are embarking upon a Yankee version of the current British experiment.

Our self-styled "liberals" thought it would be just dandy to try socialism over here in keeping with the "trend of the times." In fact, the lunatic fringe thought so-called "Democratic socialism" might ward off Soviet socialism! They wanted to cuddle up to the Russian baby bear to keep the Russian papa bear away! But the child has the potential characteristics of the parent and Democratic socalism is identical with Lenin's "Democratic centralism"—the transitional stage between capitalism and communism!

But what has socialism of any kind—British or Russian, or German or Italian—produced that makes it so hot? Why should we imitate a non-productive economy? What makes England tick, for instance, when millions of people are getting something for nothing? We, a productive economy, are providing something. That's what makes England tick! We are subsidizing socialism.

Nearly two hundred years ago, the great British philosopher, Jeremy Bentham, pointed out that that government which provides the "greatest good for the greatest number" is the most desirable.

In the machine age Bentham's statement must be amended to read, "the greatest goods to the greatest number." Capitalism provides the greatest goods to the greatest number. Compare the relative scales of living in our capitalist democracy and any Socialist country throughout all history.

The voluntary exchange of goods and services in a free competitive market provides the greatest goods to the greatest number.

A free market is outlawed by the terms of Socialist overall planning. No matter how wise the plan or how considerately enforced, compulsion is its essence and maximum productivity its despair.

Russia, England, and France are paying the price of compulsory exchange of goods and services. The incentive of personal gain for personal labor has been reduced in England and removed in Russia—a difference in degree, not in kind. Result. The people's scale of living is at subsistence level, consumers' goods are so scarce they must be rationed, and producers' goods are at the mercy of politicians.

What is there in that setup that is worthy of imitation? Yet we asked for it. Our record, if nothing else, should have demonstrated that capitalism is the most productive system and must be preserved for that reason if no other. Yet we deliberately chose a system of socialism with its inevitable by-products of compulsory labor, allocation of jobs and goods, and taxation without cessation.

Even if our socialism should prove "successful," it would mean merely an equality of poverty—as in England and Russia today. Poverty is an unworthy and uneconomic aim. Capitalism inherited poverty from its predecessors, primitive socialism and feudal socialism, wherein the top "looked after" the bottom and the bottom "looked up" to the top for its daily bread.

But capitalism has done more to alleviate poverty than any system known to mankind. It is the "wunderkind" of history. And we want to scrap it!

Sometimes we even apologize for it and, like the apostle Peter, deny our allegiance to it. "Who, me? Oh no, I'm not a capitalist, I'm a liberal!" Even businessmen have been known to say things like that—in their off moments, of course! Even businessmen's wives have been known to sabotage the very system which provides food, clothing and shelter for them and their children. They will do a marvelous job of budgeting and marketing to get the most for their dollar and then go straight down the street and vote away half their husband's entire income because they think it is fashionable to be a "liberal"!

But what is a modern "liberal"? A man who likes to play God with other people's money. Liberal with others' earnings—no relation to liberty—but first cousin to regimentation. A liberal is one who poses against special privilege for the businessman—a producer—in order to get special privilege for himself—a parasite. For privilege can never be abolished, though the personnel of the princes of privilege may change.

Finally, a liberal is one who says—and who may believe—that he does not want socialism and its derivative, communism—but who supports freedom of speech for Socialists and Communists because of a deformed interpretation of liberty.

But back to our socialism, vintage 1949—How did we get that way? What appeal could socialism, a scarcity economy, have to us, luxuriating in the economy of plenty provided by capitalism?

Well, I'll tell you. It appealed to minority pressure groups who itched to get their hands in the tax gravy and their signatures on the law books.

Some of these groups were organized—like labor and the city bosses. Some were technically unorganized but occupationally amalgamated. Some were ideologically knit, soul mates of socialism—like the penthouse pinks who sling the political slang of ragamuffins but who live the life of Riley.

The next time one of your defeatist friends shrugs his shoulders and says, "But what can we do? It's what the people want?" Please reply, "It's what what people want?" Then name the above mentioned minority pressure groups which obviously are not the people.

I doubt if all these knew what they voted for or what they want. I further doubt if the President, himself, realized the fatal implications for freedom in his messages. I have great respect for his personal integrity, and I only wish his information were comprehensive regarding socialism.

For a man's judgment is no better than his information. And the public mind has not been informed on the program upon which they are embarking. In fact, I'll go so far as to say that if an unmistakable majority of fully informed and fully aware voters had passed reasoned and sober judgment on socialism and voted for it by name, I, for one, would put up and shut up.

I emphasize by name. For, hitherto, we have been sold a Socialist bill of goods piecemeal. This time we went the whole hog and it should have been tagged, so the voter would have known the contents of the package he bought.

I have long advocated a fair trade practices act in the field of ideas. So many things are put over on us under assumed names. It might have spared us the economic cannibalism of socialism. Opponents of capitalism have called it contemptuously a dog-eat-dog economy. But for real juicy cutthroat practices the monopoly state of socialism has no equal. Under capitalism, there is always recourse to the state if the going gets too rough and monopoly rears its ugly head. But under socialism the state itself is the monopoly—the sole producer, the sole distributor, the sole employer.

But the state is not the creator. That is the unforgivable sin of socialism.

Let me tell you in a nutshell the line where capitalism ends and socialism begins. In a free capitalist economy, exchange of goods and services takes place between the two interested parties—buyer and seller. They determine the conditions of the bargain—if any. Whatever is offered, each can take it or leave it—there is no cracking down, no coercion, no hard feelings.

In a planned socialist economy, the state steps in and determines the terms of the bargain, from which there is no appeal. The case for this economic interventionism rests on the assumption that the state will enforce better terms as to price. Better terms for whom? For the poor man who may be undeserving? For the rich man who may contribute heavily to campaign funds?

No one can tell. But X marks the spot where capitalism ends and socialism begins; where a non-productive but not disinterested third party—the state—steps in, determines the conditions of exchange and enforces its decision by violence.

As for the place where socialism ends and communism begins, there is no signpost. That is the terrible danger. One merges into the other by a series of gradual changes. The qualitative break is made between capitalism and socialism. From then on, the breaks are quantitative and creep imperceptibly inch by inch upon an indifferent or ignorant people.

I could talk forever on this subject. But the time is getting short and I know you have important appointments. Let me conclude with some specific suggestions which are my answers to the question—"Now that I know where we stand, where we are headed, and who pointed our nose in that direction, what can I do about it?"

Speaking broadly, you can organize and you can become class conscious. Class warfare was not of our choosing, but our survival depends on its outcome.

Organization is inevitable in the machine age. Modern industry and agriculture demand skill. Organization is the social expression of technical skill. Labor figured that out and has acted with more dispatch than business. Take a page from labor's book. Be intolerant of those who sabotage your team by refusing to join your organization. For the only hope of survival is for business to organize from attic to cellar. Organization does not mean monopoly. Your own great associations— the least monopolistic in the nation when it comes to restricting production or influencing the market—stand as a beacon light to business in general.

Further, specifically, disabuse the public mind of the propaganda that there is any economic antagonism between so-called "big" business and "little" business. "Big" depends on "little" for parts and "little" depends on "big" for a market. They are mutually dependent, but "big" business has taken the biggest beating from the politicians who feed at its hands. "Little" business has been courted by the same men who have tried to discredit its market, "big" business.

Third, contribute money to your organization without stint. A man can't fly on one wing and an organization is helpless without a well-filled pocketbook for participation in public affairs. It is staggering to realize that "the combined legislative expenditures for all business organizations of all trades do not match the legislative appropriations of one of the two rival labor organizations."

What do you expect for a dollar—and a two-bit dollar at that?

Fourth, go class conscious. Be proud and loud about the fact that you belong to the middle class—the creators and preservers of our two-edged sword, capitalism and democracy.

When "liberals" accuse your capitalism of boom-and-bust shenanigans, remind them that the universe itself is characterized by periodicity. Why not the market? It is not an isolated phenomenon but is dependent on the physical phases of life, such as the crops, and on the social phases, such as wars and peace. Nobody can predict Mother Nature or human nature. And they are beyond control.

Fifth, speak out in meetings. When the cracker barrel Socialist yaps about profits being too high, ask him, "Too high for whom? Too high for the employer who must plow them back into the business or put them away for a rainy day? Too high for labor when employment always follows the trend of profits? Or just too high for politicians who want to make hay out of them?"

Sixth, above all, take pen in hand! Never underestimate the power of a single letter. It sounds trite to say, "write your Congressman." So I say, "Wire your Congressman and write everybody else." Much of our freedom of speech has been all freedom and no speech. Write blistering letters to forums whose "neutrality" exists in name only. Let radio stations and advertisers know when their stooges offend your class patriotism. Send love and kisses to that small lonely band of Americans who have been fighting your battles so long and with so little encouragement from you. Meaning, among others, John T. Flynn, Fulton Lewis, Jr., Westbrook Pegler, Henry J. Taylor, George Sokolsky, Isaac Don Levine, Sam Pettingill—and Ruth Alexander!

It may be too late. But it's worth trying.

If you will forget your fears which brought you to this lowly state and remember your magnificent and unsurpassed production which brought our nation to its high state you will hold your heads up once again.

It is your turn now to wake and rise. "You have nothing to lose but your chains!"

REPEAL OF THE TAFT-HARTLEY LAW [3]

HELEN GAHAGAN DOUGLAS, JOSEPH MARTIN,
SAMUEL RAYBURN, HAROLD DONOHUE [4]

The speeches below are excerpts from the debate in the House of Representatives, April 26-May 4, 1949, on the repeal of the Taft-Hartley law. The debate was prolonged but not particularly distinguished. The examples here enclosed are typical of the tone and method of argument.

President Truman repeatedly announced in his campaign that he would repeal the Taft-Hartley law. The House and Senate Committees, both administration controlled, sent to Congress on January 29, a labor bill that would repeal the Taft-Hartley Act and reenact, with minor changes, the Wagner Act of 1935 (the proposed bill was named for John Lesinski, of Michigan, chairman of the Labor Committee).

Because the two hundred and sixty Democrats in the House (as compared with a hundred and seventy-one Republicans) were divided on the issue, various bills were offered as substitutes. A Southern Democratic and Republican coalition supported the John S. Wood bill, which in the main retained the provisions of the Taft-Hartley Act.

The administration forces, seeing defeat, threw their support to the Hugo S. Sims bill—which contained comprehensive provisions intended to draw backers away from the Wood bill.

The Sims bill was voted down, two hundred and eleven to one hundred and eighty-three. The Wood bill passed, two hundred and seventeen to two hundred and three, and thus the administration was clearly defeated. At the last moment, however, Vito Marcantonio of New York, American Laborite, demanded that the bill be engrossed. This parliamentary device delayed the final vote.

On the next day, May 4th, a vote to recommit the bill to the Labor Committee passed, two hundred and twelve to two hundred and nine. The bill thus completed its round trip from the Committee chamber and left intact—for the time—the Taft-Hartley Act.

The House apparently decided to await action by the Senate.

MRS. DOUGLAS: Mr. Chairman, as we meet here today to discuss this vital issue of labor legislation, all of us realize that the subject with which we are concerned has been debated and discussed at almost incredible lengths. We know that spokes-

[3] *Congressional Record* (81st Congress, 1st session). 95:5280-81. April 27, 1949 (daily edition); 95:5602-3, 5611, 5640-1. May 3, 1949 (daily edition).
[4] For biographical notes, see Appendix.

men for both industry and labor have expounded their ideas over and over again on each minute point in the whole issue. We have literally been deluged with reports, analyses, studies, inquiries, investigations, opinions, briefs, and practically every form of written and spoken argument on every detailed phase of the issue.

I suppose we all thoroughly know the provisions of the Wagner Act and the provisions of the Taft-Hartley law.

We are not discussing these provisions. What we are discussing here is a philosophy, and the character of our discussions reveals our attitude toward the millions of working men and women of this country. A vote for the Wood bill is a vote for the Taft-Hartley philosophy. The gentleman from Virginia has made this crystal-clear.

The restrictive measures of the Taft-Hartley Act in times of full employment are repressive. They curtail and hold down the activities of labor unions. In times of unemployment, the Taft-Hartley Act, because it so clearly undermines the worker's means of self-defense, could break and destroy labor unions.

Do we believe in collective bargaining or not? That is the question we answer here. Do we believe that the men and women who turn out the raw materials and goods from our mines, factories, and mills and fields should be granted enough power by law to bargain for a living wage and decent working conditions?

When the working men and women can protect themselves against the machines of giant corporations, freedom is assured and democracy is protected. One doesn't find labor unions—independent, free labor unions—in a Fascist or Communist state.

Why is it that the first attack in a Fascist state is on the labor union? Because if working men and women who are the very heart of our society meet freely and express themselves, there can be no dictator.

There are any number of sources that one can go to to prove this point. But I quote from a document printed here in the Congress of the United States, "Fascism in Action":

The role of labor in the Fascist economic and political system is one of subservience. One of the most important changes fascism brings about is the abolition of free collective bargaining and of self-governing labor organizations. Labor policy under fascism first of all takes away from the worker all means of self-defense. It renders all militant labor action impossible.

And for the farm Representatives, I might say that in a Fascist or Communist state the co-ops are number two on the death list, because they, too, contain the deadly germ of democracy—quote from Robert Ley.

It has always seemed ironic to me that the Republicans in the Eightieth Congress wrote into the labor act a requirement that labor leaders must sign a non-Communist pledge.

While the Eightieth Congress professed to be fighting communism, actually they were following an economic pattern which if carried out logically throughout our economy could lead only to fascism or communism.

The majority of the American people live on very limited incomes. Statistics show that about 46 per cent of all families throughout the country have incomes below $3,000 and almost 30 per cent, below $2,000.

Some folks forget that. The big corporations and Wall Street, despite the tremendous economic power they possess, do not represent the desires and aspirations of Americans, whether they work in the factory or in the fields, in the ships or in the offices, whether they be doctor, teacher, or lawyer.

And that, I believe, is the greatest understatement of this debate.

That is why the four issues in the recent election were housing, farm price support program, reclamation and development of the West, and the repeal of the Taft-Hartley Act. That is why the farmer voted with labor. The farmer and labor saw the handwriting on the wall—big corporations and Wall Street, in addition to their tremendous economic power, were again to make and enforce the rules. The farmers and labor remembered what happened in 1929.

Between 1929 and 1933, auto production dropped 80 per cent but prices dropped only 16 per cent.

Between 1929 and 1933, iron and steel production dropped 83 per cent but iron and steel prices dropped only 20 per cent.

In this same period with agricultural production dropped only 6 per cent, agricultural prices dropped 63 per cent, and in this same period somewhere around 12 million consumers found themselves without any income.

Politicians and Congressmen may forget these figures, but the farmer and the laboring man cannot. He remembers them in the pit of his stomach.

In 1948, after paying taxes, profits of corporations were $21 billion. $7 billion were distributed in dividends, $14 billion were undistributed.

Labor unions are desirable not only socially but economically, if enough money is to get back into the consumers' hands to keep production rolling and maintain full employment.

It is my own feeling that because of the extraordinarily extensive debate on the details of the legislation before us, we have perhaps failed to see the forest for the trees. In other words, I have a feeling that we have failed to focus our attention on the basic question involved in the whole matter. Dare we in the face of the tremendous corporate concentration in this country, repress and hold down the activities of labor unions?

Is it fair or just for the Congress of the United States to impose, by statute, restrictions which make it almost impossible for labor organizations to grow, or even to survive while at the same time granting to big business full permission to expand until it has achieved a virtual monopoly of practically all lines of industry? . . .

MR. MARTIN: We face a serious situation not only in America but in every nation in the world. We face the possibility of a new war and we face the catastrophe of an economic depression. Either would be ruinous. We must avert both. We must keep this country sound and we must avoid bitter internal dissension if we are to come through unscathed.

In such a situation it is childish to talk about granting or denying to a Democrat patronage in accordance to their vote on the request of the executive department. That is the road to totalitarianism. It is the road to the end of representative government. It is the collapse of a government of the people, by the people, and for the people, and when it comes, labor, management, and everybody loses. God forbid that such a condition shall ever come here in America.

It is small-potato talk to rail at Republicans and Democrats voting on the same side when they think alike on certain legislation. Should a Democrat vote against his convictions simply because he finds himself walking down the aisle with a Republican instead of a Democrat? That, of course, is sheer nonsense. What good is representative government if we do not express our own convictions? And may I say right here, it is time we established real tolerance and understanding between the sections of our common country as well as between races and religions. In war and in every great crisis like the present, northerners and southerners have stood side by side. We never let the party label prevent cooperation for the welfare of the country. We are one common people in this country; we shall all go up together or we shall go down together. Let us vote on great issues as Americans and not as petty partisans, as trusted representatives of the people and not as any one man, or few men demand.

I want to help bring cooperation, understanding, and peace between labor and management. It is absolutely essential if we are to avoid a depression. It is absolutely necessary if we are to fulfill our obligations to the world. I believe the Wood amendment, as amended, and with amendments to come, will give us the best start and for that reason I am urging its adoption. I would not say it is the perfect answer, but it does make progress. I believe personally, labor and management should sit down together and study the situation and reach an understanding. That should not be impossible where there is mutual respect for the other. And both groups have so much to gain by ending class hostilities. And they might find it very easy to reach a decision. Because they have not gotten together, Congress must act.

This better understanding must be reached. Two great and powerful minorities fighting each other sow the seed of destruction. Soviet Russia can never conquer America through force of arms. It can only prevail when we are divided. This must not be allowed to come.

The one great urge of the American people at the present is for peace and jobs. They are tired of war and they want our efforts to be used to bring a real and lasting peace. There is plenty of chance for everybody in this big world of ours. And the people want peace in the industrial world to the end they can improve their position in life and give to their children more of the opportunities and comforts of life.

I sincerely believe the Wood amendment, as amended, is a contribution to that end. I hope the substitute will be rejected; several other amendments to the Wood bill be adopted and then the Wood amendment be added to the Lesinski bill.

Such a bill will strengthen the union—the union of the American States and the union of the American people in this march to progress, prosperity, and peace at home and abroad.

MR. RAYBURN: Mr. Chairman, I have sat here for several days and been tremendously interested in the remarks that have been made for and against the Lesinski bill, the Wood amendment, and the various other amendments that have been offered. I think it has been an enlightening debate.

I quite agree with my distinguished friend from Massachusetts [MR. MARTIN] that we live in a dangerous world. Crosscurrents are running throughout its length and its breadth. Many people in many sections of the earth feel that in the situations under which they must exist they are being done a grave injustice. I quite agree with them. Frankly, I do not know what kind of a world we are living in, and I do not think anybody else on the face of this earth does. Nobody can look into the mind of a dictator, no instrument has been factoried yet that would pierce his heart. So I agree that we are living in a dangerous time.

I do not want the people of the United States or any section of them, class, creed, or color, to think the Congress of the United States would do them a continuing injustice. Millions of good men and women throughout the length and breadth of this land have felt ever since the passage of the Taft-Hartley Act that they have been done a serious injustice.

We had a campaign last fall, and I shall try to steer clear of politics in my remarks. One side said the Taft-Hartley Act was unfair and unjust. The other side, when they spoke of it, defended it. It seems that we have been divided on the justice and the fairness of the Taft-Hartley Act up until today, when even the leader of the minority party, that was the majority party in the Eightieth Congress, said that he is for amendments, far-reaching amendments, to the Taft-Hartley Act. Yet he is for the Wood amendment, and most of those who have spoken against the committee bill have used the Wood amendment as their standard; and I say to you there is no difference whatever between the philosophy behind the Taft-Hartley Act and that behind the Wood amendment.

From the conversation we have heard since the beginning of the reading of the Sims substitute, it appears that we may find ourselves in a situation where it is both ends against the middle. I trust out of the good judgment of the Members of this House that they will not be swept off their feet by the arguments of either end, but the great middle, thinking membership of this House will decide that the Sims substitute is the proper approach to passing legislation the vast majority of the people will feel is fair.

So I endorse wholly and fully the provisions of the Sims substitute, and I trust that the House in its wisdom will use it as a standard and march forward to wiping from the statute books some things that I feel now, as I felt when I voted against the Taft-Hartley Act, were unfair, believing that it made good men and women throughout the length and breadth of this land feel that we had not been fair to them. Some people living in almost totally agricultural districts, like I do, feel, in all probability, that their constituents are not tremendously interested in the condition of labor. They could never be more mistaken in their lives.

MR. DONOHUE: Mr. Chairman, as I see it, the fundamental principle involved in this discussion of labor-management legislation is whether or not labor should be treated as a commodity, to be purchased in the competitive market, at a price to be determined solely by the law of supply and demand.

Two years ago, we were asked to believe that the way to American security and abundance, to peace and progress, was along the path of reaction in punitive moves directed against all forms of labor security.

The Labor Management Relations Act of 1947 was admittedly presented for the purpose of changing the whole range of national labor policy that had been built up in the previous sixteen years and reduce in every aspect the privileges and rights of labor. Its avowed objective was, in effect, to abolish industry-wide collective bargaining.

I submit that any attempt to weaken or destroy the working people's right to bargain collectively on an industry-wide basis is directly opposed to the socially progressive movement, in solid labor-management relations, that has been steadily advancing for over a century of our American democratic life.

The advantages of industry-wide bargaining manifestly outweigh the pretended disadvantages. Industry-wide collective bargaining is a natural, inevitable, and healthy step forward toward maturity in industrial relations. It is an alternative to competitive anarchy and government regulation. It is a logical development in a progressive trend from excessive individualism to group responsibility, and proper social control.

Mr. Chairman, collective bargaining has become an integral part of America's industrial structure. Most authorities agree that free collective bargaining is by far the most democratic and wholesome way of bringing about needed adjustments. It is the right way for labor and management to settle their differences and share their responsibility; it is the American way.

From the very beginning of the American labor movement, the things which unions asked for—the bread-and-butter contracts which they sought—were denounced in many corners. Then, after each gain had been won, historians and people generally looked back and agreed that labor's so-called demands were justified and necessary—because they represented the very things that gave meaning and purpose to our democracy. This fact was clear enough in restrospect and I should think it would be clear today.

Now much is being said about the need for more democratic procedures within the ranks of organized labor. I would like to point out to you that the rank and file of union members are much closer to union affairs than are the electors of most cities. I would like to remind you that union members have a much more direct interest and, indeed, a more direct voice in the way their unions are run than the average citizens in the affairs of their city.

Democracy in unions is not perfect, of course, but it compares very favorably with its counterpart in other kinds of civic activity.

Only in this country and in Canada can you find so very few in the labor movement who are tainted by some "ism" which threatens the safety of the kind of democracy we have known. Ninety-eight per cent of the American trade-unionists are not Socialist or Communist or Fascist.

The Communists, in particular, have made desperate efforts to secure a foothold in the American labor movement. Up to date they have failed utterly because the hand of American labor is against them, and will continue to be against them.

Please do not imagine I am arguing that the labor union is always right and that the employers are always wrong. I would not insult your intelligence by pressing such an argument.

There are 15 million trade unionists in the United States. With the members of their families and close relatives, they undoubtedly represent at least a fifth, and possibly a fourth, of our population. Of course, there are many shortsighted, selfish, even dishonest, men among them. If that were not true, then the labor movement of America would constitute the greatest miracle witnessed by human beings since our Lord left his sepulcher on the third day and gave His disciples concrete evidence of His divinity.

The labor movement in this country is as American as the Washington Monument or the Lincoln Memorial. Of course, it is constantly fighting to improve the condition of its members, and it will continue to do so. It is led by honorable men whose records in private and public life will bear comparison with the records of the leaders of any other group in American life. I am not apprehensive concerning the future of the American labor movement. It is not a revolutionary movement; I feel it should be regarded as an evolutionary movement, constantly progressing; the efforts being made to hold it back are practically and economically unwise.

I wish to say to the employers of labor: Extend the hand of fellowship to your workers. Recognize their right to organize unions which suit their needs. Do not be shocked when differences develop. Devise machinery to handle those differences, with a minimum of governmental or other outside interference.

If you do that in good faith, you will find that American trade unionists will meet you at least halfway. That is all you have a right to expect, and that is all the trade-union movement should concede.

I think there is a trinity in economics, as there is in religion. The trinity in economics is made up of agriculture, labor, business. They are so closely affiliated that if one is injured, the others are bound to suffer.

Impoverish the farmer, and the industrial worker will find himself without a job, and the businessman will look in vain for a market for his wares. Treat business unfairly, and labor and farmer will discover the door of opportunity is closing. Deny a just wage to the worker, and business and agriculture cannot escape the disastrous consequences.

The task of this Congress is to place our management upon a sound and workable foundation. Up until two years ago, the consistent policy of this government has been based upon the promotion and encouragement of free collective bargaining; our objective should be to restrict the accepted practice of collective bargaining and provide protective provisions for its healthy operation. Where there are admitted and demonstrated weaknesses, we must remedy and strengthen them. At the same time, we must beware of the creation of voluminous and complicated rules which can only result in transferring the conduct of industrial relations, from the parties vitally concerned, to a specially trained group of legal experts, which I submit would be a most disastrous development.

At a time when this nation and the world is entering a fateful hour of history, let us act without passion and emotion; let us judiciously avoid any threat to our national economy and security by encitement toward industrial strife. Let us reestablish the faith and confidence of both management and labor, in our government, by inspiring them to reach a commonly advantageous understanding through the peaceful processes of industry-wide collective bargaining.

EDUCATION

A NATIONAL PHILOSOPHY [1]

JAMES BRYANT CONANT [2]

President James Bryant Conant, of Harvard, delivered this baccalaureate sermon on Sunday afternoon, June 6, 1948, in Memorial Church in
the Harvard College Yard, to the senior class, their families, and guests.
This baccalaureate is a traditional service, "in which the President of the
University counsels the graduating class." It was the first Harvard senior
class for Conant to address since 1942.[3]

This address, although free from mechanically enunciated divisions,
is an unusual example of a closely knit series of logical propositions.
Note that the speaker begins with the obvious—the good fortune of his
audience and this nation in the outcome of World War II. Note further
the logical steps by which the analysis moves from the immediate and
secular to his final proposition in the series in the chains of reasoning:
The postulate of the sanctity of the individual and his duty to exercise
social justice rests upon the concept of the sacredness of human life—
"each individual is related to the structure of the universe."

The address reveals clearly President Conant's educational and religious philosophy. Assumed and implied are his concepts of education
in a free society—of universal education, equality of opportunity, the development of leadership and ability wherever they exist, the support of
practical education, frank recognition of the world as it is, but also the
recognition that educational breadth is necessary and that it is based upon
secure moral and religious foundations.[4]

President Conant, although without earlier special training in public speaking and with comparatively little experience in public address
prior to his election to the presidency of Harvard in 1933, has continually received highly favorable responses from his audiences. Through his
many and varied speaking experiences, he has also markedly improved in
his ease and general effectiveness on the platform. His direct grappling

[1] Text and permission for this reprint furnished through the courtesy of President Conant.

[2] For biographical note, see Appendix.

[3] For comment on that address and on the "Valedictory Service Address" at
Harvard on January 10, 1943, see *Representative American Speeches: 1942-1943*,
p257-65.

[4] For Conant's approach to educational problems, see his *Education in a
Divided World*, Harvard University Press, 1948.

with the mounting problems of the Hitlerian world as they affected America prior to 1941; his public defense of various war policies and programs; and his decisive position on many postwar issues, for example, aid for European recovery, gave many of his public utterances wide attention and challenged mature analysis. The weight of his ideas, the dignity and originality of his language, the clearness of his insight into American ideas and ideals, his grasp of educational goals, and his overtones of inspiration, devoid of sentimentality or triteness, explain much of his leadership as a speaker.[5]

The last time I spoke to a senior class on Commencement Sunday was in 1942. Only six years ago, and yet we were then living in a different period of world history. The United States was only just recovering from the emotional impact of Pearl Harbor and the reverses in the Philippines; the turning point of the Pacific War had not yet been reached. The Germans appeared to be still pressing the Russians so hard that many conceded a victory to Hitler's armies. Thoughtful men and women in this country talked of a ten years' war; of an iron age when civil liberties would disappear, colleges close, and the demands of the fighting services transform our democracy into a totalitarian state. There were even those who a few months earlier had declared that it was hopeless to challenge the dominance of the Axis powers outside the Western hemisphere.

June 1942 seems a long time ago, indeed—so long, in fact, that we can not readily recapture the mood which then prevailed. What was once a living nightmare is now so far behind us that we can scarcely recall the grimness with which we faced an uncertain future. Our memories are short. We forget the vividness of our former doubts and fears. We are likewise in the process of forgetting the sacrifices of those who made our bad dreams false. Failing to remember the ups and downs of a desperate period, a time of national crisis, we falsify the record in our minds and minimize the good fortune which at almost every turn favored the allied armies. I say "we" meaning that vague abstraction, the American people, a cross section of all ages made vocal through the radio, the press and public speeches. You gentlemen, a great majority of whom are veterans, hardly need to be reminded of the days and war. Many of you know from personal experience the uncertainties of battle; you know the terrible history of the war years and how fortunate are the people of the United States as compared with the inhabitants of countries which were once the scenes of action. You know how many "might have beens" on many fronts could have prolonged the war for years. To you the fourth stanza of the traditional Harvard hymn may have a special meaning:

> Let children learn the mighty deeds
> Which God performed of old.
> Which in our younger years we saw
> And which our fathers told.

At every commencement to which you will return in the coming years, this hymn will be sung as it has been for more than a century and a half. It may well be that this metrical version of the seventy-eighth psalm recommended itself to our academic ancestors because the "mighty deeds which God performed of old" was a phrase reminiscent of the miraculous success of the American Revolution. To you and your descendants, however, the overtones may be different; you may think of the 1940's and the extraordinary deliverance of the democracies from the dangers inherent in the global ambitions of the Nazis and the Japanese.

"How shall we behave ourselves after such mercies?" wrote Oliver Cromwell to an Overseer of Harvard College, describing his military triumphs in Scotland. Without necessarily subscribing to seventeenth-century Puritan theology, we must feel the force of this question. In modern secular terms, we may say our responsibilities as a nation are commensurate with our good fortune; shall we prove worthy of the opportunity presented to us by the hand of fate? Like a young man suddenly thrust into a position of leadership in time of war, shall we prove adequate to our task? These are some of the questions which I suggest may be in our minds when we survey the costly years of carnage which separate us from pre-Pearl Harbor days.

The United States has entered a new epoch in its history; our relations with other nations have been completely altered in the last half dozen years; we have no choice but to accept the responsibilities of world leadership. These basic propositions are now taken for granted by the citizens of this country, with relatively few exceptions. The contrast of the prevailing spirit today with the attitude of the 1930's will excite the wonder of future historians, but I need not dwell on it further here this afternoon. At the moment everyone is saying that we have a twofold duty: first, to make our democracy work here at home; and second, to conduct our foreign affairs with farsighted wisdom, understanding, and above all courage.

With such general statements we can perhaps all agree. But how long can we stick to these good intentions? Has a free society like ours, compounded of many cultural patterns, sufficient stamina for leadership in world affairs? If so, what are the necessary conditions for our success? The most essential is clearly a high degree of national solidarity. Unless we are united, we shall fail. Many an individual has cracked up under stress of arduous duties because he was a divided, frustrated personality. Similarly with a free nation, the factor of morale is of the first importance. Therefore, I venture to examine briefly this afternoon this matter of national solidarity. I shall attempt to explore certain of the more basic premises from which the philosophy of a nation must ultimately draw its strength. Let me begin by asking two questions: Have we in fact a national philosophy? If so, how should it be described? These have been recurring questions for many decades in this country, but they have been brought to a focus since the 1930's by the emergence of the two types of totalitarian states.

I remember fifteen years ago being asked a searching question by a member of a large audience of teachers. I had been talking about education, general education we might now say, and had been talking in rather general terms I must admit. When the time for questions came, a sincere and greatly troubled teacher threw a difficult and penetrating query at me which was essentially as follows: The Nazis and the Communists have a clear-cut philosophy of life which by its definiteness and its militancy wins many disciples, at least in other countries. What have we to offer our American youth that is equivalent in its force?

The Nazi philosophy and other forms of fascism have been defeated by force of arms, they have been driven under cover; the Soviet philosophy, however, still stands in stark opposition to the way we talk and act. Indeed, the world is now divided by the Russian version of the Marx-Engels doctrine; beyond the Eastern frontier of freedom the processes of our democracy are dismissed with derision as being but instruments of the owning class. The question of fifteen years ago is therefore by no means out of date. In one form or another we hear it repeated every week, and very often in despairing tones. For there are those who think we have no basic answer to the challenge of the Soviet or fascist view of life. They attempt to prove that we are spiritually bankrupt as a nation, and then offer to make us solvent by a free gift of their own particular set of dogmas. Needless to say, I believe all such defeatist critics of this democracy of ours are completely wrong.

I have neither the competence nor the time this afternoon to talk in terms of political or economic theory nor to address myself to the nature of the future development of this society of free men. I do believe most sincerely that by the accidents of history we today represent a form of democracy in several ways unique. I believe that our special ideals which may be summed up by such phrases as "equality of opportunity," and "social justice," still represent goals toward which we may move continuously. But rather than discuss these practical matters of collective action I would like to consider the more personal question of the fundamental faith of the more than one hundred fifty million individuals who constitute this nation. In short, I should like to examine the conditions necessary for the spiritual unity of the United States. For such a unity is a prerequisite for the solidarity we must have if our world leadership is to be commensurate with the responsibilities of the times.

We are a nation of recent immigrants. This fact must be kept in the foreground of any discussion of cultural and spiritual cohesion. In terms of world history we are all of us, except the descendants of the Indians, relative newcomers to the area we now designate the United States. We or our immediate ancestors carried across the ocean a variety of cultures, traditions and beliefs. We are all of us the products of a relatively recent process of Americanization. This process, whether conscious or unconscious, was in itself an acknowledgment of the validity of many different faiths; a wide diversity of beliefs and the tolerance of this diversity has been the bedrock to which our national unity was anchored. This historic fact is often overlooked by the woeful critics of this nation.

For example, here this afternoon many of you, perhaps the vast majority, have a theological basis for your outlook on the world which is both settled and satisfying as a guide to life. But I am certain that if we could examine the religious faiths here represented we would find not one or two but many quite different interpretations of Christianity, and other theologies as well. To those of you, whatever your religion, who have achieved a mature faith I have one and only one suggestion. However firm may be your adherence to your own theology, do not fail in your allegiance to the unifying secular doctrine of religious tolerance, for this is basic to the welfare of the United States. However zealous you may be to convert others to your own faith, remember the limits set by the historical evolution of this republic. Our public institutions are, and must remain, secular; otherwise our democratic fabric will sooner or later be torn asunder by contending theologies led by fanatic men. Our ancestors knew this; they lived near enough to the period of religious wars to recall their brutality and horror. We would do well to refresh our memories of the history of the sixteenth and seventeenth centuries from time to time.

To those of you who may be in the process of formulating or reformulating your own approach to the basic questions of the universe, I venture to speak in other terms. First of all I may remind you that there can be no doubt that the Hebraic-Christian tradition with its emphasis on the sanctity of each human soul was one of the mainsprings of the development of democracy in this land of pioneers. The point has been made so often since the outbreak of World War II and so carefully documented that there is no need to argue the case again. The moral basis of our culture rests on the dual postulate of the sacrosanct nature of the individual and the duty of each person to do unto others as he would have others do unto him.

I am well aware that up to a point a satisfactory system of ethics can be derived solely from a consideration of the welfare of the community. Granted certain premises as to the nature of the free society we wish to perpetuate on this continent, definitions of right and wrong can be formulated in terms of the social consequences of an individual's deeds. I am the last one to minimize the importance of emphasizing this broad ethical base of our culture. But most of us will not be satisfied unless we dig deeper to find a more solid foundation. To be sure, the agnostic and the liberal Protestant, for example, can go hand in hand in stressing the Christian virtues; the one privately justifying the ethical teaching by reference to the growth of a "normal" individual and a smooth-working society, the other by his belief in the significance of his own interpretation of the Christian dogmas. In most situations the ideal behavior of an American citizen will be identically assessed by these two men. But it is not difficult to envisage cases where the divergence in basic philosophies leads to different judgments. May I give an illustration of what I mean.

Let us imagine two or three individuals on a raft or a desert island with death certain in their eyes within a few days or weeks. Under these conditions which by definition are isolated and mortally terminal can an individual's conduct be said to be right or wrong? Where by hypothesis there are no social consequences of action, is there any standard of reference for what occurs? Is betrayal of a friend or even murder under these highly unusual circumstances to be regarded only as a physiological reflex and described as merely pleasing or offensive to one's taste? Is behavior under these conditions to be judged as right or wrong or merely regarded as similar to that of an insane person or an animal?

To my mind these questions probe deeply into a man's outlook upon the world. They throw a revealing light on the common denominator which unites many Americans of otherwise highly divergent views. For I am convinced that all but a very small number of honest and intelligent citizens of this nation of all ages will answer these questions almost instinctively in just one way. They will affirm that the universe is somehow so constructed that a sane individual's acts are subject to moral judgments under all circumstances and under all conditions. The nature of the "somehow" is the door by which one passes into a vast edifice of philosophical and theological discussion—a mansion in which there are many chambers.

The reasons given for a belief in the significance of the actions of even an isolated individual would be many; but whether Protestant, Catholic or Jew, active church member or non-conformist, almost every American believes that human life is sacred. This fact is the answer to those Cassandras who would have us believe that there is no spiritual unity in the United States. When face to face with the question, is the dignity of man determined solely by the fact that man is a social animal, we automatically would say no. In short, our practical democratic creed turns out on analysis to be an affirmation of the common basis of our many faiths.

Theological and philosophic warfare between contending churches and rival groups obscures too often the unity of our culture. Instead of seeking to find broad terms in which to express the moral basis of our society, controversialists all too often argue as if their phrases alone had meaning. We quarrel about words which have different overtones for descendants of immigrants of different centuries and from different lands. This is unfortunate to say the least. For these are days when we must meet an aggressive Soviet ideology on the one hand, and face the possibility of a recrudescence of fascism on the other. We endanger our political and social solidarity if we close our eyes to the nature of the spiritual unity of this nation. The questions I have just posed to those of you who are now examining your philosophy of life, therefore, seem to me to point to a central issue of our times. The answers separate the believers in a free democracy from the adherents to the Soviet or Fascist doctrines. In defending our unique brand of democracy, we must never lose sight of those goals toward which we strive by collective action; we must continue to think in terms of the welfare of the community as well as of the individual. But unlike the totalitarians, we do not believe that the collective end justifies the means; we do not assert that the good of mankind demands that an individual be sacrificed to the community. We hold the opposite to be true; for us each individual is related to the structure of the universe. This belief is both widespread and firmly rooted, however divergent may be its formal expression in many philosophies and creeds. If we recognize this fact we are ready to answer all doubting Thomases who are skeptical of our capacity as a nation to remain unshaken in troubled times. Holding fast to the principle of tolerance of diversity, the descendants of immigrants of many faiths may proclaim their basic unanimity. With confidence in the soundness of the national spirit they may humbly accept the burdens placed upon them by the defeat of the Axis powers: may history prove that they are not unworthy of the challenge of the times.

THE ART OF CONTEMPLATION [6]

VIRGIL M. HANCHER [7]

President Virgil M. Hancher gave this charge to the candidates at the Commencement exercises at the State University of Iowa, Iowa City, Iowa, on Saturday, June 5, 1948.

At each of the University convocations, held in February, June, and August, since his appointment at Iowa in 1940, the President has delivered such final remarks to outgoing classes. This one is typical in its brevity, its direct appeal to the graduating audience, and especially its identification of high educational purpose and endeavor with wisdom, perspective, and motive.

The structural completeness of the speech is based upon a problem-solution pattern. The vocabulary is strikingly effective in its oral quality, repetition of key words, figurative phrases, diction appropriate to the academic audience, contrast and comparison, analogies, epigrams, direct address, Biblical allusion, restrained humor, and sentence variety and rhythm.

President Hancher, although he occasionally uses a manuscript, is primarily an extempore speaker, at home before both university and community audiences. His method of composition is to jot down central ideas, and then write and rewrite the discourse. On the platform he uses few or no "speaker notes." His voice is excellent, his manner conciliatory yet forceful. He is an excellent example of one who demonstrates the three sources of credibility in orators, as suggested by Aristotle: "There are three things apart from demonstrative proofs which inspire belief, viz. sagacity, high character, and good will." [8]

The staccato tempo of modern life has made difficult the art of contemplation. The days pass, they gather into weeks and months, arteries grow old and reactions slow down without the acquisition of that wisdom which comes only from the distillation of experience. Cynicism may also be the distillation of experience; but it is a bitter brew. The wise man, no less than the cynic, will not be taken in by life; but neither will he let the

---

[6] Text furnished through the courtesy of President Hancher. The talk was printed in *Vital Speeches of the Day*, 14:590-1. July 15, 1948, and was later distributed as a brochure by the City News Publishing Company, New York City.

[7] For biographical note, see Appendix.

[8] J. E. C. Welldon, Aristotle's *Rhetoric*, London, 1886, p10. For further comment on Hancher as a speaker see *Representative American Speeches: 1943-1944*, p319-28.

weaknesses and frailties of men blind him to their aspirations. Wisdom knows that men's eyes can be, and are, sometimes turned toward the stars, even though at other times they may be turned toward the gutter.

"Instinct, Intelligence, Wisdom" are the categories named by Whitehead, and they arrange themselves in an order of progression. If life is to have meaning, if the things we do are not illusion, if there is reality in our efforts and our undertakings, the freedom of choice and of action, which we appear to possess, is more than appearance. It is a real freedom, and the choices which we make are real choices.

To come to such a decision is in itself an act of faith. It assumes that the universe is not driven by blind, mechanistic forces which we can neither resist nor understand—and, indeed, of which we are a part without our knowledge. Our ultimate view of the universe is always an act of faith, rather than of reason, because our ultimate view of the universe rests upon a first postulate which cannot be proved.

The ancients said that there could be no dispute in matters of taste. "De gustibus non disputandum." Men differ in matters of taste, but there are no absolutes. Perhaps the same might be said of postulates, although this will be disputed and disputed vigorously. For with one postulate you will become a religious orthodox and with another you will become a dialectical materialist.

I do not mean to imply that it is a matter of indifference that you become one or the other, or that you arrive at any one of the infinite number of destinations between the two. Neither do I mean to imply that all postulates are equally valid. What I do mean to imply is that with the infinite variety of men, there will be diversity of outlook, and now, and for a long time to come, one man's meat will be another man's poison.

What I would desire for you is an apprehension of the postulate upon which your faith is founded. Because you do have a faith, or at least a working hypothesis of your relation to the entire scheme of things, on which your life is founded. Whether this hypothesis is formulated or unformulated in your consciousness, it still exists—and your actions, if not your declarations of faith, are witness to it. Indeed your actions may be the true witness.

Your hypothesis may range all the way from a belief that life has purpose to a belief that it is utterly without purpose —that nothing can be done to give it sense or meaning. But your hypothesis exists. Do you know what it is?

The staccato tempo of modern life makes difficult the contemplation necessary for self-knowledge. I make no plea for the good old days. Most of us would not be here if the good old days had not been changed for the better. Disease or famine would have cut off us or our ancestors, and of those who survived only a fortunate few would have achieved the luxury of an education. The triumphs of science and of scientific method are not to be overlooked. Nevertheless the balance sheet has its debit side.

Somewhere along the pathway of progress, the art of contemplation has been lost. The Society of Friends, certain Roman Catholics, an occasional mystic or band of mystics have preserved the art. They retain an anchorage in a sea of ceaseless motion, of disquiet, of drifting. They posses an integrity, a calm and assurance, a wholeness of mind and body that is a kind of holiness. This wholeness, this holiness, I crave for you.

It will be difficult to achieve. All the forces of modern life conspire against it. The church which once exercised such great dominion over the bodies and souls of men now competes with a thousand secular rivals. Competition, activity for its own sake, the lust for success and power make difficult the art of self-mastery. We are slaves and not masters. "Things are in the saddle and they ride mankind." The newspaper, the radio, and now television interrupt our days and disturb our nights. Everyone is a little tired, a little distraught, a little below par, a bit inaccurate in judgment.

Yet this need not be so. It is so, because others have willed that it be so, and we have let them have their way. Mark Twain has been quoted as saying that he once stopped reading the newspapers for seven years and they were the seven happiest years of his life! This remedy for our modern distemper seems a bit drastic, but perhaps nothing less than a radical remedy will now halt the disease. Until the radio and the newspapers have learned that men cannot survive in perpetual crisis, they are in danger of reprisal. A populace made schizophrenic by perpetual crisis and inaccuracy may well construe "the freedom of the press" and the radio to mean freedom to publish the truth—and nothing less.

But nothing compels you to give up your sanity, even though the world conspire to drive you mad. You can make it a rule of your life to withdraw each day into quiet and contemplation—religious quiet and contemplation, if you will, but quiet and contemplation, in any event—so that you may put aside the pressing and temporal things, and look upon those which come out of the deep places of human experience. "The heavens declare the glory of God," said the psalmist, "and the firmament showeth his handiwork." Modern man cannot afford to lose the sense of wonder. Perhaps it has been recaptured by some in the fission of the atom; but, for most of us, this must remain as great a mystery as the origin of life or the nature and destiny of man. Yet against this mystery we pit our intellect and our wills, however feeble they may be, confident that the unexamined life is not for us, but that out of our struggle we shall apprehend the postulates of our faith, and achieve that distillation of experience which is wisdom.

History records the ebb and flow of civilizations, the aspirations and failures of men and nations. Whether it possesses a rhythm or pattern is still a matter for dispute—yet, as one surveys the record, the trend has been upward. There is little evidence that modern man has a better brain than the prophets of Israel or the sages of Greece or Rome, but modern man is the inheritor of ideas and instrumentalities without which our modern civilization could not exist.

These ideas and instrumentalities have come to us because men have believed that they were free to make choices, and that the choices were real. They have believed that what they did, as individuals and collectively, made a difference in the long history of mankind, even in human destiny itself. They counted it the better part of wisdom to be on the side of the angels.

You, too, have a choice, and the choice is real. It should be made, not in response to the staccato drum-beat of temporality but in the quiet and contemplation of eternity. You have but one life, and a short one, at your disposal. There is not time to squander it hastily. Only in leisure can you savor it to the full. "Be still and know that I am God," said the voice to the psalmist long ago. "Be still and know the good" is as modern as tomorrow's television set.

Wise choices are the distinguishing mark of an educated man. You, too, can be on the side of the angels. Can you afford to be anywhere else? With what greater wisdom can you be wise?

ARE WE EDUCATING FOR THE NEEDS
OF THE MODERN MAN? [9]

GEORGE V. DENNY, JR., PAUL H. DOUGLAS,
GEORGE D. STODDARD, CLIFTON FADIMAN,
AND JAMES R. KILLIAN, JR. [10]

This debate-discussion, in the Academy of Music, Philadelphia, Pennsylvania, was heard on Tuesday evening, January 25, 1949, from 8:30 to 9:30, E.S.T., over the American Broadcasting Company Network. It was also televised over WJZ-TV, New York City, and WFIL-TV, Philadelphia.

The program included (1) introductory remarks by Moderator Denny, (2) six-minute "set" talks in turn by each of the guest speakers, (3) informal colloquy by the four speakers, (4) an audience participation period, "Questions Please," of some fifteen minutes (because of the limitations of this volume the questions from the audience have been omitted), and (5) summarizing speeches by each speaker.

These programs have been given continuously since 1935, "the oldest series of this type on the air." Several million usually listen. The program has been highly successful in presenting to the public "both sides" of highly controversial problems. Only highly experienced speakers and those with special background and knowledge of the topic for discussion are scheduled.

On this program were four outstanding platform personalities and national leaders. Paul Howard Douglas has been professor of industrial relations at the University of Chicago, has served on many important educational and administrative committees, and was a major in the Marine Corps in World War II. He has an unusually good radio voice, and had recently completed a highly extensive political campaign for election as Democratic Senator from Illinois.

George Dinsmore Stoddard, President of the University of Illinois since July 1946, and previously Commissioner of Education for the State of New York, was in 1949 a member of the Executive Board of the United Nations Scientific and Cultural Organization. A former college debater and speaker at many educational conferences, President Stoddard is at his best in informal extemporaneous discussion. His more formal discourses probe issues to their philosophical bases; his oral style is per-

[9] Reprinted from *Bulletin of America's Town Meeting of the Air*, 14, no. 39, January 25, 1949. By permission of the speakers, and by special arrangement with Town Hall, Inc., and the courtesy of the American Broadcasting Company.

[10] For biographical notes, see Appendix.

sonal, unhackneyed, and persuasive. He is outstanding as a speaker among educational leaders.[11]

Clifton Fadiman has contributed widely to magazines and has had much editorial experience. He had extensive experience as lecturer for the People's Institute and elsewhere. Master of ceremonies on the "Information Please" program, he attained a nationwide reputation as radio speaker. He is witty, intellectually highly alert, versatile in language, energetic and stimulating in his delivery. His pronunciation and articulation are those of cultivated New York City.

James R. Killian, Jr., was former president of the American Society for Engineering Education, and was educated at Duke and Massachusetts Institute of Technology. For several years he was editor of the *Technology Review* and before his inauguration as President of the Massachusetts Institute of Technology on April 2, 1949, served in various administrative and executive positions at that institution. His educational breadth, as reflected in his brief contribution to this radio program, aroused considerable audience applause. Engineering education, to him, calls for much more than high specialization.[12]

MODERATOR DENNY: Good evening, neighbors. It's fitting that tonight's program should originate here in the famous Academy of Music in Philadelphia under the auspices of the Philadelphia Forum, an institution dedicated to the education of adults.

Now let me assure you at the outset that this is not going to be a theoretical discussion. When we speak of modern man here tonight, we are referring to you and me—the men, women, and children who live in America today.

We can't take in the problems of education throughout the world in one program. Indeed, we can only scratch the surface of our problem here in this hour. Our needs are many and varied, but we propose to center tonight on the one most urgent need of all the citizens of this nation of ours in this Year Four of the Atomic Age: our need to meet the responsibilities of citizenship in the richest, the most powerful, the most productive nation in the world, the nation to which the greater part of the rest of the world is looking for leadership and aid.

Our educational system has helped us to attain a greater material prosperity than any other nation in the world, but

[11] For further comment on President Stoddard, see *Representative American Speeches: 1947-1948*, p169-78.
[12] For additional examples of the Town Meeting of the Air programs, see *Representative American Speeches: 1947-1948*, p188-205.

this golden crown rests uneasily upon our heads. Because we fear war, we spend billions for national defense, economic aid, and propaganda.

As modern man seeks for solutions to his most urgent problems, he turns invariably to education for help and guidance. Education has given us the tools with which to conquer material forces that were once our enemies, and turn them into slaves to do our bidding.

Through education we've conquered time and space and transformed our world into a neighborhood of more than two billion neighbors. But what of our capacity for neighborliness? We can destroy a million people at one blow, but what can we do to rid our neighbors and ourselves of the appalling fear of another world war?

Earnest men have dealt with this problem for centuries without success. Here, we submit, is modern man's most urgent need. In a very real sense, this is our day of judgment.

In our terms, the day may last for ten, fifteen, or twenty years, but the problem is in the hands of modern man. Yes, in our hands.

To help us explore this subject, we are to hear from two college presidents, a literary critic, and a United States Senator who was formerly a teacher and more recently a fighting Marine. We will hear first from that Senator—Senator Paul H. Douglas of Illinois. Born in Salem, Massachusetts, he spent his boyhood on a Maine farm. He chose the teaching profession after getting his Ph.D. from Columbia University, then government service, then back to teaching at the University of Chicago, where he became professor of economics. He was always active in politics. When the war came on, he joined the Marines and saw active service in Palau and Okinawa where he was severely wounded, and decorated for his bravery.

Last year, he was elected president of the American Economic Association. On November 3 of this year, he was elected to the United States Senate on the Democratic ticket. Senator Paul Douglas, may we have your views on tonight's question? Senator Douglas.

SENATOR DOUGLAS: Mr. Denny and friends. The answer to this evening's question is that we are still only educating in part for the needs of modern man. Before we express our discontents, however, let us acknowledge the progress we have made. A half century ago, the average American left school at the end of the sixth or seventh grade, and only a comparative few ever went on to high school.

Today, the average American boy or girl finishes at least two years of high school, while about a third finish high school, about a quarter go to college, and about a sixth graduate from college. There are, indeed, approximately two and a half million students in our colleges today, or sixteen to every one thousand of the total population. This is proportionately fifteen times as many as in England.

In addition, the quality of instruction is improved. The length of the school year has been greatly extended, and quality of our teachers has been raised, our school buildings are much better, children are being treated more as human beings whose interest should be enlisted, rather than as passive sausages who should be stuffed.

But there is still much to be done. First, on the financial side we need a broader base for financing our schools. Since education is primarily financed by the localities, the regions where children are many and taxable property is scanty, are not able to give their youngsters even a basic minimum of training, try as they may.

We need, therefore, a larger degree of central financing both within and between states so that the wealthier regions may help to raise the level of education within the poorer ones. This is necessary because men and women are entitled to at least a more even start in life. It is also necessary because a large proportion of the children who grow up in the poorer regions later migrate to the wealthier sections.

It is better for the wealthier regions to help pay part of the immediate cost of educating these children, than for them to inherit men and women who are badly trained. That is why I believe our Federal Aid for Education bill, which will shortly be reported out of committee, should be passed by Congress.

Secondly, schools, along with families, churches, and individuals, need to help us all develop a greater sense of emotional, intellectual maturity to match the technological maturity of our times, and the terrible strains to which we, as a people, are exposed.

We have developed, as Mr. Denny has said, at once the greatest productive power and we are in temporary possession of the most frightening discovery in the history of the world. At the same time, we are faced with the fact that Soviet Russia has declared its open hostility to us and is seeking, by national policy, and by its fifth columnists in every country, to undermine us and to institute a police state both over us and over the world.

We need to be firm in our resistance in this cold struggle of ideas and acts which may endure for many years.

We must be physically prepared to defend our country and to help the free nations of the world to defend theirs, and yet our defense must be more than physical. We must equally defend the ideas and practices of freedom, and the practice of consent rather than of brute power in the making of decisions.

Similarly, while properly on guard against false peace overtures, designed to lull us into a careless sense of security, we must be ready for cooperation if and when Russia, by tangible deeds, shows its readiness to undo past errors and to live cooperatively.

This, as I have said, calls for emotional maturity of a high order to be calm and determined; resolute, but not provocative; firm, but without hatred.

But we also need to educate ourselves more both about current events and about the great past world of human thought. If one, for example, really understands the Marshall Plan, or the workings of the United Nations, one understands international affairs of today. And if one is able, to follow intelligently the current discussion over the Taft-Hartley law is to give oneself, indeed, an education in industrial relations.

We should not be provincial either in place or in time. There is every reason why we should know something at first hand about the conflicting theories of Plato and of Aristotle; of

Pascal, Spinoza, and Descartes; of Hobbes, Milton, and Locke; of Calhoun, John Stuart Mill, and Lincoln. All this will give a third dimension to human history.

Finally—and this may seem to be ending on a minor note, but even as a freshman Senator, one becomes aware of how important it is—we must as individuals moderate group pressures upon society if we are to preserve national welfare unity.

Men find protection and fellowship in organized groups, but all too frequently modern groups make demands upon the community which are both grossly unjust to others and harmful to the commonwealth itself.

There is simply not enough wealth, even in this wealthiest of countries, to satisfy all the demands of all the groups. It is not safe to let the leaders of economics and of government carry the sole burden of arbitrating these claims, for such decisions as theirs are at best forced and do not spring from consent. If we are to prevent our nation from breaking up into bitter and conflicting classes, men themselves must observe restraint in their group activities. To group power must be added group responsibility and group selfishness must be made to be as bad form [as] individual selfishness.

MODERATOR DENNY: Thank you, Senator Douglas. I am glad you don't agree with that college graduate who, when he got his degree, went to Western Union and telegraphed his parents, "Educated, thank God."

We'll hear next from the president of the University of Illinois and a native of this great state of Pennsylvania, a psychologist, and an educator, who has always maintained an active interest in world affairs. He served as a delegate to UNESCO meetings for the past four years, was formerly Commissioner of Education of the State of New York and is well qualified to speak on tonight's question. Dr. George D. Stoddard.

DR. STODDARD: Mr. Denny and friends. I agree with Senator Douglas. Education has made progress, but it still has a long way to go. It is unequally available and it lacks top. Something is missing, something has gone wrong—and not just in the deep rural South.

The modern man must absorb change and rise above it. So far, change has bewildered him. He mut stop fighting science and start using it, not for gadgets, but as a marvelous means of understanding himself and his world.

Modern man, like the status quo, may be defined as "the mess we are in." There is no other kind of man really, although men alive today may work, dress, and think much like their protypes of twenty centuries ago.

Last month, when I was in Syria, I saw thousands of men working with donkeys and camels, without much evidence of change on the part of either man or animal. Let us call modern, then, the man who reads and writes and worries about local, national, and state affairs. By the time his mind is made up, his emotions have been aroused.

Modern man has not lost the deep layers of his past, but he has added something. As in the earlier family tribe he needs a basis of exchange with his fellowmen, but now the basis is found in the common culture. Are we educating for the needs of such a man?

If I were defending my profession, or my university, I should say loudly, "Yes, we are"—meaning, of course, that we try to, that we do sometimes, in some places, perhaps by degrees.

At least, I know teachers who are educating for men more modern than those on the streets today. Generally, their work is contained in what is called liberal education, and education is as likely to spring from great experiments as from great books. I was glad to hear the Senator recommend both scientists and philosophers.

Liberal education, as I see it, is an education that contributes to mental power in situations that cannot be predicted in detail. It is abstract, but not unreal. Without this generalizing power, the human mind would run over its problems like an insect, understanding nothing, but trying only to get away. Not all knowledge is of equal worth. Learning proceeds by selection and imagination.

There is not much education unsolved when children or men are taught what to memorize, what to think, or what to expect. Hence, the Nazis and the Japanese, while literate and expert, were not truly well educated.

The educated modern man develops human relations and values that endure under stress. He is not a machine, nor a cog in a machine.

The question is then, What are we educators doing to free the mind? Well, we place the student in a ferment of ideas. His mind is exposed to outside stimuli. A little community on a college campus, perhaps only a few hundred yards square, brings to the most reluctant learner the problems, discoveries, and failures of all the ages.

The aim of any school or college is to give students a living fund of knowledge from which they may generate ideas. The aim is to improve human relations. There is a place, too, for daring enterprise. The men in our medical clinics are free and immensely resourceful in what they do to, with, and for the human body.

The nuclear physicist abhors the bomb, but he will go right on unraveling the secrets of nature. It is up to all of us to put such unheard of power to work for human welfare.

My own field of psychology illustrates the whole process of education. We psychologists work on three of the greatest problems in human culture—the problem of learning, the problem of behavior aberrations that lead to crime and insanity, and the problem of wars that, according to UNESCO, begin in the minds of men.

We know already that frustration may lead to aggression. If tensions exist among leaders who are symbolic of their people, they penetrate to all levels, and generate a massive war action. The best antidote, it seems to me, is an abiding sense of freedom—the freedom to ask questions, to criticize, to vote against, as well as for.

The loss of freedom means the loss of thinking, and without thinking man ceases to be modern. If we fail to practice what we preach, we ruin the lesson in the classroom. Information is not enough. Technology is no fit substitute for the human spirit. It reduces drudgery, but it does not guarantee liberty.

Since education, in this sense, is one of the great hopes of the world, and since the world obviously is in a hurry toward destruction or toward salvation, I believe that education should fast get its own house in order.

MODERATOR DENNY: Thank you, Dr. Stoddard. Since Dr. Stoddard has pointed out that technology is not enough, I am sure we are glad to hear from a man who is president-designate of one of the most famous educational institutions in America, the Massachusetts Institute of Technology, which was headed for so many years by Dr. Carl Compton. Dr. James R. Killian has been in educational work since he graduated from M.I.T. in 1926. He is president of the Board of the Boston Lying-in Hospital, Director of the American Unitarian Association, and other organizations in and around Boston. We are happy, indeed, to welcome to Town Meeting the president-designate of the Massachusetts Institute of Technology. Dr. James Killian.

DR. KILLIAN: Mr. Denny and friends, Senator Douglas has cited the steadily increasing proportion of our young people who are going beyond the grammar school in their education. Let me give you a startling contrast.

At M.I.T. we were recently comparing notes with a distinguished British educator. He was astonished to learn that nearly two and a half million students are enrolled in American institutions beyond the high school level.

Since the comparable enrollment in the United Kingdom is nearer seventy thousand, he estimated that twenty times the proportion of young people are going to college in America than are going to college in Great Britain.

I cite these enrollment figures to point up one of the great achievements, and one of the great problems of our educational system. We are seeking to give more education to more people than any free nation has ever before attempted. In our preoccupation with numbers, it is not surprising that our education while growing has not, as Dr. Stoddard says, grown up.

But when Walter Lippmann argues that American education creates "no common culture, no common faith, no common body of principle, no common body of moral and intellectual discipline," I would disagree.

As I see it, certain common objectives are already beginning to emerge which are designed to meet the needs of modern man more fully than they have in the past.

Let me state these goals briefly: First, we must give an understanding of our American heritage and of the sacredness of individual liberty in a free society. Here, I believe, we are teaching common principles, at the present time.

Next, we must prepare men to grow in moral and spiritual stature. Our people must not only be literate; they must harness literacy to ideals and to a sense of the first rate.

We must follow the precepts of the philosopher, Whitehead, that "moral education is impossible without the habitual vision of greatness."

Third, we must prepare men to be skilled and creative in their share of the world's work. Since I come from an institution devoted to professional education, my part in this discussion is to support the validity of this third objective. This I do enthusiastically, but with the conviction that specialized education must be, and can be, fused with the other two objectives.

Again, Whitehead drives a point home when he remarks that "a merely well-informed man is the most useless bore on God's earth." He must be able to do something.

I also believe that our specialized institutions, as, for example, our schools of science and engineering, have made important contributions, aside from their professional training, to the education of modern man. They have benefited from the liberalizing influence of science and its record of freeing men from superstition and crippling fears.

Here in Philadelphia, Benjamin Franklin's experiments with lightning were once criticized because they were taking away from the Lord the power of frightening His children by thunderstorms for the good of their souls.

Our professional schools give their students the inner satisfaction of being able to do something useful and do it well. Their curricula have pointed the way to a unity, a discipline, and a creative attitude that largely were lost when the classical curriculum became outmoded.

Here especially for your benefit, Mr. Fadiman, let me emphasize that science and engineering should not be confused with gadget-making. Science gives us penicillin and it also gives us the understanding of the laws of nature. Engineering helps us to harness nature for useful purposes, to replace, as it has, slave labor by machine labor. They both give you and me more freedom to be socially responsible citizens, to be good neighbors, to pursue the good life.

So far I have suggested some of our educational goals and achievements. We still have much to accomplish. We must find ways of financing our private institutions so that they may remain free and independent parts of our educational system. We must find ways of attracting and keeping great teachers and of giving them a position of dignity in our communities.

We must find ways of encouraging the exceptional student and of letting him advance at his own fast pace. We must not let our preoccupation with numbers of students result in quantity overwhelming quality.

We must encourage and support creative scholarship, minds "forever voyaging through strange seas of thought alone."

If we can continue our progress in achieving these goals, Mr. Denny, we can educate for the needs of modern man.

MODERATOR DENNY: Thank you, Dr. Killian. Few radio listeners need an introduction to our next speaker. Well-known for so many years as the Quiz Master of "Information, Please" and book critic for *The New Yorker* magazine, Clifton Fadiman has taught high school, and was for many years Chairman of the Lecture Division of the Peoples' Institute of New York City. He served as editor-in-chief of a New York publishing house and has edited two volumes called *Reading I've Liked* and *The Short Stories of Henry James*. He is now on the board of judges of the Book-of-the-Month Club. Mr. Fadiman, are we educating for the needs of modern man? Clifton Fadiman.

MR. FADIMAN: Mr. Denny and friends. Senator Douglas has stated the necessity of providing better financial support for our schools and also the necessity of improving their instruction. Dr. Stoddard reminds us that our goals, perhaps, stack up a little better than our achievements. And Dr. Killian points out that specialized education must be infused with the humane viewpoint.

This is all true. But what worries me, mainly, is the meaning of our question.

First, is there such a single thing as modern man? To my mind, there is not. But I do believe that, at will, we can become, in the near future, either one of two kinds of modern man.

Now, the first kind is, perhaps, not a modern man at all. He is simply a man—that is, a whole and rational being; a citizen, as Chancellor Robert Hutchins of Chicago University puts it, "able to use rational processes in relation to all other men in the human community."

There is also a second kind of modern man that we can become if we wish. This second kind is not interested in justice or reason. What is he interested in? In the manipulation of gadgets—from can openers to atom bombs, in the accumulation of objects or wealth, and, finally, in wielding power over his fellowman.

This second kind of modern man is called under various aspects technological man, acquisitive man, aggressive man. Most of our so-called successes, our "men of distinction" are men of this type. They do not seem to me whole human beings or good citizens. To my mind, on the contrary, their pursuit of gadgets, objects, and power leads straight to the antheap state of which we have a rough pattern in Soviet Russia.

Now, if we wish to be gadget-object-power men, we will have certain educational needs. If we wish to be just and reasonable men, we will have other and entirely different needs.

The gadget-object-power man needs very little education it seems to me. What he does need is the training which will help him to use gadgets, accumulate objects, and exercise power over his fellow man. Well, this comes down mainly to getting and holding a job, except during those periods when he is efficiently killing his fellowmen in war.

Now if the job is the main object of human life—if, as one of our Presidents once said, the business of America is business

—then I propose the revising of our education so that the emphasis is laid on the three R's, technological training and learning how to sell a lot of objects to a lot of people.

But suppose, instead, we aim to produce just and reasonable men. Then our educational needs will revolve around the attainment of justice and reason, and will produce a different kind of education altogether.

Are we educating for the needs of modern man? Maybe that's not the way to pose the question. Education is not so much a method of satisfying needs, it is more a method of questioning needs. It should teach men to need and want those things that are really important, among them universal peace, universal law, and universal respect for our fellowmen.

To me this is the only kind of education that is really practical, for it is the only kind of education that will enable the human race to do that most practical of all things—survive. A knowledge of hog-calling, business administration, and the relative industrial merits of different alloys—these are all good things, but such knowledge will not produce citizens capable of preventing the human race from committing suicide in a series of atomic and bacteriological wars.

One more point. It is an error to talk about our education as if it were entirely in the hands of the school and in the hands of such gentlemen as Dr. Stoddard and Dr. Killian—better if it were—for the education of all of us, particularly the child, is increasingly in the hands of those who own or control the movies, the comic books, the sports column, the advertising agencies, the radio and television transmitters, the newspapers and the picture magazines. If we wish the child to become the just and rational man that all four of us on this platform have been talking about, we must either induce the owners and controllers of these instruments of communication to become just and rational themselves—and some of them are, or would like to become so. Or if they refuse to become just and rational men, we must try by democratic means to reduce their influence and return education to those to whom it belongs—to the educators.

Now this involves, of course, a revolution in our thinking. It means making teachers what they should be in any rational society; that is, the most inportant and respected people in the United States. If we can affect this revolution in our thinking, we can save ourselves from destruction. But if we cannot effect this revolution in our thinking, we cannot save ourselves from destruction, no matter how many great football teams we produce, how many new school buildings we erect, or how much money we spend.

I think we're beginning to realize this. Being the kind of people that we Americans are, I think we have at least a fighting chance of creating within a generation, perhaps, the kind of education which may begin to produce the finest citizens history has seen since the Athens of Pericles. Only then will education really begin to meet the needs of the modern man.

MODERATOR DENNY: Thank you, Mr. Fadiman. Well, these other three educators weren't quite as bold as Mr. Fadiman was in pointing a finger at certain things. Maybe, now that Mr. Fadiman has broken the ice, Paul Douglas here, who is a good name-calling politician, will step up here and get mad at somebody. How about it Senator?

SENATOR DOUGLAS: I don't believe in getting mad at anybody, and I find myself in very large agreement with what Mr. Fadiman has said. I would like to say, however, that I think he has drawn a somewhat false antithesis between technical science and humanism. I should like to point out, if I may, that in the Orient, the average coolie, overburdened as he is with toil and racked by disease, working fifteen to eighteen hours a day, does not have time to pursue the idea of justice or to practice the pursuit of reason, and that in this world of ours, even with those gadgets, people are released for time to pursue reason and even to seek justice. Therefore, science lays a material basis upon which the pursuit of the good life can be waged by all of us and not merely by a few. (*Applause.*)

MR. DENNY: Thank you, Senator. Mr. Fadiman do you have any comment to make on that?

MR. FADIMAN: I agree entirely that science does enable us to gain and attain leisure and what we do with it, it seems to me, is involve ourselves with the doings of Mr. Shmoo and Li'l Abner. (*Laughter and applause.*)

MR. DENNY: Too bad Al Capp is not here tonight to speak for himself. Dr. Killian?

DR. KILLIAN: Senator Douglas has really made my speech for me because he has made the most effective statement I know in the defense of my position. But I'd also like to point out that I think Mr. Fadiman has greatly over-simplified the problem of education, however much I agree with his general principles. That is, that we cannot educate for the objectives he has set forth unless we educate people who can do something. We must enable them to perform some useful service in our society if we're going to have any society. He seems to overlook that aspect of the problem. (*Applause.*)

MR. DENNY: Mr. Fadiman do you care to comment?

MR. FADIMAN: No, I don't think I quite overlooked it. I think it is quite possible, for example, to be a good chemist and a just and rational man. I think it is quite possible to be a good taxi-driver, or a good farmer, and a just and rational man. I assume the necessity of technical education; I assume the necessity of training. I merely say that it should be subservient and subordinate to our possession of a general set of human principles. There, I believe that I am in thorough accord with Dr. Killian, because that's what he said in his own speech much more effectively than I did. (*Laughter and applause.*)

MR. DENNY: All right. Thank you. Dr. Stoddard.

DR. STODDARD: It's hard to disagree with Mr. Fadiman, except that I agree that he oversimplifies the problem. I don't know what college catalog he picked hog-calling out of—I've been around a good deal and I never saw that one, but you can find almost anything in a college catalog. But if by that he also means hog-breeding and hog-feeding, then I must differ from him, because that's just another word for agriculture. One of the reasons we have wars is that people are hungry, and one reason why they're so hungry is they're so primitive, so stupid, so uneducated. We've learned how to grow food in the desert, and we'd better keep on doing it. Much of the food that we grow in the desert is exported to countries that have much rich land and have never known how to take care of it.

So all I would say is that we shouldn't eliminate the agricultural man, nor the technological man, nor the economic man, but we should build upon him. I think Mr. Fadiman gets over the line a little bit when he thinks you can be civilized, and like Virgil simply contemplate without ever plowing or ever eating. (*Applause.*)

MR. DENNY: Thank you. What was that, Senator?

SENATOR DOUGLAS: I say that Virgil, if you may believe his poetry, did a great deal of drinking. (*Laughter.*)

[Question period]

ANNOUNCER: Now for the summaries of tonight's discussion, here is Mr. Denny.

MR. DENNY: For our first summary, here's Mr. Fadiman.

MR. FADIMAN: All I've tried to stress is one simple point. First, we must decide what kind of citizens we wish to produce. Then we can figure out the kind of education best fitted to produce them. I am convinced that these citizens must be men and women in whom live the principles of justice and reason. If we do not produce fairly large numbers of such men and women quickly, the world will fall into the hands of the men and women who worship power.

As a result, the human race will either commit suicide in a series of planetary wars, or else stagger backward into chaos. If you tell me that history has never produced large numbers of just and rational men, I reply you are right because it has never had to. Now it has to—we have no choice. We must, or else! (*Applause.*)

MR. DENNY: Thank you, Mr. Fadiman. And now, Dr. Killian.

DR. KILLIAN: May I stress again that education must provide for the full man—men who are fit to live as well as fit to live with, as some one has said. Let us also, in our education both general and vocational, stress some of the liberal values of science: its search for truth, its search for an understanding of natural laws, its internationalism, its belief in the dignity of the human mind and its capacity to grow.

Finally, I urge a more positive approach to education than the defensive objective of mere survival. Great education has higher goals than survival. If we can teach these goals, survival will probably take care of itself. (*Applause.*)
(*Applause.*)

MR. DENNY: Thank you, Dr. Killian. And now a word from Dr. Stoddard.

DR. STODDARD: I think we should give up the idea that what is abstract or general is, therefore, unimportant. Great ideas, old or new, in books or in laboratories, enable modern man to get beyond gadgets and above narrow details. They give him a sense of direction, how to teach the young, how to strengthen the family, how to become ethical and stable, and how to keep wars from beginning in the minds of men.

These are the great problems of our day. Education alone cannot solve them but if education ignores them, as is its habit, we shall never find a solution. Hence, the call is for more education and for better education at every level.

MR. DENNY: Thank you, Dr. Stoddard, and now Senator Paul Douglas.

SENATOR DOUGLAS: For the immediate future, our need is for men and women who will have sufficient intellectual and emotional maturity so that they will be able, at the same time, to resist the efforts of a police state to conquer the world, yet to maintain a free and liberal America—to be humanists in a world of strife.

MR. DENNY: Thank you, Paul Douglas, Dr. Killian, Dr. Stoddard and Mr. Fadiman. Well, gentlemen, you all seem to agree on the essential point that education should provide modern man with the ability to answer the basic problems of human relations if he is to survive in today's world.

THE NEW BIRTH [12]

JOHN TYLER CALDWELL [13]

Dr. John Tyler Caldwell delivered this address on the occasion of his inauguration as Sixth President of Alabama College, the State College for Women, at Montevallo, Alabama, on December 11, 1948, in Palmer Auditorium, Alabama College.

At Mississippi State College, Dr. Caldwell had a course in speech and one in parliamentary law. For a time, he was a member of the debating club. His teaching and professional duties have been accompanied by constant speaking.

States President Caldwell: "All teachers must have a great deal of faith in words. Indeed, our civilization is built on ideas and ideas can take form only in words. Furthermore, we are living in what Walter Bagehot has called—'The Age of Discussion.' Democratic processes require much discussion, much writing, much speaking. To the extent that we can refine the practice of oral communication so that ideas are expressed concisely, accurately, pleasingly and persuasively, we will have made a tremendous contribution to the success of discussion as a social process. The speech departments in all colleges are doing a wonderful job and need all the encouragement they can get from administrators and colleagues." [14]

May I express my appreciation for the honor done to Alabama College by the presence of you delegates and visitors here today.

This ceremony, in which a new President of Alabama College is formally acknowledged and tendered the responsibilities of his office, touches me profoundly. I accept humbly the honor and responsibility. I pledge the Board of Trustees and the people of Alabama at this moment my high intent and earnest effort to administer the affairs of the College to the very best of my ability, as honestly as I can and as nearly as I am able in accord with the principles of our great spiritual heritage of Christian living. More than this I cannot attempt. A lesser goal would be unworthy and would be a discredit to

[12] The text was furnished through the courtesy of President Caldwell.
[13] For biographical note, see Appendix.
[14] Letter to this editor, May 10, 1949.

the hopes, faith and labors of my distinguished predecessors, to these students, and to this faculty.

Delaying an inauguration for more than a year is not too good an idea from several standpoints. I do not commend it to Presidents Draughon, Gallilee and Norton.

But it affords me the opportunity of saying truthfully that I shall never be able to thank enough the wonderful Staff and student body of this College for the tolerance, understanding and earnest effort to help me get my sea legs on this voyage. They have been tolerant, they have been understanding, they have been invaluable in their help and advice. As my sea legs grow steadier I have every confidence we shall retain the fine standards established under the leadership of Captain Reynolds, President Peterson, President Palmer, President Carmichael and finally by my able and distinguished immediate predecessor, Dr. Arthur Fort Harman, who passed away on Founder's Day, October 12, this year. Let me not forget, I pray, that what Alabama College now proudly is, is the product of every girl, every teacher, every trustee, every gardener, every dean, every taxpayer, every president, who passed this way and did his bit.

I have chosen as a subject for my remarks: "The New Birth, or, Alice in Wonderland." Any resemblance of the subjects to recent events or newly arrived persons to this campus is entirely deliberate and premeditated on my part. If the recent arrival objects to having her name used here, she may sue her father when she comes of age in October 1966, A.D.

All here recall Lewis Carroll's sprightly and gentle classics, *Alice in Wonderland* and *Through the Looking Glass.* Alice, a little blonde-headed child, grown drowsy from picking daisies, was not greatly surprised to see a Rabbit walk by, nor to hear him speak plain English. But when the Rabbit pulled a watch from his waistcoat pocket, Alice, burning with curiosity (natural for a woman) just had to follow him to his hole.

At this point, as one who so recently has accepted a college presidency, I find myself sympathizing with Alice. For the story records, "In another moment down went Alice after it (the rabbit), never once considering how in the world she was to get out again." President Draughon, President Galilee and President Norton (and our wives, God bless them) are among the more recent sympathizers who surely join me in a fellow feeling for Alice's venture down the hole.

I cannot refrain from saying here how much Alice in Wonderland at one place reminded me forcefully of Alice of Flowerhill. Shortly after Alice arrived in Wonderland, she wept a lake of tears and flooded the surrounding area. Then after she, the mouse and others had arrived on dry land and sat for a time, the mouse asked Alice, "How are you getting on now, my dear?" "As wet as ever," said Alice. "It doesn't seem to dry me at all."

But I must begin soon what I have to say. You will remember that the Mock Turtle began his personal history with the command to Alice and her companion, "Sit down, both of you, and don't speak a word till I've finished." Then when nobody spoke for some minutes, Alice thought "I don't see how he can ever finish, if he doesn't begin." So, as the Mock Turtle finally did, I shall begin. (Not with his words, however, for he began, "Once I was a real Turtle.")—All I can say is, with some nostalgia, "Once I was a teacher. . . ."

"The new birth" has reference first of all to the scriptural passage in which Jesus said to Nicodemus, "Except a man be born again, he cannot see the kingdom of God," and that, "Except a man be born of water and of the Spirit, he cannot enter into the Kingdom of God. . . . Marvel not that I said unto thee, ye must be born again."

Secondly, "the new birth" refers to a passage in Lincoln's Gettysburg address, when he said: "That this nation, under God, shall have a new birth of freedom, and that government of the people, by the people, for the people, shall not perish from the earth."

Nations are reborn when its citizens are reborn, that is, when its people as individual men and women discover their innate sense of spiritual values, revamp their aims in terms of moral and ethical achievement, and assert their faith in the validity of kindness, gentleness, goodness, mercy, love, honesty, peace and so on.

Finally, then, "the new birth" refers to the purpose and process of education which to all who participate in it, to teacher as well as learner, and at all levels, is the continual unfolding in the mental horizons of men and women of broader horizons, new insights, deeper meaning, purer loves, loftier ideals, better reasons for courage, more significant skills.

Such are the potentialities of education which make it worthy. A great head of this institution, Dr. O. C. Carmichael, now President of the Carnegie Foundation for the Advancement of Learning, said recently that "education represents the cutting edge of progress." Indeed it is. If the findings of the physical sciences and social sciences are true, they will undoubtedly lead on and on, progressively, to man's high destiny toward which the humanists have already penetrated and dimly defined. But if these heights are to be reached by mankind, all men and women must see the goal clearer and find the paths more surely.

Goals are important; Alice found it so when she was confused and asked the Cheshire cat, "Would you tell me please, which way I ought to go from here?"

"That depends a good deal on where you want to get to," said the cat.

"I don't much care where—," said Alice.

"Then it doesn't matter which way you go," said the cat.

"—so long as I get somewhere," Alice added as an explanation.

"Oh, you're sure to do that," said the cat, "if you only walk long enough."

Since education must take its goals from the society which it serves, let's have a look at our American society's goals. Or do they exist? And who established them? I know they do not exist alike in all of our thoughts. And I doubt that agreement is sufficiently widespread for the nation as a whole to claim them. Perhaps the goals will just unfold as we go along. Perhaps. But I prefer not to adopt the Alice in Wonderland policy of just walking long enough to get "somewhere." I like to see a goal ahead. Let it be an ideal, if you please. Thus we come squarely up to the question of who is to take the lead in establishing our goals. And, clearly enough, the answer is: We are! You and I, each generation of us, will make some contribution to defining the goals, be they high ones or low ones. So those we educate today in our colleges will be setting goals tomorrow, or else we will just drift to "somewhere." What then are our ideals here at Alabama College?

Let me speak for myself and trust that my friends and colleagues will not be too much offended.

Our goals here, as I see it, are: *First,* to assist each young woman who comes to us to find herself a beautiful creature of the Most High God endowed with many wonderful and special talents. *Second,* to assist her to find that her fellowman, regardless of race or creed, is her brother man, possessing dignity and inherent goodness, and that her most important talent to develop is her power to love that fellowman as she herself would be loved. *Third,* to assist her in discovering that no part of existence is insignificant, but that each contributes to the unity which constitutes being. *Finally,* to bring to her consciousness a sharper awareness of a universal cause, a universal order, and a universal destiny in which she is obliged to participate. This is a big job. But it *is* our job.

These are the goals of a liberal education. In the proportions they are achieved in our students, our society will be improved. Sometimes it might be wondered how with our secularism and scientism we can work toward these goals in our institutions of higher learning. The answer is again found in the essential unity of all true knowledge. If the physical and biological sciences appear to delve only into the secrets of the material universe, we can take reassurance from the fact that the more we learn about that universe the closer we come to the truths about universal cause and universal order.

If the frontiers of psychology are progressively pushed back and its findings made known to men and women for everyday living, those who learn of it will discover perhaps but the ancient preachings of Jesus and Paul and John who admonished their hearers that the best psychology of all was to love one another, and who knew that hate, false pride, false knowledge, self-love and selfishness were the real demons of man's life, doing injury to his mind and body and society.

If the sciences of society—sociology, anthropology, political science, and economics—are properly pursued, they will reveal the mechanics of a more orderly society, here and now, where the Golden Rule can hold sway, in which man meets brother man and common objectives are worked out harmoniously and peaceably, in which wealth rewards honesty, nobleness, moral courage, and unselfishness and base motives are penalized. Here too the truths about mankind will begin to destroy the divisions in men's minds which separate people by artificial and superficial devices created out of selfishness, pride, ambition, hate, and most of all, by ignorance.

The pursuit of man's ideals, hopes, joys, tragedies and triumphs, in the literature, the drama, and poetry of our own and other tongues, inspires the student to formulate his own philosophy, inspires him—if truly taught—to identify his destiny with that of other men and seek a reconciliation of conflict. These accomplishments are not un-Christian. It is in the best tradition of our Hebrew-Christian heritage that these disciplines were developed and are available in order to free men's minds of ignorance, prejudice and hate.

The arts help Jane and Ellen and Sylvia find the thrill of creating something meaningful and beautiful, and of doing it themselves. Jane yearns to link her individual achievement with the possibilities of all men who are in the business of reflecting their Creator. She learns the thrill of producing beauty and grace in form or movement or sound or speech or color. These attributes are mental and spiritual, not materialistic. It is no accident that artists are passionate in their love of freedom. They know they would never have discovered themselves except in an atmosphere of freedom.

Do I omit the vocationalist? No, indeed not. To become an effective member of our economy is a worthy accomplishment and an obligation which educational institutions must support. I hasten to point out, however, that the "liberally" educated man or woman is best equipped to pursue successfully any vocation chosen and trained for. There is no home economist, no pianist, no laboratory technician, no physiotherapist, no social worker, no administrator, no teacher, who wisely will omit the liberalizing value of the sciences and humanities from her formal education.

On all this I should say more. But I move on to ask: What kind of society then will these girls so educated want to establish? What will this kind of education cost? Will it be worth it?

I am amused as I lay out before you my ideas of society, for I think of Alice's saying to the White Queen, "There's no use trying, one can't believe impossible things." To which the Queen replied, "I dare say you haven't had much practice. When I was your age, I always did it for half-an-hour a day. Why, sometimes I've believed as many as six impossible things before breakfast. . . ." (Some older heads here may be thinking that of me now.)

The kind of society our Alabama College education is calculated to produce will have several characteristics.

First, it will be a *free* society, in which the individual's personality is the most important consideration. Happy, well-adjusted persons will be the principal objective of public and private endeavors. Freedom to worship, think, read, investigate and to speak will not be questioned.

Second, it will be a *just* society, in which the standards of success and reward will be honesty, service, intelligence, unselfishness and responsibility.

Third, it will be a *secure* society, in which a wife and husband can build a family and a home free from fear, secure in the knowledge that theirs and their children's future will not be penalized because of society's failure to function with reasonable order and responsibility.

Fourth, it will be a society of *opportunity,* in which a person with intelligence, initiative, energy, skill, courage and foresight will be rewarded for his useful accomplishments that benefit his fellowman.

Fifth, it will be a society at *peace,* in which the growth of international understanding will have overshadowed the divisions among men and the psychology of love will have supplanted fear, ignorance and hate.

Finally, it will be a *happy* society shaken loose from sordid-ness, tawdriness and shallowness, finding inner resources more joyous, more sustaining, uplifting and relaxing than what today passes too often for entertainment and which is really a spoila-tion of character and standards.

I do not know whether the government of our new so-ciety will have three branches or not. I do not know whether or not there will be a National Labor Relations Board or a TVA or a Federal Trade Commission or a State Utilities Commission or Federal Aid to Education or a United Nations organization or not. I do not even know whether individual enterprise capitalism will be part of the new society or not. These are all devices which one generation of citizens has thought neces-sary and later generations may retain, modify or abolish. I happen to believe them all to be extremely useful devices now for moving toward our ethical goal, which is not well defined. What is important, and perhaps the only thing about the organized social order that really matters, is that the people of each generation always must be free to change it and adapt it to their chosen ends. This is the *sine qua non* of democratic accommodation, adjustment and progress. This, incidentally, is what a free people will demand. And it places on the people a great responsibility.

The kind of education which free people require is, there-fore, the very best the society can afford—no less. Chiefly we need our share of the ablest people of our society on the teaching staffs of our educational institutions from the kindergarten through the graduate schools. Faculties are at the core of the educational process. We cannot in our highly advertised so-ciety, where material well-being has become the standard of prestige and success, expect our ablest sons and daughters to choose a profession which requires its members to spend years and money in preparation, only to find it difficult to raise and educate a family on the average expected income, much less to enjoy the ordinary material advantages of a car, home owner-ship and some travel. It would perhaps be well to have every teacher of economics and related social sciences spend some time in the workaday world of business for maturity of viewpoint. But those who complain that the teachers of economics for example, are "not practical" and that they are "undermining our system" cannot expect to purchase maturity, poise, wide knowledge, experience and intensive training for from twenty-five hundred to four thousand dollars a year under the present circumstances. We can be grateful that we have as little as we do of the wrong kind of criticism of the present social system.

Ladies and gentlemen, I put it to you as a proposition that if this state will dig deeper into its taxable jeans and plan better the overall application of their dollars for higher education in the state, your sons and daughters tomorrow will call you blessed as will their sons and daughters. We want industrial and agricultural progress in this grand State of Alabama and in this great region of opportunity and we are getting some of it. But we constantly are tempted to talk and act as if education were just another cost of government. My friends, if you would reduce the breadlines of the future, if you would obliterate the Communist of the future, if you would eliminate the ugliness of your cities and rural slums, if you would raise the standards of your public servants, if you would increase the capitalization of your banks, if you would extend the number of home owners, if you would curb delinquency, if you wish this region to boom as it blossoms into the full splendor of a new day, educate the people.

I rather think, finally, that if we strive to do a proper job at Alabama College, and at all our sister and brother institutions, public and private, in bringing about a continual rebirth in the minds of each student of this generation, we shall bring about also a new birth of freedom and prosperity to this whole blessed land. How much will it cost? I did not ask. I only ask my hearers today if there is any task more important, or if there is any need more urgent. I only ask if we are doing all we can. Or whether we think education is just another item on which we can practice "economy."

The words of John in *Revelations* are applicable here:

I know thy works, that thou art neither cold nor hot: I would thou wert cold or hot. So then because thou art lukewarm, and neither cold nor hot, I will spue thee out of my mouth.

This generation cannot afford lukewarmness toward the moral issue of whether or not education is our most important public endeavor. "Through the Looking Glass" contains the final answer to the importance of education in today's battle of ideas. Tweedledee and Tweedledum were preparing themselves for their personal battle with each other. Alice was arranging a neck protector for Tweedledee "to keep his head from being cut off." "You know," he said gravely, "it's one of the most serious things that can possibly happen to one in a battle—to get one's head cut off."

RELIGION

THE CHURCH AND INTERNATIONAL DISORDER [1]

JOHN FOSTER DULLES [2]

John Foster Dulles gave this address before the first Assembly of the World Council of Churches, at Amsterdam, Holland, on August 24, 1948. A hundred and forty-five churches were gathered to consider problems of implementing interdenominational unity in the face of international disaster. This speaker, at that time said to be candidate Thomas Dewey's choice for his Secretary of State, and widely experienced in negotiations with the Soviets, addressed a capacity audience in the Concertgebouw Hall. He at once set up the premises of Western civilization: (1) belief in a moral law, and (2) recognition of the dignity of every "human individual." He then logically attacked Marxian communism as destructive of these principles. "There is, says Stalin, no such thing as 'eternal justice.' . . . Human beings have no rights that are God-given and therefore not subject to be taken away by men."

The conclusion from his carefully and closely reasoned argument was that the churches must "create a world organization that will go on working daily to mobilize Christian power." According to reporters, the speaker "stood in an easy stooped slouch and spoke rapidly and vigorously." [3]

Joseph L. Hromadka, of the Evangelical Church of Czech Brethren, professor of theology of the John Hus faculty of Charles University in Prague, followed with a speech that directly contradicted the principles and detailed arguments of Dulles. Thus a full-fledged debate ensued.

This Assembly of the Churches has worldwide significance. That is because we represent both great diversity and great unity. Such a combination attracts the attention of men everywhere, for it is the combination that is needed to save mankind from disaster.

We are here from over forty lands; we are of many races, nationalities and classes; we represent many different branches

---

[1] Text and permission to reprint furnished through the courtesy of Dr. John Foster Dulles.

[2] For biographical note, see Appendix.

[3] For further comment on Dr. Dulles as a speaker, see *Representative American Speeches: 1947-1948*, p58-67.

of the Christian Church. Yet we are here organizing for continuing association and we are doing so freely and in fellowship. We are showing that moral and spiritual forces can overcome differences that usually divide men into hostile camps.

This illustration comes at a fateful hour, for, in the world, division is assuming an ominous character. Tension mounts, means of mass destruction are being feverishly developed and there is conceded risk that mankind may be plunged into an awful abyss. So, Christians and non-Christians alike are anxiously looking to what we do here. They hope that we may perhaps show the way of deliverance from the terrible fate that impends.

We shall not ignore those expectations. We do not forget that we belong to a generation that has already subjected countless human beings to incredible horror and we know that millions were sustained in their agony by the hope that the very intensity of their suffering would make a total of suffering so immense as to compel those who survived to find the way to live at peace. Also, we know the dread and frustration that grip the living, as they see their leaders becoming ever more competent in ways of destruction, but apparently remaining incompetent to break the cycle of recurrent war.

So, this Assembly is confronted with the responsibility of moral leadership, knowing that mankind is doomed but for the saving grace of the spirit.

We shall not, of course, attempt to prescribe detailed political solutions, for that is not the function of spiritual leadership. But we shall, I hope, identify the evil, arouse men to combat it and point out the moral principles that are needed to win that battle. The churches can prescribe broad strategy, leaving to political and lay leadership responsibility for tactics.

This is a time for the churches to expose the evil of war and its futility. Many are talking about war as though it were an unpleasant, but necessary, remedy for existing ills. The fact is that another world war would engulf all humanity in utter misery and make almost impossible the achievement of the good ends for which, no doubt, the combatants would profess to be fighting. At times, war may have to be risked as the lesser of two evils. But there is no holy war.

War is evil. Over the ages violence has repeatedly been invoked for noble ends. That method is dramatic and exciting. It seems to promise quick and decisive results and, at times, it inspires fine and sacrificial qualities. But violent methods breed hatred, vengefulness, hypocrisy, cruelty and disregard of truth. Because of such evils, wars have seldom accomplished lasting good and there is no reason to think that a new war now would accomplish any good.

The churches can and should say these things and develop a stronger public opinion against war. But that part of the churches' task is the easier part. War has been recurrent throughout the ages, despite its generally acknowledged evilness and most men's preference for peace. For that there must be some basic cause. The churches' further and harder task is to discern that cause and show how it can be overcome.

The Oxford Conference of 1937 pointed out the most basic cause of war. That is the fact that, in a living world, change is inevitable and unless there are political institutions that make provision for peaceful change, there is bound to be violent change.

It is possible to have a peace of exhaustion or a peace of tyranny. But such peace is not true peace and it seldom lasts long. If peace is to be durable it must be organized on the basis of laws that are made peacefully and that can be changed peacefully.

That is a basic conclusion; but nothing practical can be done about it unless certain other matters can be settled. If the organization of peace is dependent on law, it is necessary to have some understanding as to the nature of law. Are laws merely what the most powerful want, or are they an effort to carry into effect moral principles of right and wrong? And if law-making is relied upon to effect change, who are to control that process and how are non-assenters to be treated? Without agreement on these matters there can be no adequate organization of international peace.

At this point the churches can make a decisive contribution. Two great principles are here involved. One is recognition that there is a moral law and that it provides the only proper sanction for man-made laws. The other principle is that every human individual, as such, has dignity and worth that no man-made law, no human power, can rightly desecrate.

Both of these concepts rest on fundamental religious assumptions. Belief in a moral law flows from the assumption that there is a divinely ordained purpose in history, that moral considerations are ultimate and that man, through his laws, cannot disregard the moral law with impunity, just as he cannot disregard the physical laws of the universe without wrecking himself.

Belief in the dignity and worth of the individual flows from the assumption that the individual is created by God in His image, is the object of God's redemptive love and is directly accountable to God. He therefore has a dignity and worth different than if he were only a part of the natural order. Men, born to be children of God, have rights and responsibilities that other men cannot take from them.

Experience shows that when men organize a society in accordance with these two basic beliefs, they can, within such society, have peace with each other.

The Western democracies have never created, internationally, adequate institutions for peaceful change. But domestically they do have institutions that, to a large extent, reflect the two principles to which we refer. For many years their governments have, in the main, been governments of law. The laws have been made and changed by representative processes that assume that men generally have a perception of right and wrong and will seek what seems right. But it is also recognized that popular majorities are not infallible and so majorities have been bound to respect minorities. Neither rulers nor majorities have been allowed to do anything they wanted merely by the device of giving their desires the label of "law." Every man, however alone or however humble, has been entitled to follow the dictates of his own reason and conscience and peacefully to seek to persuade others to agree with him. Thus, views originally held by only a minority have come to prevail peacefully. Justice has been considered to be an eternal verity, existing apart from and above any human will, however powerful, and the administration of justice has been separated from politics.

Under those conditions, social and economic changes have been immense and they have, in the main, been peacefully effected. Human beings have less and less been treated as mere tools of production. Women have been freed from grave disabilities. Infant mortality has been greatly reduced, health generally improved and the span of life lengthened. Education has become general and the development of spiritual life has been freed of political inhibitions. Individual initiative has worked, experimentally and competitively, to find new ways for men to produce more. At the same time there has developed an increasing sense of social responsibility. No longer can the social order be described as "each for himself and the devil take the hindmost." Social security has rapidly expanded in scope, and works of public utility have come to be owned or regulated in the general interest. Graduated income taxes and death duties effect a very considerable distribution in accordance with need.

To say these things is not to be self-righteous or complacent. All societies are un-Christian in many respects, and no society is without practices that promote human welfare. But where political institutions have been designed to reflect the moral law and to respect the dignity and worth of the individual, it has proved possible to organize peaceful change. Also, where society is organized in conscious denial of these two moral principles, force and violence are conceded to be inevitable.

Marxian communism is atheistic and materialistic. Its leaders reject the concept of moral law. There is, says Stalin, no such thing as "eternal justice"; laws are merely the means whereby those in power carry out their will, and human beings have no rights that are God-given and therefore not subject to be taken away by man. So, while some good things have been done for the proletariat, both theory and practice involve coercing, terrorizing and liquidating those whose reason and conscience compel them to reject the order sought to be imposed. There are some similarities between the social and economic ends that Communists profess and those that Christians seek. But the methods taught are utterly dissimilar and the present methods of communism are incompatible with peaceful change.

The Soviet Communist regime is not a regime of peace and, indeed, it does not purport to be. It may not, and I hope that it does not, want international war. But if so, that is a matter of expediency, not of principle. Violence and coercion are the accepted methods, class war being, however, usually preferred to national war. Within the Communist-controlled states leadership has periodically been determined by violent purges and it is fanatically taught that there is, for communism, no peaceful path of development. The recent Cominform indictment of the Communist Party in Yugoslavia charged as a grievous offense that that party believed that there could be a "peaceful growth" of communism in relation to capitalism. That, it was pointed out, was the heresy of Bukharian, who had been executed in the purge of 1938. The true doctrine was that there must be "ever sharpening" conflict.

It is inevitable that orthodox communism should reject peaceful ways, except as a matter of temporary expediency, because it rejects the moral premises that alone make possible the permanent organization of peace. Peace can never be stabilized except by institutions that seek to reflect the moral law and that respect the dignity of the individual. There always have been, there always will be, human spirits that will rebel against totalitarian dictatorship and that fact, in turn, requires such dictatorships to be violent and coercive.

Communist parties control governments in sixteen countries and through them rule nearly one quarter of the world's population. Their leadership is dynamic and it has world-wide ambitions. That, of itself, makes it impossible to create at once a universal organization of peace through law, and it confronts those who seek peace with a difficult problem.

It is not a problem that can be solved by abandoning those faiths that clash with the Communist creed. That is morally unthinkable and practically impossible. Also, that could not advance us toward the desired goal, for it would mean abandoning precisely those principles that are needed to organize peace on a stable basis.

Also, the problem cannot be solved by trying to crush communism by force. Collective action may, at times, be required pursuant to the United Nations Charter, to protect member states or individual human beings in their charter rights. But it would be wrong and stupid to use violence in order to convince people that violence ought not to be used.

There is a way of solution. It assumes that we can have a little time, but that, I think, is a reasonable assumption. The solution is for those who have faith to exert themselves more vigorously to translate their faith into works. Those who believe in the moral law and human dignity must be more concerned to make social institutions reflect those ideals. In that way they can provide an example that others will follow and a unifying process will be begun.

That is not just a speculative possibility; it is a probability. History shows that men everywhere are always attracted to an effort that combines idealism and realism. Consider, for example, the so-called "Christian" or "Western" civilization. For several centuries it had influence that was world-wide. That was partly due to coercion, but in the main it was because it seemed that the Western peoples were intent on creating institutions that would better promote human welfare. Out of that creative effort came opportunity that could have been used for the organization of world peace. If now that opportunity has receded and the world is seriously divided by the Communist challenge, that is most of all because even the good practices of the West no longer seem to be the expression of a great faith. Arnold Toynbee, in his recent volume *Civilization on Trial*, says that Western civilization has "been living on spiritual capital. Practice, unsupported by belief, is a wasting asset, as we have suddenly discovered, to our dismay, in this generation."

Once the connection is broken between faith and practices, practices, however good, lose their moral significance and seem to be matters of expediency. As such they are vulnerable to attack by those who inject strong belief into different practices. Today, many who defend the institutions of the West do so on purely materialistic grounds, such as that they have developed mass production. Such reasons are inadequate. No political or social system should prevail unless it is the means whereby men are consciously trying to bring human conduct into accord with moral law and to enlarge the opportunity of men to exercise their human rights and fundamental freedoms.

There is a vast field for such creative action. I know that there is much to be done in my own country. I assume it is the same elsewhere. Internationally, there is much to be done in the United Nations and its subsidiary organs and groupings. If many will engage themselves actively and intelligently in this task, their spirit will be contagious, the results will be good and that combination will draw men into unity that will recreate world-wide opportunity.

We are not in a world where "all or nothing" is a healthy rule for living. Some put down on paper the theoretical ideal and then feel frustrated if it cannot at once be realized. The alternative is to get to work wherever that is practically possible and to rely on creative spirit and its good results to open up new areas of opportunity. Of course, Communist power now limits what can be done internationally. But also it is the fact that we have not nearly approached those limits. If we will do what now is possible, in a spirit of universal brotherhood, we can be sure that present limits will constantly recede. They cannot withstand such unifying influences as we can thus set in motion.

The world situation is serious because of a sharp division. On the one hand are those who claim to be seeking the welfare of the masses but who reject the moral premises necessary to make their efforts peaceful and fruitful. On the other hand are those who accept the moral premises necessary for the organization of peace but who have allowed their practices to seem routine, materialistic and spiritually unfertile. That division will gradually become less sharp if those who believe in moral law and human dignity will make it apparent by their works that their political practices are in fact being made to serve their faith.

As we thus analyze the world situation, Christian responsibility emerges as an inescapable fact. The moral principles that need to be put to work are implicit in all the great religions. But Christians believe that moral truth was uniquely revealed by Jesus Christ. Also, Christianity emphasizes not merely the relations of man to God, but also the relations of man to man. So the Christian churches should feel a special responsibility. If they do not discharge it, political leadership can scarcely hope to succeed.

That is a conclusion that ought to lead to practical consequences. The Christian influence is considerable but as yet wholly inadequate. If, in the international field, Christians are to play their clearly indicated part, the churches must have better organization. They should be able to speak more impressively with greater unity. They should be able to act with greater coordination. They should put more emphasis on Christianity as a world religion, remembering that God gave His Son because He loved the World, not merely the West.

It is for such reasons, I take it, that we are here. We are not here merely for a single inspiring experience. Rather, we are here to create a world organization that will go on working daily to mobilize Christian power to break down the walls of division. Thus we shall serve Him who was lifted up that He might draw all men unto Him.

HIGHER RELIGION FOR HIGHER EDUCATION [4]

RALPH W. SOCKMAN [5]

Dr. Ralph W. Sockman delivered this address at the annual conference of the Association of American Colleges at Cincinnati, Ohio, on
January 12, 1948. Pastor of the Church of Christ (Methodist), New
York City, he has long held a reputation as one of the half dozen outstanding preachers of the Protestant church. Since 1937 he has been a
speaker on the *National Radio Program* and has steadily added to the
number of his radio listeners. He has also been in constant demand as
a lecturer before educational groups.

The present address reflects his sermonic habit of close organization,
effective audience adjustment, and conciliatory mood. He uses contemporary, sometimes personal illustrations, with frequent quotations from
literary, Biblical, and historical sources. His oral style is concrete, lively,
idiomatic, figurative. The speech printed below is one of Dr. Sockman's
best.

His thesis, the necessity of religion in any concept of general education, was under special examination at this time by representative educators. The reanalysis of the liberal arts program in many colleges raised
again the question of whether courses in religion should be required or
strongly recommended. Publicly supported institutions, in viewing the
role of religion in education, were raising the old question of the separa-
tion of church and state and were attempting to define the limits that
might be necessary in including such courses in the curriculum. [6]

The presence of ecclesiastical representatives on your program year after year attests your recognition that religion has a
place in higher education. How to meet the religious needs of
the student without impairing the freedom of study is the common problem of the churches and the colleges.

Confession is good for the soul—even of a clergyman. And
speaking as a representative of the church may I say that religion
must be more educational if it is to ask education to be more religious. We must confess that the pulpit has often flogged the

[4] Text and permission to reprint furnished through the courtesy of Dr. Sockman. Reprinted from *Vital Speeches of the Day*. 14:304-8 March 1, 1948.

[5] For biographical note see **Appendix**.

[6] For further comment on Dr. Sockman as a speaker, see *Representative American Speeches: 1942-1943*, p267-75; *1946-1947*, p271-8.

will rather than fed the mind. We have frequently blamed the universities for destroying the faith of our youth when in reality we had sent them to you with very little faith to shake. It is hardly surprising that a young man should stop praying when higher education awakens his mind to the immensities and processes of the physical universe if the only prayer he has ever learned is, "Now I lay me down to sleep."

We of the pulpit have too often given the impression of handing down our doctrines of creed and our rules of conduct in dogmatic fashion. It is little wonder, therefore, that our youth sometimes lose respect for our intellectual acumen and integrity when they are introduced to the project method of the college classroom with its impression of professors and students as open-minded fellow-seekers after truth. The conclusion drawn is that the pulpit is concerned in presenting data to prove its preconceived thesis while the professor seeks only to follow where the facts may point.

Furthermore, the popular mind has been impregnated with the idea that ecclesiastical bodies are almost hopelessly divided by their sectarian and denominational differences. Youth are naturally repelled by what appears to them as narrowness and provincialism. This repulsion is increased by their courses in the liberal arts, which studies, if true to their intent, tend to emancipate the mind from prejudice and parochialism. We of the churches can hardly expect to lead the young or their thoughtful elders in this day when all are longing for a united world unless we manifest a deeper and wider spirit of unity.

Having admitted these weaknesses on the ecclesiastical side, may I ask if there are not some confessions which could be made from the college side?

University circles tend to identify religion with its institutional implementation rather than its spiritual motivation. They see the shell and miss the seed. Taking this external and superficial view they overemphasize the sectarian divisiveness and overlook the central unities.

Colleges in their desire for freedom resist the indoctrination by religion and accept the indoctrination by secularism. By ignoring the religious element in the treatment of formative cultural factors, the impression is given that religion is an irrelevant elective, all right for those "who like that sort of thing." Sometimes this silent treatment of religion is replaced by a supercilious attitude on the part of professors, who make the student feel that only the intellectually unemancipated still go to church. Quite frequently these criticisms of church policies and beliefs are based on observations made by the professor in some little provincial parish of his boyhood. Those who are wise do not take too seriously the shadows cast on the church by those who have not darkened its doors for twenty-five years. Students, however, are not so discriminating.

University teachers do not always accord religious leaders the respect given to specialists in secular fields other than their own. A professor of psychology would not presume to pass judgment on the findings of the physics department; but religion is commonly regarded as a realm in which one man's opinion is as good as another's—if not a little bit better.

When we get beyond this desultory sniping, we find that there is no war between the American church and the American college. Both are on the side of decency and democracy. Both are fighting for freedom and fullness of life. Both are awake to the dangers which threaten our ideals and institutions from atheistic and autocratic ideologies. Both know that the best defense against Communist and Fascist propaganda is a better cultivation of the wholesome features of our religious faith.

Both religious and educational leaders, however, are aware that this cultivation of our historic faith is sadly deficient. C. S. Lewis has posed the issue in his new book, *Miracles*.

If we are content to go back and become humble plain men obeying a tradition, well. If we are ready to climb and struggle on until we become sages, better still. But the man who will neither obey wisdom in others nor adventure for her himself is fatal. A society where the simple many obey the few seers can live; a society where all were seers could live even more fully. But a society where the mass is still simple and the seers are no longer attended to can achieve only superficiality, baseness, ugliness, and in the end extinction. On or back we must go; to stay here is death.

A religiously illiterate people eventually become an irreverent people. And when reverence is lost, all virtue becomes unstable.

The person who reveres nothing lacks high incentives. When we cease looking up to something higher than ourselves, we start going downward. When we take away all the "no trespass" signs from life's garden and hold no spots as sacred, then the landscape soon is transformed from beauty to barrenness. Goethe put it not too strongly:

There is one thing no one brings with him into the world, and it is a thing on which everything else depends, that thing by means of which every man that is born into the world becomes truly manly. That thing is reverence.

Reverence is easier to recognize than to define. But may we not regard it as the profound feeling of awe stirred by something regarded as of supreme reality and value. Reverence can be inculcated without sectarian rivalry. Roman Catholic, Protestant and Jew recognize and cherish the truth of the Hebrew proverb "The fear of the Lord is the beginning of wisdom," or as Moffatt translates it, "Reverence for the Eternal is the first thing in knowledge." Without reverence knowledge never becomes wisdom.

Higher education seeks wisdom rather than mere knowledge. While uncritical reverence has often been the foe of free inquiry, enlightened reverence is the only atmosphere in which freedom is safe and true tolerance is possible.

As I understand it, theories of higher education are roughly classified into three groups, which for lack of better terminology may be called, the "liberal," the "classical," and the "progressive." Certainly the "liberal" theory with its concern for "value" must recognize the need of the reverent spirit in safeguarding the ends of all our striving. And surely the "classical" theory in its accent on "truth" and the purely intellectual disciplines emphasizes objectives which can be reached only through a reverent spirit. To quote President Hutchins: "The aim of education is wisdom and goodness. . . . We must reconstruct education, directing it to virtue and intelligence. . . . The great problem of our time is moral, intellectual and spiritual".

And even the "progressive" theory of education with its emphasis on "adjustment," by which is meant both adaptation to one's world and willingness to change it—even this theory in the most recent books of its exponents shows a profound, almost reverent allegiance to the democratic ideal.

Therefore, cannot the three groups of educators, liberals, classical and progressive, and the three groups of churchmen, Jewish, Roman Catholic and Protestant, agree that "reverence for the eternal is the first thing in knowledge?" And from that premise may we proceed to consider how and where religion can serve America's program of higher education.

Education shows its progressive spirit by its repeated efforts to reappraise its achievements and redefine its goals. Recently there appeared the first report of President Truman's Commission on Higher Education. Since the findings of this commission have not yet been fully published and since we are met here in Senator Taft's city of Cincinnati, I thought it might be more politically tactful to go for guidance to a commission which antedates the Truman administration.

About nine years ago the National Educational Association appointed a commission on secondary schools to redefine the aims of education. This commission came forth with four goals so simply stated and yet so comprehensive that they seem to me a suitable framework for the consideration of religion's contribution to the American college, for while given to secondary schools, they are equally applicable to higher education.

The first goal is self-realization. While students are struggling for a multiplicity of ends, many of which are undefined, the general drive might be described as the desire to be somebody, to do something and to get somewhere. If religion can be seen as contributing to such self-realization, it will receive attention.

Too many young people have the idea that religion is a straitjacket put over on them by their elders to make them "be good." They must be helped to see that religious faith has developed findings which are like formulas of living tested in the laboratory of long experience and that instead of being limitations they are enlargements of life, just as are the experiences of former scientists and the experiments of present students.

The word good has connotations of varying appeal. The youth who resents being told to "be good" is eager to find the "good life." Henderson in his volume *Vitalizing Liberal Education*, asserts that "education for the good life" is the ethical aim of the college. But he says that "what the good life is must be determined experimentally." But do we not have to admit that the individual student's span of years is too short for him to determine experimentally for himself what is good for him, and if he sets out to try all the experiments he will probably make his life even shorter? A neighbor of mine in a New York apartment house came into possession of a cornet at Christmas time. He seems to be trying all the possibilities of expression resident within that cornet. I am hoping that he will soon learn that some of the experiments on that instrument have been tested in the past and found wanting and that wisdom will prompt him to procure a teacher who will save him futile trouble and safeguard his neighbors' peace of mind.

Similarly the teachings of religion must be seen as a time-saving aid to what "progressive" educators call "the good life," even if they are not temporarily interested in religion as a soul-saving essential for the good life hereafter.

Also, religion should be recognized as a frame of reference for the student's whole outlook and not as merely another campus "activity." At one of our leading woman's colleges a year or two ago I found that the religious organization was regarded as one of the seven or more activities for which a girl could go out. There seemed to be no conception of it as a formative factor in shaping one's philosophy of life. It is little short of tragic when our liberal arts colleges allow mental departmentalization and fragmentation to infect even the freshmen.

Have we not a right to expect a liberal arts education to provide youth with a realistic frame of reference adequate to give meaning and worth to human personality? Self-realization requires some ultimate value from which the individual's value is adduced. Polonius' counsel to young Laertes, good as it is, is not good enough: "To thine own self be true, and it must follow as the night the day, thou canst not then be false to any man." Suppose Polonius had given that advice to young Hamlet.

Would the young Dane in his agonized state of mind have known which aspect of himself was the norm to which he should be true? A man needs to be true to himself; he also needs to be shown and shown repeatedly what his true self is. And this is a function of religion.

President Eliot of Harvard was wont to say that the strongest incentive he could use with wayward boys was to remind them of the sacrifices made for them by their parents. Religion lengthens that retrospect of sacrifice. This gives a new appreciation of one's own worth. We cannot hold ourselves cheaply. These bodies of ours are no mere bundles of senses to be indulged selfishly as if their treatment were our own business. They are to be handled with reverence. These minds of ours are no mere flashes of sensation in a brain which will soon burn out and be no more. They are candles of the Eternal Light which "lighteth every man coming into the world."

The recent Report of the Harvard Committee, *General Education for a Free Society*, states: "The true task of education is so to reconcile the sense of pattern and direction deriving from heritage with the sense of experiment and innovations deriving from science that they may exist fruitfully together." Accepting the soundness of this statement, may we not infuse campus life with a religious spirit which enriches the pattern of heritage without impairing the freedom of science? Can we not awaken the student to see that he can hardly call himself cultured unless he knows something of the faiths by which men have lived? Religion is a factor of culture which has produced the greatest masterpieces of painting, music and literature, and can a person be regarded as educated if he does not explore the sources of such inspiration? Let us appeal to what they are missing rather than to what they mustn't.

Religious art and music provide channels of spiritual stimulation not blocked by doctrinal differences. These resources have been only very partially developed both in secondary and higher education. Our industrialized world, scarred by war, has left youth hungry for beauty. And beauty is one attribute of godliness.

After James Russell Lowell heard Emerson deliver the Phi Beta Kappa address at Harvard in 1867, he wrote these words: "Emerson's oration . . . began nowhere and ended everywhere and yet as always with that divine man, it left you feeling that something beautiful had passed that way—something more beautiful than anything else, like the rising and setting of the stars." One contribution of religion is such a total, indefinable effect, like that which Emerson's speech had on Lowell. It creates a climate which stimulates the whole being; it disturbs us with the joy of elevated thoughts; it lures us toward a beauty beyond the ranges of routine living and toward values beyond the marketplace; it humbles one's egoism and heightens one's self-respect; it gives us standing in the universe.

Having considered religion as an aid to self-realization let us turn to the second aim of education as listed by the NEA Commission. This is training in human relations. In the recent report of President Truman's Commission on Higher Education appears this paragraph:

Today's college graduate may have gained technical or progressive training in one field of work or another, but is only incidentally, if at all, made ready for performing his duties as a man, a parent, and a citizen. Too often he is educated in that he has acquired competence in some particular occupation, yet falls short of that human wholeness and civic conscience which the cooperative activities of citizenship require.

Our emphasis on specialization has led Alfred Noyes to declare that we are "misled by small clever minds." We exalt the specialist and very often he knows his own field without seeing or caring how his specialty fits the general pattern. The liberal arts college must help the student to see life steadily and to see it whole.

Harmony in human relationship is not guaranteed by merely "getting together." The closer we get together physically the more conscious we become of our differences, as witness the sharpness of racial, cultural, religious and economic tensions in the crowded cities.

Training in human relations calls for more information about those of different racial and religious background. How much the present tension between Roman Catholics and Protestants could be lessened if each group had more authentic information about the other. As it is, most of the reported facts which a Roman Catholic reads about Protestantism or a Protestant reads about Roman Catholicism come from writers affiliated with the reader's own group. Or worst yet, the reputed information comes from spurious or anonymous sources.

But information about religious values and factors should and can have much wider scope. Secular college courses make the student aware of the part played by spiritual forces. My graduate study was done in Columbia under such men as Shotwell, Robinson, Beard and Dunning. References to religion were woven into the studies of European and American culture. How clearly we saw the impact of ecclesiastical policy on political theories. Courses in the social sciences, as well as in history, and literature, should give credit to the contribution made by religion.

Information can only make for happier human relations if it is inspired by the spirit of truth. The Master Teacher said: "Ye shall know the truth and the truth shall make you free." In the foggy atmosphere of our propaganda-beclouded day, we must clean the lens of our personal vision with the spirit of truth, so that we are willing to follow the facts as we find them. Only such truth-seekers can resist the pressure of the professional propagandists who make profit from playing on the fears and prejudices and hatreds of people.

And if the search for information is inspired by the spirit of truth, it reveals such a vastness of truth about God and Christ that no one group can claim to have a monopoly. When we have the modesty of seekers, we shall have a spirit of tolerance which is not condescension.

But training in human relations calls for imagination almost more than for information. Cold facts can make for "cold war." We must sensitize the imaginations of men so that they can see and feel how life is to those whose skin is of a different color, those whose racial backgrounds differ from their own, those who live in London or Moscow or Calcutta. This sensitizing of the imagination comes when we truly worship the God and Father of all mankind. Such worship is like looking up into a mirror in the ceiling and thereby being enabled to look down into other persons' places.

Our task now is to rise above the discussion of racial and class problems into the experience of fellowship, to translate our world outlooks into world brotherhood. And toward this, true religion is of immeasurable help both through information and imagination.

The third aim of education as given by the NEA Commission is *economic efficiency*.

Work is essential to vital living. Without work, human energies turn in on themselves destructively. Work gives a man courage. It is an anodyne to grief. It links a person with his comrades. And higher education in America deserves credit for doing a superb job in vocational training. However, does not economic efficiency call for more than vocational training?

We must give something to live *for* as well as something to live *on*. What sustains a person in worthwhile activities after his retirement from vocation? Medical science has lengthened the normal period of human activity, while organized industry has shortened the period of employability. What an economic waste is found in those post-employable years if the individual does not have resources and interests to give him zest! Religion, broadly conceived, should help to supply these.

Then, too, economic efficiency calls for growth without displacement. The other day I engaged a taxi-driver in conversation. I asked him whom his friends favored for president. After naming his favorite, he ventured a view about the presidential office which had a touch of originality. He said: "That's a job I wouldn't want. It don't offer no chance for advancement." No doubt it was a joke, but it carries a point. No job, however high, is satisfying if it offers no chance for advancement.

But what do we mean by advancement? Promotion from place to place, each with a larger salary and wider powers? Such a conception of progress makes for tenser competition and often leaves a trail of bitter disappointment. Furthermore, our colleges are no longer training a few select youths to be leaders. We have democratized higher education for the many. Obviously they cannot all become commissioned officers. Some must be great in the rear ranks.

We must teach youth that true advancement consists in growth rather than in change. We must Christianize the popular pattern of success at this point.

Religion regards man as a creature of God; science regards man as a creator. Perhaps this is one basic reason that religion has come to seem irrelevant in education, dominated as it is by the scientific spirit. We have so focused our study on what man can do through scientific processes that we disregard what is done for him. But man's highest creativity comes only when he also recognizes his creaturehood. Man's own productive capacities are expanded when he feels One "who is able to do exceeding abundantly above all that we ask or think according to the power that worketh in us."

Perhaps the nearest human analogy to this divine experience which I can suggest is an occasion when Toscanini was applauded by his orchestra after an unusually inspired rehearsal. Modestly silencing them he said, "Remember, gentlemen, it's not myself. It's Beethoven."

We are most economically efficient when our creative work is inspired, enlarged and sustained by a sense of the Creator within us.

The fourth task of education, according to the Commission whose findings we have been following, is training in *civic responsibility*.

We are here as representatives of American churches and American colleges. As such we are responsible to America, the land by whose laws we are protected, by whose bounties we are supported, the land that we love. Yet as churches, true to the Hebrew-Christian tradition, we are responsible to God for America. We worship One who is sovereign ruler of the universe. And you as college educators share the same responsibility if you are loyal to the principles of our Founding Fathers. Basic to the whole political philosophy of those who established our Constitution and our institutions was the doctrine of divine sovereignty.

This fact is shown by the practice of requiring our president to take his oath or affirmation on the Bible, by the opening of our legislatures with prayer, and in various other ways. As Lincoln put it, America is "this nation under God."

In fulfilling our joint responsibility to "this nation under God," colleges and churches must train citizens adequately for a free nation. As Lord Moulton pointed some years ago, unless we have sufficient citizens who will "obey the unenforceable," we must expect increasing regimentation until our free societies go the way of dictatorships. We need those inner sanctions which will restrain man when there are no laws or police to hold him back. We need to inculcate those ideas of right which rest not on expediency or the latest Gallup polls but on what mediaeval jurists and theologians called "the law of nature," which is the law of God. We need to remind the public that our much vaunted rights rest on the religious doctrines of man's divine sonship, regardless of race, creed or color. We need to clarify our concept of freedom so that any minority group which calls for tolerance will grant the same in case it should come to power.

We are opposed to the totalitarian state which treats the citizen as cannon fodder. We should also be opposed to any conception of democratic state which treats the government as a pork barrel.

We must train citizens for a free world as well as a free state. Granted that America looks today like a garden spot in the wilderness of the world. How do you keep a garden when weeds are in the air from the surrounding wildness? You cannot keep them out by taking youth out of school, putting uniforms on them and marching them up and down the road. No, the only way to keep a garden is to cultivate it.

Our task is to cultivate our principles of freedom so that they apply to minorities as well as to majorities; to develop free enterprise so that it is as free for the one-talent man as for the ten-talent man; to revere human personality under whatever color so that life is worth so much more along the Ohio and the Mississippi that the race-conscious Orient will look to us as the apostle of liberty. Our task, in short, is to discern the differences between bigness and greatness and to make America so truly great that the world will come to love her for what she does rather than to fear her for what she might do.

Let us so serve "this nation under God," that we shall be serving the whole world.

THE WANT OF THE WORLD [7]

ROBERT I. GANNON [8]

The Very Reverend Robert I. Gannon gave this address at the second session of the Fourth Annual *New York Herald Tribune* Forum for high schools, held at the Waldorf-Astoria on Saturday, March 5, 1949.

Father Gannon, recently retired after thirteen years as President of Fordham University, is a strong defender of high scholarship and liberal education. He opposed the "progressive" movement in education and strongly supported graduate research. His own academic background is unusually complete. He has an A.B. degree from Georgetown, M.A. from Woodstock, Doctor of Sacred Theology from the Gregorian University, Rome, and has pursued further advanced study at the Sorbonne, Oxford, Cambridge (M.A.), and other European universities.

Father Gannon has become one of the foremost speakers in this country on ecclesiastical and educational subjects. He has frequently talked over the radio. In 1943, he delivered a series of Lenten sermons at Westminster Cathedral in London. With his rich background of learning, his power of analysis, his ability to play a subject against a background of language, emotion, and knowledge, with a personality in which dignity is combined with rare humor, President Gannon has the essential qualities of Cicero's Orator. [9]

This address is a highly interesting example of thought well-adjusted to the high school group. The speaker selects language and illustrations to secure effective response from the high school audience. Nevertheless, the speech reflects the mature philosophy and wide cultural background of the speaker.

It is often remarked that a man in Denmark can understand a man in Java more readily than he can a woman in his own household, and something similar can be said for men themselves in different age groups. As American boys and girls, it is easy for you to understand the general sense of values that prevails at your age in any part of the world, together with the hatreds and loyalties that are based on it. Only an exceptional man, however, can remember why some things seemed

[7] Text from the New York *Herald Tribune*, March 7, 1949, reprinted by permission of the New York *Herald Tribune* and the Very Reverend Robert I. Gannon.

[8] For biographical note, see Appendix.

[9] See *Representative American Speeches: 1941-1942*, p191-200.

so vital to him thirty years ago. That is the reason why fathers and sons are often so far apart; why one generation under-estimates another. The underestimation, of course, is usually mutual. To the youngsters, the elders are hopelessly stupid, and to the elders, the youngsters are crazy (and much can be said for both points of view). But old and young should remember that the passage of years has two inevitable effects on mortal man.

It dulls his perception and deepens his understanding. So that in planning for the future you fresh recruits can help us by showing us your visions—visions that for some of us have faded in the light of common day—and we can help you by telling you how veterans interpret them.

Now, in every discussion preliminary to the blueprint of your brave new world, there is always the assumption that your fathers were to blame for getting us involved in World War II and your grandfathers in World War I. In this you are playing favorites. You are sparing the real culprits, your grandfathers' grandfathers and maybe their grandfathers before them. For all this horror which we old orange pulps have lived through twice and which is entirely too familiar to these visiting students sitting on the stage today, did not result even principally from the willfulness of tyrants or the stupidity of messianic democrats. Our plight is much more the result of the philosophy that made it possible for our supermen to arrive at their fatal decisions. So it is not going to do you or the world any good to talk about freedom from this, that or the other thing as long as we are enslaved by this stulti-fying philosophy.

It is called Naturalism—an innocent name for an appalling affliction. Through it we have inherited the intellectual arro-gance of the nineteenth century and with it a spirit of despair. William James was right when he wrote, "Sadness lies at the heart of every natural philosophy." For naturalism teaches that there is nothing supernatural, nothing spiritual, nothing to hope for. It has a kind of a catechism all its own, for it is in the last analysis a kind of perverted religion. Its first question reads, "Who made man?" and the answer, "Nobody. He just

happened." To the second question, "What, then, is his purpose in life?" there are two answers, one for each side of
the Iron Curtain, but both of them leading to the same sad
conclusion. On one side, the Eastern side, the answer reads,
"Man lives to promote the state." On the other side, our side,
"Man lives to promote his own health, culture and comfort."

To us it is clear enough without proof and clearer still to
the poor wretches who live in the Soviet and its dependencies,
that life lived for the state is not worth living. Now it is
beginning to dawn on us here in the free part of the world,
that the same is true of a life that is lived for our own health,
culture, and comfort. For if that is all we have to aim at, few
can hope for even a shadow of happiness. For most of the
human race, health is precarious, culture is on the wane and
comfort has vanished. Even the favored few cannot enjoy
all three for long. Besides, how can we expect the happiness
of fulfillment when we are living for something that is dead;
something that was dead from its beginning; something that
was still-born? I mean the world. Not the world of the good
green earth; the world of the fjords, of the Cote d'Or, of the
Delectable Duchy and the Rocky Mountains. Not the world of
human souls which is the world you are planning for today.
I mean the world that Christ refused to pray for; the world
which symbolizes self. I mean human society in so far as it
ignores God's claims, treats God's creatures as its playthings
and makes health, culture and comfort the rule of life. That
world is dead. As Martha said of her brother Lazarus when
he had been in the tomb four days "Jam foetet." By this time,
it stinketh. You may call in the smart young moderns to strew
the house with lilies and gardenias but you cannot hide the
odor of inner death. The stench of a dead soul has gone all
through society; a stench more pungent than the stench of
last week's battlefield. It began by poisoning the air which
a spiritual people must breathe to live. It ended by condition-
ing the people through despair for the absolute state.

So as you sit here today in the ballroom of this great
hotel planning the world you want, be sure you begin with
the want of the world, the world of human souls. What that

world wants most of all is hope and the will to live; not merely to endure but to live a full and healthy intellectual and spiritual life, a life that will help it to come finally to grips with the spirit of naturalism, the spirit of despair.

It is easy of course to exaggerate in a time of crisis. After all we are not the first generation to have smelt decadence in the air. If we think we are, it is reassuring to read the Old Testament occasionally and sermons that run back to the time of St. Augustine. In them we shall find that the prophets and preachers have always liked to begin with the words "There never was a time when . . ." before describing a condition that existed a dozen times before they were born. Fortunately, or rather providentially, there is always an element in society too young for discouragement. Some of us knew Europe before World War I. I paid my first visit forty-two years ago. The conditions we found were not perfect, of course. They never are. There were social injustices, discrimination and poverty, more in some countries than in others. But to the casual observer, that is to the average man, there were culture and beauty and charm and above all there was order, an order largely entrusted to the keeping of an empire which hardly realized that Victoria was dead. There was a tranquility of order known as peace which had not been disturbed, except locally, since the Congress of Vienna. Here in America the prospect was so comfortable and dull that we who were in college at the time used to lament our fate that we lived too late to see history in the making. With such a background, it requires a conscious effort on our part to realize that something can be salvaged from the wreck of civilization. Your generation has a different point of view. You were born into chaos. It is part of the Providence of God that you, our sons and daughters who have to pick up the pieces of the Modern Age, should look on disorder and uncertainty as a normal condition to be faced without surprise or fear.

Your elders perhaps have seen more disaster than you have, but if you can free yourselves from the philosophy that paralyzed their resistance, if you can realize your own absolute and relative value, that is, if you can understand the reason for your dignity as persons, if you can see clearly how you fit into the pattern of creation and why you are here, you will know more about disaster than your grandfather did, for you will be able to see through disaster. You will be able to hope.

For you there will be no delusion that "all's right with the world" but merely the conviction that "God's in His heaven," which is a very different thing. You will expect the times to be frequently out of joint. You will expect as much regress as progress in the affairs of men. You will be prepared to find that there are some clouds that have no silver lining except what comes to them from the white light of eternity; that there are some roads that have no turning this side of the grave. You will not have the heart to tell every poor man you meet that his ship will surely come in some day because it probably will not. Most ships never do. And yet you will keep your souls alive and keep society alive with hope. You will look life squarely in the eye and say "life is bitter." Of course it is, stupid. What did you expect? Life is a warfare. But who ever said that this little round of weeks and months and years, with its monotony, its disillusionments and its heartbreaks—who ever said this was the whole story? Only the fool who hath said in his heart, "There is no God."

When you go to the university, you may run into a Spengler, for some historians can be very gloomy indeed, but you will find that history itself is full of hope; full of dawning and of turning tides; full of recurring springtime and of youth. You are the dawn of the world and the turning of the tide. We need you not for what you know but for what you are. You can supply the want of the world. It is the only way you will ever get the world you want.

APPENDIX

BIOGRAPHICAL NOTES [1]

ACHESON, DEAN G. (1893-   ). Born in Middleton, Connecticut; B.A., Yale, 1915; L.L.B., Harvard, 1918; honorary M.A., Yale, 1936; L.L.D., Wesleyan, 1947; private secretary to Louis D. Brandeis, 1919-21; practiced law, 1921-33; Under Secretary of Treasury, (resigned) 1933; practiced law, 1934-41; Assistant Secretary of State, 1946-47; Under Secretary of State, 1947; practiced law, 1947-48; Secretary of State since January 1949; Ensign, U.S. Navy, World War I; member, Delta Kappa Epsilon, Scroll and Key. (See also *Current Biography: February 1949*.)

ALEXANDER, RUTH. Born in Chicago, Illinois; B.M., Kidd Key Conservatory of Music, Sherman, Texas; A.B., *summa cum laude*, Northwestern, 1920, M.A., 1921, Ph.D., 1932; concert pianist, 1929-30; lecturer on economics since 1927; associate editor, *Finance*, since 1941; editorial columnist, New York *Mirror*, since August, 1944; editorial columnist, Hearst Newspapers since 1945; radio debater on "Wake Up, America" and Town Hall programs; "Award of Merit," Northwestern University, 1945; member, Phi Beta Kappa. (See also *Current Biography: 1943*.)

BARKLEY, ALBEN WILLIAM (1877-   ). Born in Graves County, Kentucky; A.B., Marvin College, Kentucky, 1897; studied at Emory College, and at the University of Virginia Law School; practiced law since 1901; member of the Sixty-third to the Sixty-ninth Congresses, 1913-1927; United States Senator 1927-49; reelected Senator in 1939 after a strenuous primary

[1] The chief sources of these notes are *Who's Who in America, Current Biography, Religious Leaders in America, International Who's Who, Who's Who in American Education, Directory of American Scholars,* and *the Congressional Directory*.

campaign against A. B. Chandler, of Kentucky; Senate leader of the Administration party, 1937-1948, resigned on February 24, 1944, and was unanimously reelected to that position; elected Vice President of the United States, November 1948. (See also *Current Biography: January 1949.*)

BROWN, HARRISON S. (1917-   ). Born at Sheridan, Wyoming; A.B., University of California, 1937; Ph.D., Johns Hopkins, 1940; instructor, Johns Hopkins; research assistant in plutonium project, University of Chicago, 1943; assistant director of chemistry, Clinton Laboratories, Oak Ridge, Tennessee; assistant professor, Institute of Nuclear Physics, University of Chicago, 1946, associate professor, 1948; $1000 prize, American Association for Advancement of Science, 1948.

CALDWELL, JOHN TYLER (1911-   ). Born at Yazoo City, Mississippi; B.S., Mississippi State College, 1932; A.M., Drake, 1936; Wisconsin, 1938; Ph.D., Princeton, 1939; Economist, Resettlement Administration, 1936-37; Economist, Bureau of Agricultural Economics, U.S. Department of Agriculture, 1939; instructor in political science, Vanderbilt, 1939-48; president of Alabama State College for Women since 1948.

CHURCHILL, WINSTON SPENCER (1874-   ). Educated at Harrow and Sandhurst; entered the army, 1895; served with Spanish forces in Cuba, 1895; service in India, 1897-98; with Nile army, 1898; correspondent with *Morning Post*, South Africa, 1899-1900; in various battles of the Boer War, 1900; Member of Parliament, 1900-22; an officer in the British Army of France, 1916; First Lord of Admiralty, 1911-15, 1939-40; Minister of Munitions, 1917; various ministerial offices, 1918-22; Chancellor of the Exchequer, 1924-29; Prime Minister, First Lord of the Treasury, and Minister of Defense, 1940-45; leader of Opposition in Parliament since 1945; visited the United States in 1941, 1943, 1946, and 1949; author of a long list of books, including *Marlborough* (4 vols.), 1933; *Blood, Sweat, and Tears,* 1941; *The End of the Beginning,* 1943; *Onward to Victory,* 1944; *Gathering Storm,* 1948; *Their Finest Hour,* 1949.

CONANT, JAMES BRYANT (1893-   ). Born in Dor-
chester, Massachusetts; A.B., Harvard, 1913, Ph.D., 1916;
LL.D., University of Chicago, 1933; New York University,
1934; Bristol University (England), 1941; Sc.D., Cambridge
University, 1941; D.C.L., Oxford University, 1936; honorary
degrees from many other universities at home and abroad; instructor, assistant professor, professor of chemistry, Harvard,
1916-17, 1919-33; President of Harvard since 1933; lieutenant,
Sanitary Corps, U.S. Army, 1917; major, Chemical Warfare
Service, 1918; member of the atomic bomb project under Office
of Scientific Research and Development, 1941 and after; Chairman, National Research Defense Committee, 1941-46; member
of Sigma Xi, Phi Beta Kappa, and many learned societies; author of *The Chemistry of Organic Compounds,* 1933; *An Understanding of Science,* 1947; *Education in a Divided World,*
1948; and other books and articles.   (See also *Current Biography: 1941.*)

DENNY, GEORGE VERNON, JR. (1899-   ). Born in
Washington, North Carolina; B.S., University of North Carolina, 1922; LL.D., Temple University, 1940; instructor in dramatic production, University of North Carolina, 1924-26; actor,
1926-27; manager of W. B. Feakins, Inc., 1927-28; director, Institute of Arts and Sciences, Columbia University, 1928-30; associate director, League of Political Education, 1931-37; founder
and director, America's Town Meeting of the Air; treasurer,
Economic Club of New York; member of executive board,
American Association for Adult Education; president, Town
Hall, Inc.; served Students' Army Training Corps, 1918.   (See
also *Current Biography: 1940.*)

DEWEY, THOMAS EDMUND (1902-   ). Born in Owosso,
Michigan; A.B., University of Michigan, 1923, LL.M., 1937;
LL.B., Columbia University, 1925; honorary degrees at Tufts,
Dartmouth, and other institutions; admitted to New York bar,
1926; chief assistant, United States Attorney, 1931-33; special
prosecutor, Investigation of Organized Crime, New York City,
1935-37; elected District Attorney, New York County, 1937;

Republican governor of New York since 1942; defeated as candidate for the presidency, Republican ticket, November 1944 and 1948; author, *The Case Against the New Deal, 1940*. (See also *Current Biography: 1944*.)

DONOHUE, HAROLD D. (1901-   ). Born in Worcester, Massachusetts; student, Northeastern, 1925; admitted to Massachusetts bar, 1926; lawyer, Worcester, since 1926; member, House of Representatives, as a Democrat, since 1946; United States Navy, 1942-45 (lieutenant commander).

DOUGLAS, HELEN GAHAGAN (1900-   ). Born in Boonton, New Jersey; studied at Barnard College, New York, 1920-22; married Melvin Douglas, 1931; appeared in many Broadway plays, including "The Cat and the Fiddle," "Moor Born," "Mary, Queen of Scotland"; also in motion pictures and operas; toured Europe in concerts; member of 79th, 80th, and 81st Congresses, 1945-49; prominent in Democratic national politics; member of Foreign Affairs Committee, House of Representatives. (See also *Current Biography: 1944*.)

DOUGLAS, PAUL H. (1892-   ). Born in Salem, Massachusetts; A.B., Bowdoin, 1913; A.M., Columbia, 1915, Ph.D., 1921; instructor in economics, University of Illinois, 1916-17; Reed College, 1917-18; associate professor of economics, University of Washington, 1919-20; successively, assistant professor, associate professor, and professor of industrial relations, University of Chicago, since 1920; service on many commissions related to unemployment; Guggenheim fellowship, 1931; member Advisory Committee to U. S. Senate and Social Security Board, 1937; private, later major, in Marine Corps, 1942-45; wounded, battle of Okinawa; awarded Bronze Star for heroic service; elected U. S. Senator from Illinois, 1948; member, Phi Beta Kappa, and other learned societies; author of *Wages and the Family*, 1925; *Theory of Wages*, 1934; and some dozen other books.

DOUGLAS, WILLIAM O. (1898-   ). Born in Maine, Minnesota; private in United States Army, 1918; B.A., Whitman

College, 1920; LL.B., Columbia, 1925; honorary M.A., Yale, 1932; honorary LL.D., Whitman, 1938; with law firm in New York City, 1925-27; member of faculty, Columbia Law School, 1925-28; Yale Law School, 1928-39; active as a member of various governmental agencies, including Securities and Exchange Commission; appointed by President Roosevelt to Supreme Court, 1939; author of various works, including *Cases and Materials on the Law of Management of Business Units* (with C. M. Shanks), 1931; member, Delta Sigma Rho. (See also *Current Biography: 1941.*)

DULLES, JOHN FOSTER (1888-   ). Born in Washington, D.C.; B.A., Princeton, 1908, LL.D., 1946; Sorbonne, Paris, 1908-09; LL.B., George Washington University, 1911; LL.D., Tufts, Wagner, Northwestern; began law practice, New York City, 1911; director, Bank of New York; trustee, Rockefeller Foundation; chairman, Carnegie Endowment for International Peace; chairman, Federal Council of Churches Commission on a Just and Durable Peace; secretary, Hague Peace Conference, 1907; captain and major, United States Army, 1917-18; counsel, American Commission to Negotiate Peace, 1918-19; member, Reparations Commission and Supreme Economic Council, 1919; member, United States delegation, San Francisco Conference on World Organization, 1945; Council of Foreign Ministers, London, 1945; General Assembly, United Nations, 1946; Meeting of Council of Foreign Ministers, Moscow, 1947; London meeting of "Big Four," 1947; United States Senator from New York, appointed July 1949 (to complete term of Senator Wagner); Phi Beta Kappa; writer and speaker on international affairs. (See also *Current Biography: 1944.*)

EISENHOWER, DWIGHT DAVID (1890-   ). Born in Denison, Texas; B.S., United States Military Academy, 1915; Army Tank School, 1921; graduate, War College, 1929; 2nd Lieutenant, U. S. Army, 1915; Lt. Colonel, Tank Corps, World War I; advanced through grades to General of the Army, December 1944; Chief of Operations Division, Office of Chief of Staff, 1942; Commanding General, European Theatre of Operations, June 1942; Allied Commander in Chief, North Africa, November

1942; Supreme Commander of Allied land, sea, and air forces in Western Europe, November 1943; Chief of Staff, United States Army, 1945-48; elected President of Columbia University, 1948; author of *Eisenhower Speaks,* 1948; *Crusade in Europe,* 1948. (See also *Current Biography: 1948.*)

FADIMAN, CLIFTON (1904-   ). Born in New York City; A.B., Columbia, 1925; lecturer, People's Institute, 1925-33; contributor to newspapers and magazines since 1924; editor, Simon and Schuster, 1927-35; book editor, *New Yorker,* 1933-43; "Information Please" radio program, 1938-48; member Writers War Board; Book-of-the-Month Club Board. (See also *Current Biography: 1941.*)

GANNON, ROBERT I. (1893-   ). Born at St. George, Staten Island, New York; A.B., Georgetown University, 1913, Litt.D., 1937; A.M., Woodstock College, 1919; S.T.D., Gregorian University, 1927; M.A., Christ's College, Cambridge University, 1930; LL.D., Manhattan, Holy Cross, and other colleges; instructor in English and philosophy, Fordham University, 1919-23; dean of St. Peter's College, 1930-36; dean of Hudson College of Commerce and Finance, 1933-35; president of Fordham University, 1936-49; author of *The Technique of the One-Act Play, After Black Coffee.* (See also *Current Biography: 1945.*)

HANCHER, VIRGIL M. (1896-   ). Born in Rolfe, Iowa; A.B., Iowa State University, 1918, J.D., 1924; Rhodes Scholar, Oxford (England), 1920-22, B.A., 1922, M.A., 1927; LL.D., Grinnell, Augustana, Northwestern, University of Southern California; attorney at law, Chicago, 1924-40; president, State University of Iowa, since 1940; Naval Reserve Force, 1918-19; Phi Beta Kappa; Delta Sigma Rho; chairman, Committee to Study Postwar Educational Problems of the National Association of State Universities.

HOOVER, HERBERT CLARK (1874-   ). Born in West Branch, Iowa; B.A. in engineering, Stanford, 1895; honorary degrees from Brown University, Columbia, Johns Hopkins, Oxford, Prague, and other institutions here and abroad; United States Food Administrator, 1917-19; director of various relief organizations for the war-stricken nations of Europe; appointed Secretary of Commerce in 1921; President of the United States, 1929-33; coordinator of food supplies to thirty-eight countries, 1946; chairman of Committee on Reorganization of the Executive Branch of the Government, 1947-48; author of *American Individualism*, 1922; *The Challenge to Liberty*, 1934; and numerous addresses on government. (See also *Current Biography: 1943*.)

JACKSON, ROBERT HOUGHWOUT (1902-   ). Born in Spring Creek, Pennsylvania; educated at Albany (New York) Law School, Union University; admitted to New York bar, 1913, and began practice at Jamestown; appointed general counsel, Bureau of Internal Revenue, 1934; Assistant Attorney General of United States, 1936-38; Attorney General, 1939-41; Associate Justice of the United States Supreme Court since 1941; Chief Counsel, International Tribunal to try Axis war criminals, 1945-46.

KILLIAN, JAMES R., JR. (1904-   ). Born at Blacksburg, South Carolina; student at Duke University, 1921-23; B.S., Massachusetts Institute of Technology, 1926; Sc.D., Middlebury, LL.D., Union College, 1947; assistant managing editor, *The Technology Review*, 1926-27; managing editor, 1927-30, editor, 1930-39; executive assistant to the president of Massachusetts Institute of Technology, 1939-43; executive vice-president, 1943-45; vice-president, 1945-49; inaugurated as president, April 1949; member and officer of learned societies; contributor to professional magazines.

LILIENTHAL, DAVID ELI (1899-   ). Born in Morton, Illinois; B.A., DePauw University, 1920, LL.D., 1945; intercollegiate orator; LL.B., Harvard Law School, 1923; admitted to Illinois bar, 1923; practiced law, Chicago, 1923-31; edited "Public Utilities and Carriers' Service" for the Commerce Clearing House, 1931; director of the Tennessee Valley Authority,

1933-46; appointed chairman of Board of Directors, 1941; appointed Chairman of the Atomic Energy Commission, 1947; reappointed, 1948-   ; Phi Beta Kappa, Delta Sigma Rho; author, *T.V.A.: Democracy on the March,* 1944. (See also *Current Biography: 1944.*)

MARTIN, JOSEPH (1884-   ). Born in North Attleboro, Massachusetts; high school, North Attleboro, 1902; reporter, *North Atlantic Sun* and Providence *Journal,* 1902-08; publisher, North Attleboro *Evening Chronicle* since 1908; Massachusetts House of Representatives, 1912-14, Senate, 1915-17; member of 69th to 81st Congresses, 1925-1949; Republican leader, House of Representatives, 1939; Speaker, House of Representatives, 1947-48. (See also *Current Biography: 1948.*)

RAYBURN, SAM (1882-   ). Born in Roane County, Tennessee; B.S., East Texas College; studied law, University of Texas; began practice, Bonham, Texas; member, Texas House of Representatives six years (speaker last two years); member of Congress since 1913, representing 4th Texas District; speaker, 77th-79th, and 81st Congresses. (See also *Current Biography: 1940.*)

SAYRE, FRANCIS BOWES (1885-   ). Born in South Bethlehem, Pennsylvania; B.A., Williams College, 1909; LL.B., Harvard, 1912, S.J.D., 1918; various honorary degrees; instructor in government at Williams, 1914-17; law faculty of Harvard University, 1919-34; adviser in foreign affairs to Siamese Government, 1923-25; later represented Siam on various treaty commissions; director of Harvard Institute of Criminal Law, 1929-34; Assistant Secretary of State, 1933-39; U. S. High Commissioner to the Philippines, 1939-42; representative of the United States in the Trusteeship Council; member of the United States delegation to the Third General Assembly, United Nations, 1948-49; long list of honorary awards by various nations; member of Phi Beta Kappa; author of *Experiments in International Administration,* 1919; *Cases in Criminal Law,* 1927; *America Must Act,* 1935, and other books. (See also *Current Biography: 1940.*)

SOCKMAN, RALPH WASHINGTON (1889-   ). Born in Mount Vernon, Ohio; educated at Ohio Wesleyan University, B.A., 1911, D.D., 1923; Columbia University, M.A., 1913, Ph.D., 1917; Union Theological Seminary, graduate, 1916; numerous honorary degrees; minister, Madison Avenue Methodist Church (now Christ Church) New York City, since 1917; preacher, National Radio Pulpit, since 1937; Lyman Beecher lecturer at Yale, 1941; trustee of a number of colleges and universities; member of Phi Beta Kappa, Delta Sigma Rho; author, *Live for Tomorrow,* 1939; *Now to Live,* 1946; and numerous other volumes on religion.   (See also *Current Biography: 1946.*)

STODDARD, GEORGE D. (1897-   ). Born in Carbondale, Pennsylvania; B.A., Pennsylvania State College, 1921; diploma, University of Paris, 1923; Ph.D., University of Iowa, 1925; LL.D., St. Lawrence, Hobart, New York, Union, and various other colleges and universities; associate in psychology and education, University of Iowa, 1925-26, assistant professor, 1926-28, associate professor of psychology, 1928-29, professor, 1929-41; director, Iowa Child Welfare Research Station, 1928-41, and dean of the Graduate College, 1936-42; second lieutenant, Field Artillery, Reserve Corps, 1918-23; member of Delta Sigma Rho; executive officer of various educational societies; president of the University of the State of New York and commissioner of education, 1942-45; president, University of Illinois, since July, 1946; United States representative, UNESCO, 1947-48; author, *Tests and Measurements in High School Instruction* (with G. M. Ruch), 1927; *Study Manual in Elementary Statistics* (with E. F. Lindquist), 1929; *Child Psychology* (with B. L. Wellman), 1936; *The Meaning of Intelligence,* 1943; *Tertiary Education,* 1944. (See also *Current Biography: 1946.*)

THOMAS, LOWELL (1892-   ). Born in Woodrington, Ohio; B.Sc., University of Northern Indiana (Valparaiso) 1911; B.A., M.A., University of Denver, 1912; M.A., Princeton, 1918; Litt.D, Grove City College, 1933; other honorary degrees; reporter, various newspapers, Cripple Creek, Colorado, and with Chicago *Journal* until 1914; professor of speech, Chicago Kent College of Law, 1912-14; instructor in English, Princeton, 1914-

244 REPRESENTATIVE AMERICAN SPEECHES

16; chief of civilian mission to Europe to prepare records of
World War I; lecturer after 1919; two-year trip around the
world; National President, Tau Kappa Alpha, honorary forensics society; news commentator since 1930; commentator for
20th Century Fox Movietone since 1935; Television commentator since 1940; author of many boys' books, and of *Wings Over
Asia* and other travel books.

TRUMAN, HARRY S. (1894-   ). Born in Lamar, Missouri; student, Kansas City School of Law, 1923-25; captain,
Field Artillery, World War I; judge, Jackson County Court,
1922-24; presiding judge, 1926-34; United States Senator from
Missouri, 1935-41, reelected for the term 1941-47; elected Vice
President of the United States on the Democratic ticket, November 1944; sworn in as President on the death of President Roosevelt, April 1945; elected President in 1948. (See also *Current
Biography: 1945.*)

VANDENBERG, ARTHUR HENDRICK (1884-   ). Born in
Grand Rapids, Michigan; studied law at the University of Michigan, 1901-02, honorary A.M., 1925; LL.D., Hope College,
1926; editor of Grand Rapids *Herald*, 1906-28; United States
Senator from Michigan, since 1928; Chairman of Republican
Senate Legislative Committee, 1933-34; received seventy-six
votes for Republican presidential nomination, 1940; American
delegate, United Nations Organization Conference, San Francisco, 1945; United States Delegate to United Nations, 1945-47;
chairman, Senate Committee on Foreign Affairs, 1947-48; member, Authors' Club, London, England; author, *Alexander Hamilton, the Greatest American,* 1921; *If Hamilton Were Here Today,* 1923; *The Trail of a Tradition,* 1925. (See also *Current
Biography: 1948.*)

WALLACE, HENRY AGARD (1888-   ). Born in Adair
County, Iowa; B.S., Iowa State College, 1910, honorary M.S. in
agriculture, 1920; editor of *Wallaces' Farmer* since 1910; Secretary of Agriculture in cabinet of President Roosevelt, 1933-40;
Vice President of the United States, 1941-45; visited Latin

America, 1943; defeated for nomination for reelection as Vice President on the Democratic ticket in 1944, but campaigned actively for Roosevelt; appointment as Secretary of Commerce confirmed in March 1945, after vigorous Senate opposition; resigned, September 1946; spoke in England, France, and other European countries, April 1947, in opposition to Truman policies; candidate for the presidency on the Progressive party ticket, 1948, but carried no state; author of books and articles on agricultural, political, and religious topics. (See also *Current Biography: 1947.*)

CUMULATED AUTHOR INDEX

An author index to the volumes of *Representative American Speeches* for the years 1937-1938 through 1948-1949. The date following the title of each speech indicates the volume in which it appears.

SPEECH AND DEBATING

Competitive Debate: Rules and Strategy. By G. M. Musgrave. 128p. 1945. $1.25.

Extempore Speaking: A Handbook for the Student, the Coach, and the judge. By D. L. Holley. 115p. 1947. $1.50.

High School Forensics: An Integrated Program. By A. E. Melzer. 153p. 1940. 90c.

Oral Interpretation of Literature in American Colleges and Universities. By M. M. Robb. 242p. 1941. $2.75.

Representative American Speeches. By A. C. Baird, comp. Published annually in The Reference Shelf. Prices vary.

Each volume contains representative speeches by eminent men and women on public occasions during the year. Each speech is prefaced by a short sketch of the speaker and the occasion.

Selected Readings in Rhetoric and Public Speaking. By Lester Thonssen, comp. 324p. 1942. $3.